OF GHOSTS AND GODPOLES

THÉODISH ESSAYS PERTAINING TO THE RECONSTRUCTION OF SAXON HEATHEN BELIEF, BOTH OLD AND ANGLO

ÞÓRBEORHT LÍNLÉAH

OF GHOSTS AND GODPOLES

THÉODISH ESSAYS PERTAINING TO THE RECONSTRUCTION OF SAXON HEATHEN BELIEF, BOTH OLD AND ANGLO

BY
ÞÓRBEORHT LÍNLÉAH

EDITED BY
CYNEWYNN TÍWES

HÆÐENGYLD BOOKS
2014

Interior Art: Anglo-Saxon 'Bracteate-Faced' Disc Brooch 016347. Circa 6th-7th century. Discovered in Wiltshire along the Wansdyke. The design is that of two intertwining, zoomorphic swastikas, also referred to as fylfots.

Copyright © 2014 Þórbeorht Línléah

All rights reserved. This book or any portion thereof may not be reproduced or used in any manner whatsoever without the express written permission of the publisher except for the use of brief quotations in a book review or scholarly journal.

ISBN: 978-0-578-15159-5

HÆÐENGYLD BOOKS
PO Box 13961

Richmond, VA 23225

BETÆCUNG/BETEACHING/DEDICATION

This book is dedicated to Gárman Lord, the founder of Théodish Belief, whose article, "The Mystery of Heathen Sacrifice," first set me upon the way of the Heathen.

INNUNGA/INNINGS/CONTENTS

	Gecnáwnessa/Knownesses/Acknowledgments	i
	Fórspæc/Forespeech/Preface	iii
1	Inlád/Lead In/Introduction	1

Old Saxon Lorework

2	Layers in the Well	5
3	Searching for Sahsnôt	29
4	Poles, Pillars, and Trees	45

Anglo-Saxon Lorework

5	Betwixt Blood Bespattered Benches	71
6	Dragons among the Dead	87
7	Lore and Landscape	119

Bæc Andweorc/Back Andwork/Back Matter

8	Hóhinga/Hangings/Appendices	133
9	Bóchord/Bookhoard/Bibliography	175
10	Endemarc/Endmarks/Endnotes	189
11	Fórefinger/Forefinger/Index	225

GECNÁWNESSA/KNOWNESSES/ACKNOWL-EDGMENTS

The author would like to extend his deepest and most heartfelt thanks to the following friends who have, over the years and throughout its various stages, reviewed and/or edited the work found within these pages:

Hildiwulf Ritter for reviewing the original publications of "Layers in the Well," "Searching for Saxnôt," and "Poles, Pillars, and Trees" and for writing the "Preface" to this work.

Arrowyn and Henry Lauer of *HEX* magazine for re-editing and republishing both "Layers in the Well" and "Searching for Saxnôt," which appeared in issues 11 and 8 of that much missed magazine.

Darren Hobbs, for proofing an early draft of this book, and for catching many of my innumerable inconsistencies. Those which remain are entirely my own.

Cynewynn Tíwes for the initial editing of "Dragons among the Dead" as well as the overall editing of this book. Had this Farlearner not wandered upon the path that I was traveling, this work would most certainly not have taken shape. Thank you for keeping me out of the woods.

ÞÓRBEORHT LÍNLÉAH

FÓRESPÆC/FORESPEECH/PREFACE

In your hands, reader, you hold a book of some importance – a heady read, a deeply dolven lore-trove. This is what many heathen publications aim to be; in short, this is a work of scholarship.

I suppose you can be forgiven if you skip over the rest of this Preface in order to dive into the work. I am usually the sort that does that myself, being little interested in some third party's impressions of the book I'm starting, and generally eager to begin forming impressions of my own. If, however, you are that other sort of reader, exhibiting a patience that I admire but am so rarely able to emulate, then I suppose I must tax your patience a bit further with some words about who I am, how I know the author, and why precisely I feel this book to be worthwhile enough to not merely stand proudly upon your bookshelf, but to be dog-eared, highlighted, scribbled with marginalia, and rarely far from the place where you read the good stuff.

I am Théodish and have been since January of 1996 when I entered into *þrældóm* to Gerd, then lord of Frêsena Thiâd and currently *Forsta* of Axenthof Thiâd. It was in Frêsena – then a part of the Winland Ríce under Gárman Lord – that I received my education in religious scholarship from Gerd, my training in *wéofodþegnscipe* (priesthood) from Gárman, and that I founded the Théodish Scops' Gild. These three intertwined pursuits of scholarship, priestcraft, and poetry were, I think, what led Þórbeorht to seek me out in 2002. From the start, he struck me as an intelligent man with a driving interest in improving his understanding and practice of Heathenry.

Over the years that we have corresponded, discussed, and debated scholarly theories, collaborated on verse, and honed rituals, Þórbeorht has shown himself to have a particularly agile mind, coupled with a diligent intensity in study and an encyclopedic memory for detail. He has shown a great aptitude for exploring and testing theories, implementing them in his own practice, discarding them when they prove ill-founded, and building upon them when they prove firm.

The book that you hold in your hands is a result of this mental agility and diligence, offered up as a resource for your benefit. Three of his earlier works are contained herein: His "Layers in the Well" is particularly valuable for the heathen scholar looking for information on the origins and conversion of the Old Saxons; "Searching for Saxnôt" employs the powerful tools of comparative mythology to uncover the identity of this enigmatic god; "Poles, Pillars, and Trees" casts a much-needed light upon misunderstandings surrounding the Irminsûl of the Saxons, as well as upon the entire subject of images of the gods in the pre-Christian Germanic religion and the symbolism therein of the World Pillar / World Tree.

Three of his newer works are also published here for the first time. "Betwixt Blood Bespattered Benches" is an attempt to get inside the head of Hengest – one of history's least known and most misunderstood figures – by looking at his actions through the lens of his own culture. "Dragons among the Dead" is an analysis of *Beowulf*, the role played in it by the (un)dead therein, and their connection to sovereignty, providing unique and valuable insights into this poem. "Lore and Landscape" is a fascinating exploration of the transformative effect of landscape and climate on Germanic ideology over time.

All in all, this is a fascinating and valuable book. You would do well to read it, I think, in further pursuit of deepening your understanding of the ancient Heathen religion and our Théodish efforts to reconstruct it.

Nicholas "Hildiwulf" Ritter
Winterfylleð 2014 C.E.

INLÁD/LEAD IN/INTRODUCTION

The reader who is new to Heathen belief and who is hoping to find within in these pages an easily accessible introduction to Saxon Heathendom or Þéodisc Geléafa would do well to first procure a copy of Swain Wódening's *Hammer of the Gods* and/or Gárman Lord's *The Way of the Heathen*. To date you will find no finer works with which to begin your journey into what has been called "The Undiscovered RetroHeathenry."

The book that you now hold in your hands is a collection of essays, some previously published, some appearing for the first time in print, which delve deep into Heathen lore to touch upon topics arcane and obscure. Each essay stands on its own as a separate work of Heathen scholarship. Together, as chapters within a larger work, they represent my effort to push the boundaries of reconstruction further and to demonstrate just how much of our once lost lore can be rediscovered.

The first three chapters, "Layers in the Well," "Searching for Sahsnôt," and "Poles, Pillars, and Trees," pertain to the reconstruction of continental Old Saxon Heathenry. They were originally self-published as separate booklets between 2007 and 2008 yet went out of print shortly thereafter. Alas, self-publishing was a far more peril-fraught venture in 2008 than it is today.

Over the next few years, interest in each of these works, particularly "Searching for Sahsnôt" and "Poles, Pillars, and Trees," began to increase among Anglo-Saxon Heathens. As it were, I began to receive requests to make them available once more. In 2011 "Searching for Sahsnôt" was republished as an article by *HEX* magazine with "Layers in the Well" following it in 2012. Sadly, *HEX* magazine closed its covers in 2012, one issue before "Poles, Pillars, and Trees" would have been republished.

The next three chapters, "Betwixt Blood Bespattered Benches," "Dragons among the Dead," and "Lore and Landscape," either pertain to the reconstruction of Anglo-Saxon Heathenry or, in the case of "Lore and Landscape," were written from the perspective of an Anglo-Saxon Heathen. "Betwixt Blood Bespattered Benches" was penned in 2013 as my Master degree's penultimate work. Likewise, "Dragons among the Dead" served as my Master's thesis. "Lore and Landscape" is a curious work, penned with an emphasis on environmental science as it relates to the Teutonic migrations and the various religious and political changes which unfolded whilst our folk were wandering.

"Layers in the Well" is a work of historical method, a gathering of scattered knowledge gleaned from primary source material and the rendering of those disparate odds and ends into a cohesive historical narrative. Until fairly recently, it was nigh impossible for the English reader to find a comprehensive and coherent history of the Continental Saxons. At the time that this chapter in its original booklet form was penned, its purpose was to fill that void. Yet, unlike most contemporary histories which pretend to be impartial and objective, this work makes no such attempt to disguise its bias. It is a work of Heathen history written, without apology, from a Heathen perspective.

"Searching for Sahsnôt" is, through and through, a work of comparative mythology. As a Saxon Heathen, it seemed important to me to understand just how the god known to the Old Saxons as Sahsnôt and to the Anglo-Saxons as Seaxnéat fit into their Heathen religion. Was his worship unique to the Saxons or rather was Sahsnôt/Seaxnéat a regional byname for a god known by another, more familiar, name?

"Poles, Pillars, and Trees" invokes both archeological evidence and textual analysis to not only explore the significance of the sacred tree in the Heathen religion but to specifically address various misconceptions held by contemporary Heathens regarding the Irminsûl (OE: *Eormensýl*). It may very well be that some will find the discoveries presented herein to be a challenge to what they have heretofore held to be true. To such readers I can but offer the following Anglo-Saxon maxim for reflection: *Tréo sceolon brædan ond tréow weaxan*, "Trees shall broaden and the truth shall wax."[1] The truth is its own consolation.

"Betwixt Blood Bespattered Benches" is, much like "Layers in the Well," a work of historical method as applied to the life of Hengest. Beyond this, however, it falls into the realm of leadership studies, drawing upon psychology, ethics, and sociology to re-evaluate Hengest's mores and motivations as a *dryhten*. For those mindful enough to read the endnotes, there is a second, unfinished essay tucked away in the citations.

"Dragons among the Dead" is a work of textual analysis and linguistic anthropology. Unlike my other works, wherein I only occasionally provided my own translations, for this essay I undertook the daunting task of providing original translations for each of the primary sources cited therein. At its heart, "Dragons among the Dead" is a re-examination of *Beowulf* which, surprisingly, reveals itself to be a Heathen ghost story.

"Lore and Landscape," while included among my Anglo-Saxon writings, delves deep into Proto-Germanic pre-history yet ultimately finds its final expression in the Heathendom of the Norse "Viking" kings. Among Heathen-wrought literary works, it is a rare specimen, drawing upon environmental science and climatological change to provide further insight into the shifting of cultic practices from the Proto-Germanic period through the Viking Age.

As an author, it is my hope that you, as the reader, will find something of worth within these pages, something that will speed you in your own rediscovery and reconstruction of the elder trow. And, should you disagree with the conclusions contained herein, may you at least be the more lore-wise for having been introduced to primary sources seldom seen and perspectives heretofore hardly considered in contemporary Heathendom.

On the Term Théodish as It Appears in the Title

Þéodisc Geléafa, more commonly called Théodish Belief, is a religious movement rediscovered on the night of July 4th, 1976 C.E, in Watertown, New York. Unlike other present-day Pagan movements, Théodish Belief constituted contemporary Heathendom's first truly earnest effort to reconstruct, as authentically as possible, the ancient, ancestral Teutonic religion, and that of the Anglo-Saxons in particular.

Over the years Théodish Belief has waxed and waned, working out its own *wyrd*, yet worthing itself all the same. As such, it is difficult for any Théodsman, as its adherents are oft called, to completely pinpoint what is Théodish Belief. Simply put, those who are in thew with Théodish Belief, i.e. those who have inherited its traditions, recognize it when they see it.

The use of the term Théodish in this book's subtitle is of paramount importance in understanding the nature of the work contained herein. That this book is rooted in academic tradition should be apparent in its pages, particularly as the chapters progress. Yet, throughout its wendings, *Of Ghosts and Godpoles* is an entirely Théodish wrought work, written from the *weltanschauung* of a Retro-Heathen who practices much of the religion described herein. This said, this is not a work of Théodish holy writ. The conclusions drawn herein are the author's own, though other Théodsmen, wiser even, might find them favorable.

Þórbeorht Línléah
Whitthenge Heall
Richmond, Virginia
Midsummer 2014 C.E.

HÉAFODCWIDE/HEADQUIDE/CHAPTER I
LAYERS IN THE WELL: RECONSTRUCTING THE HISTORY OF THE CONTINENTAL SAXONS

Forward

Information on the Continental Saxons, or Old Saxons as they are often called, is scarce and difficult to come by for English speaking readers. Early on in my own study of the Old Saxons, I found the lack of an English history regarding the Old Saxons to be no small source of frustration. Having at one time spearheaded the efforts to revive the Old Saxon Heathen religion here in America, I found myself coming across others who shared my frustration. It is for such readers and for such a purpose that this history is written.

Origins

In his tenth century history of the Saxon peoples, *Res Gestae Saxonicae*, Widukind of Corvey proffered three explanations for the origin of the Saxon peoples.[2] His first, that the Saxons were remnants of Alexander the Great's armies, can be ruled out without further consideration; it was common for Germanic ecclesiastics and historians to attempt to tie the history of their people to Classical and Biblical history. The Saxons were no more a displaced Greek army than the Franks were the descendants of Troy, even though monks thought both lineages desirable for their people.

Widukind of Corvey's second explanation was that the Saxons were descended from the Danes or other Northmen. The close proximity of Saxony to Denmark does make this plausible.[3] Scandinavian goods are not unknown among Saxon grave finds, and the two peoples both allied and warred against one another throughout the centuries. Yet, linguistically, the Saxons were much closer to the Salian Franks and the Frisians, indicating a West-Germanic rather than a North-Germanic origin. That said, it would be ridiculous to think that there was not some familial and cultural blending between the two. In 777 CE and again in 782, the Saxon duke, Widukind Heritogo sought sanctuary in Denmark, then known as Nordmannia, from the Christian armies of Emperor Charlemagne. That the Danish court would aid Widukind against Charlemagne's Frankish hordes speaks to the bonds that must have existed between the Saxons and the Danes.

There are those, however, who believe that the traces of a more northern language can be detected in Old Saxon, perhaps the language of a Scandinavian people who came to conquer and rule over the Germans of the ancient North coast.[4] The Saxons themselves preserved, according to Widukind of Corvey in his third explanation of their origins, a tradition wherein they had originally arrived by ship along the shores of Northalbingia, a place considered by most scholars to be the homeland of the Saxons.[5] There they landed at a place along the mouth of the Elbe, known as Hathalaon (Hadeln), just beneath the Jutish peninsula and Denmark.[6]

At Hadeln the Saxon wanderers, having been driven from their home by overpopulation and famine, found themselves the unwelcome guests of the Thuringian inhabitants.[7] Unable to gain even enough hospitality to disembark from their vessels and set up camp, the Saxons resorted to guile. As relayed in the *Res Gestae Saxonicae*,

> At that time it happened that a certain young man well adorned with gold disembarked from a ship; for he was wearing a golden necklace as well as golden armbands. A certain Thuringian meeting him said: "What do you want with so much gold around your starved-looking throat?" "I am looking," he replied, "for a buyer, and I am wearing this gold for no other reason; for when I am threatened with starvation what value can I place on gold?" The Thuringian then enquired as to the quality and price. "There is no question of price

with me," replied the Saxon, "I will take whatever you wish to give me." The Thuringian then laughed at the young man: "What if," he said, "I were to fill your lap with this dust?" For there was in that place a large heap of earth [sic]. The Saxon did not delay but made a fold of his garment and took the soil, and gave the gold to the Thuringian at once; each man then joyfully hastened to his own people. . . When [the Saxon's] companions met him and realized what he had done, some of his friends began to laugh at him, while others censured him, but all agreed that he was out of his mind. But he demanded silence, and then cried out: "Follow me, brave Saxons, and you will prove to yourselves that my madness will be useful to you." Thereupon, even though they were still dubious, they followed him as if he were a leader. But he, taking the soil in his hands, scattered it in very small amounts throughout the neighboring fields, as far as it would go, and then occupied the ground by posting a camp.[8]

The Thuringians called the Saxons to Þing on the matter, quite sure they had received the worse end of the bargain. Knowing that they would receive no good from the Thuringians, the Saxons hid beneath their cloaks long knives known as *sahs (OE: seax). During the assembly the Saxons drew their weapons and slew the multitude of Thuringians, taking by force what the Thuringians would not afford them by peace. These Northern wanderers were given the name *Sahsono, "warriors with long knives."[9]

Though no date is given for this event, the Saxons (*Sahsono) must have established themselves during the late first century and early second century. They are not mentioned by Tacitus in his *Germania,* and the first written record of the name "Saxon" appears in the mid-second century treatise *Geography* by the Greek cartographer, Ptolemy.[10] Thus, it was between 98 CE and the middle of the next century that the original Saxons came into their own.

If this account is indeed true, the original Saxons were a Northern people who conquered the coastal Thuringians and Northalbingians. This may account for the vast difference in social status between Saxon nobility and freemen. Arguing in favor of later Saxon nobility being descended from the original Saxons and the nobility of the Chauci, Orrin Robinson claimed in his work *Old English and its Closest Relatives*,

> First, the nobility was a far more numerous class in Saxony than elsewhere. Second, in the proposed original homeland of the Saxons, Northalbingia, the class of nobles appears to not have existed; neither did that of bondsmen. . . . Third, the place of the nobility as against the freemen was much higher in Saxony than elsewhere: the wergild, or death price, of a noble was six times that of a freeman.[11]

The Saxon Confederation

In Ptolemy's *Geography*, it is said that the Saxons held the land between the Chalusus (Eider) and Suevian (Elbe) rivers.[12] Yet sometime in the third century, the territory of the Saxons expanded westward beyond the Weser river, stopping just short of the Rhine.

The root of this expansion lay in the formation of a great tribal confederacy. With the beginning of the Migration Era, the political landscape of Northern Europe changed rapidly. It became increasingly difficult for smaller tribes to hold their own during this turbulent time. Thus, a number of Suebic tribes, already bound by the language, the gods, and the customs they shared, came together under the banner of the confederation of the Saxons.[13]

Aside from the original, possibly Nordic, Saxons, this Saxon confederation consisted of several tribes mentioned as early as the first century by Tacitus in his *Germania*.[14] Chief among these were the tribes of the Chauci,[15] who occupied the land between the lower Ems and Elbe rivers;[16] the Cherusci,[17] whose lands included the Teutoburger Wald and the land along the middle of the Weser River;[18] and the Angrivarii,[19] who dwelt on both banks of the Weser River.[20]

The Cherusci

The history of the Cherusci, and their role in the battle of the Teutoburger Wald, is one that has been celebrated for countless generations. In September of the ninth year of the Common Era, Arminius, a Cherusci chieftain, who like many Germans of his time had once served in the Roman army as a commander of auxiliary forces, sent news of a Cherusci uprising to Varus, a Roman general. Varus marched the Seventeenth, Eighteenth, and Nineteenth Legions – accompanied by several auxiliary cohorts of cavalry and infantry – out from the Roman camp, located west along the Weser River, to quell the supposed revolt. It was a massive force numbering some twenty thousand soldiers. Varus' path lay through unfamiliar territory along a treacherous and narrow road on the edge of the Teutoburg forest between wooded hills and marshland.[21]

Little did Varus know that the Cherusci awaited him, concealed in the dark forest. Having learned Roman battle tactics firsthand, Arminius knew that the Roman forces could not effectively fight in the wooded marshland of the Teutoburg forest. The Romans were accustomed to fighting on open fields where they could advance and defend in formation; the marshy earth and wooded surroundings of the Teutoburg forest would allow for none of that.

Arminius had gathered under his command the various tribes of the Cherusci in an attempt to halt Roman encroachment into Germany, a slow and steady advancement which had begun in 58 BCE when Julius Caesar first led his armies against the Suebic tribes in Gaul.[22] Emperor Augustus continued the Roman expansion into the Rhineland with the building of new fortifications. In the years preceding the battle of Teutoburger Wald, General Drusus and General Tiberius both led their armies across the Rhine, deep into the heart of Germania, where they dealt the Germanic tribes a number of stinging blows. To numerous Cherusci, Arminius included, it became apparent that the Roman advance must be decisively dealt with lest all of Germania be subjugated to Roman rule.

Under Arminius' war-kingship, the Cherusci united. The trap was set and the Roman legions marched directly into it. Pinned between a hill, behind which the Cherusci had concealed themselves, and a marsh that offered no escape, the Roman forces found themselves ambushed. In the battle that ensued, the entire Roman force was nearly slaughtered. In 30 CE, the Roman historian Velleius recounted the battle's outcome in the second book of his *Roman History:*

> Hemmed in by forests and marshes and ambuscades, [the Roman army] was exterminated almost to a man by the very enemy whom it had always slaughtered like cattle, whose life or death had depended solely upon the wrath or the pity of the Romans.[23]

Varus fell upon his sword, taking his own life rather than face capture. Arminius had his corpse beheaded and sent to Marobuduus in an attempt to foster an alliance with that Chieftain of the Marcomanni. Thus, in one day three Roman legions fell, and the Roman advancement into Germania was forever halted along the boundary of the Rhine River.

Unfortunately, when Tacitus penned his *Germania* some eighty-nine years later, the Cherusci were in decline. Such was the sorry state of the Cherusci in his day that Tacitus wrote

> . . . the Cherusci have been left free from attack to enjoy a prolonged peace, too secure and enervating – a pleasant but perilous indulgence among powerful aggressors, where there can be no true peace. When force decides everything, forbearance and righteousness are qualities attributed only to the strong; and so the Cherusci, once known as 'good and honest,' now hear themselves called lazy fools . . . .[24]

The Chauci

We now move to the Chauci, the tribal group which came to constitute the largest portion of the Saxon confederation.[25] During the first century these people flourished. However, a fourth century text attests that by the third century their name nearly disappeared as they had become part of the Saxon confederation.[26] Of them Tacitus spoke highly:

> They are the noblest people of Germany, and one that prefers to maintain its greatness by righteous dealing. Untouched by greed or lawless ambition, they dwell in quiet seclusion, never provoking a war, never robbing or plundering their neighbors. It is conspicuous proof of their valor and strength that their superiority does not rest on aggression. Yet every man of them has

arms ready to his hand, and if occasion demands it they have vast reserves of men and horses. So their reputation stands as high in peace as in war.[27]

The Angrivarii

The Angrivarii, or men of Enger, were a Suebic tribe which dwelt along the banks of the Weser River. In his *Annals* Tacitus recorded that the Angrivarii initially fought against the Romans but eventually surrendered to Stertinius and allied themselves with Rome.[28] In *Germania* it is said that they and the Chamavi occupied the lands which once belonged to the Bructeri before that tribe was almost eradicated by a coalition of other tribes, of which it is not unreasonable to suspect the Angrivarii may have been a part.[29]

Other Tribes

In addition to the original Saxons, the Cherusci, the Chauci, and the Angrivarii, it is quite likely that various other Suebic tribes took part in the Saxon Confederation. There is even an indication that non-Suebic tribes may have fallen in with the Saxons. Around 400 CE the bulk of the Langobards began to move southward, leaving the region of the lower Elbe behind. Of the Langobards who remained, there is evidence that they joined the Saxon Confederation, adding to its already diverse and impressive constitution.[30]

In time, the various tribes of the Saxon Confederation came to be associated with their own *gâ* (NHG *gau*), or tribal district, each led by its own *aldarman* (chieftain). Of these *gâ* the names of the following have come down to us through the ages: Agradingun, Angeron, Aringon, Astfalon, Bardongavenses, Buki, Derlingun, Dragini Firihsetan (Virsedi), Guddingen (Gotingi), Hluini, Holtsaeten, Nordalbingi, Nordliudi, Nordsuavi, Norththuringun, Sahslingun, Scopingun, Scotelingun, Steoringun, Sturmarii (Sturmera), Thiadmariska, Waissagawi, Waldseton, Waledungun, Wigmodia (Wihmodi), and Westfali.[31]

The administration of the Saxon Confederation was shared by the *aldarmen* of each confederate *gâ*. Together, these *aldarmen* and their respective *gâ* would meet yearly at Marklo, along the Weser River, to hold *Þing*. Of this government, Hucbald of St. Amand's ninth century *Vita Lebuini Antiqua* stated,

> In olden times the Saxons had no king but appointed rulers over each village; and their custom was to hold a general meeting once a year in the centre of Saxony near the river Yser at a place called Marklo. There all the leaders used to gather together and they were joined by twelve noblemen from each village with as many freedmen and serfs. There they confirmed the laws, gave judgment on outstanding cases and by common consent drew up plans for the coming year on which they could act either in peace or war.[32]

With this, the origin and constitution of the Saxon peoples will now be set aside as we begin our journey into their recorded history.

Toward Britannia

With the Saxon Confederation thus established by the third century, the Saxons soon began to cast their gaze across the North Sea toward the Roman province of Britannia. In his fourth century work, *Res Gestae Libri XXXI*, Ammianus Marcellinus recorded that by 364 CE the Saxons had begun to raid Britannia. Shortly thereafter, in 367 CE, the Saxons would add to their intentions another Roman province, "losing no opportunity of raiding the parts of Gaul nearest to them by land and sea . . . ."[33]

All was not well with the Roman Empire. In 376 CE the Gothic tribes crossed the Danube, defeating the Roman forces at Adrianople in 378 CE in a battle which would claim the life of Emperor Valens. With instability in the empire, the sudden presence of the Goths, and the looming danger of the Huns, Magnus Maximus withdrew most of the Roman troops quartered in Britannia and moved them to the continent in 383 CE. By 407 CE the last of the Roman regulars would be called back. In 410 CE, the same year that Alaric, King of the Goths, captured Rome, what was left of the Roman Empire was no longer able to afford Britannia any aid against the Irish and the Picts, who had far surpassed the Saxons in the trouble they had heaped upon the Britons.[34]

A band of Saxons led by the brothers Horsa and Hengest were

received by King Vortigern of Britannia in 449 CE on the condition that they would defend the Britons from the Picts and Irish.[35] However, as the Saxon forces continued to multiply, the Britons realized the error of inviting a foreign army inside their borders. As Nennius wrote in his eighth century *Historia Brittonum*,

> After the Saxons had continued some time in the island of Thanet, Vortigern promised to supply them with clothing and provision, on condition they would engage to fight against the enemies of his country. But the barbarians having greatly increased in number, the Britons became incapable of fulfilling their engagement; and when the Saxons, according to the promise they had received, claimed a supply of provisions and clothing, the Britons replied, "Your number is increased; your assistance is now unnecessary; you may, therefore, return home, for we can no longer support you;" and hereupon they began to devise means of breaking the peace between them.[36]

The Saxons did not take kindly to this gesture. In the years that followed, the Saxons, along with the Angles, Jutes, and other Germanic peoples, began to press further and further into Britannia, carving out their own kingdoms from its remains. These people would in time come to be known as the Anglo-Saxons, whereas the Saxons of Germany came to be known as the Old Saxons.

A Return to Saxony

During this time most of Saxony was abandoned as more and more Saxons sailed to Britannia to partake in the spoils of war.[37] However, by the early sixth century, the Britons had begun to offer some resistance to the Anglo-Saxons under the banner of a military commander known as Arthur, whose legacy would later be embellished in the stories of King Arthur. Arthur managed to temporarily unite the Britons under his command and to lead them in twelve successive victories until, after the battle at Badon Hill circa 516 CE, many of the Saxons were forced to return to the homeland they had left to gather and refurnish their forces.[38]

By 531 CE a number of Saxons had returned from Britannia under the leadership of Hadugato, sailing into Hadeln just as they had done more than four hundred years earlier. There they found themselves once more at war with the Thuringians. Adam of Bremen recorded the following account:

> Theodoric, the king of the Franks, was at war with his brother-in-law, Irminfrid, the duke of the Thuringians, and was cruelly devastating their land with fire and sword. But when after two engagements, in which he suffered grievous losses, the fighting was still indecisive and victory hung in the balance, Theodoric, his hope of conquering frustrated, sent messengers to the Saxons whose leader was Hadugato.[39]

Together, Hadugato and Theodoric defeated the Thuringians, splitting the lands and peoples of Thuringia between Saxon and Frank alike.

Toward Italy

Having been back in their homeland for less than forty years, the Saxons once again departed in 568 CE, aligning themselves with the Langobards in the conquest of Italy and rekindling the ancient ties that had existed between the two tribes. Of this Saxon-Langobardic venture into Italy, Paul the Deacon wrote that

> Alboin, being about to set out for Italy with the Langobards, asked aid from his old friends, the Saxons, that he might enter and take possession of so spacious a land with a larger number of followers. The Saxons came to him, more than 20,000 men, together with their wives and children, to proceed with him to Italy according to his desire. Hearing these things, Chlothar and Sigisbert, kings of the Franks, put the Suavi and other nations into the places from which these Saxons had come.[40]

A Second Return to Saxony

With Italy conquered, the Langobards began to set down their own laws. The Saxons, not wanting to live under Langobardic rule, departed Italy and began to make their way home, crossing through Gaul. There they were routed by the army of King Mummulus and were forced to purchase their passage through Gaul by paying Mummulus in gold for the trouble their crossing had caused. In keeping with the Saxon reputation for guile, however, their gold was nothing more than brass overlaid with gold.[41] Thus, the Saxons returned to their homeland and, after several difficult battles, retook their homeland from the Suavi (Suebi, OE: *Swǽfe*) who had occupied it in their absence.[42]

Conflict with Christianity

"But those mine enemies, which would not that I should reign over them, bring hither, and slay them before me."[43] With this commandment to his followers, Jesus of Nazareth ended his sermon before entering into the city of Jerusalem in 30 CE. There his followers came, armed with swords,[44] expecting to crown him king "that the kingdom of God should immediately appear."[45] While he would fail to incite a rebellion to drive out the occupying Roman forces, Jesus' followers would spiritualize his intentions, deifying him as a god. Thus, the religion of Christianity was born, which would turn the world upside down,[46] promising to "set a man at variance against his own father, and the daughter against her mother, and the daughter-in-law against her mother-in-law."[47] And so it did.

Though the intentions of Jesus might have been spiritualized, the followers of the religion founded in his name held true to his original designs for increasing the fold. The history of the Christianization of the Germanic and Slavic peoples is largely the history of slaughter and subjugation. Nowhere was this more evident than in the coerced conversion of the Saxon peoples. Seven hundred forty-five years after Jesus exhorted his followers to bring his enemies before him and slay them, the spirit of his words was echoed in those of King Charles of the Franks, who would be known as Emperor Charlemagne. As recorded in the *Royal Frankish Annals*,

While the king spent the winter at the villa Quierzy, he decided to attack the treacherous and treaty-breaking tribe of the Saxons and to persist in this war until they were either defeated and forced to accept the Christian religion or entirely exterminated.[48]

Trouble with Charles Martel

Tensions began to rise between the Heathen Saxons and the Christian Franks by 714 CE. Neustria, the western region of the Frankish kingdom, had revolted, entering into an alliance with King Radbod of the Heathen Frisians, who had expelled the Christian mission in Frisia. At the same time, the Saxons marched on the Frankish lands of Hattuaria and Austrasia looking for their share in the bounty of war. The Frisian/Neustrian rebellion was crushed by Charles Martel, Mayor of the Palace, over the next few years.

Once Neustria had been subjugated, Charles Martel looked toward the land of the Saxons, eager to repay them for the havoc they had caused in Austrasia. In 718 CE and again in 720 CE, Charles Martel led his army as far as the Weser River, where he fought against the Saxons.[49]

There was nothing spectacular about these battles. They were, like most battles between Germanic tribes, little more than "wife and cattle raids" or political affairs. Such was the norm in Germanic society. Such would not be the case with Charles Martel's sons, Carloman and Pepin. During their reigns, the conflict between the Franks and the Saxons would transform into something altogether different.

The Rise of the Carolingians

Carloman, son of Charles Martel, entered Saxony in 743 CE, took the fortress at Horhensee, and forced the Saxon leader – possibly a war-king named Theodoric – to surrender. It was at this time that Carloman issued the infamous *Capitulary of Carloman* which, under Frankish law, required the Saxons to convert to Christianity. It required them to renounce in particular, the worship of Þunar (OE: Þunor), Uuôden (OE: Wóden), and Sahsnôt (OE: Seaxnéat).[50] Clearly, the Saxons did not accept the terms of this surrender for very long since Carloman was forced to invade Saxony once more with his brother Pepin in 744 CE, this time capturing Theodoric.

The years that followed marked a period of great change within the Frankish kingdom. In 746 CE Carloman took up the habit of a monk, leaving his brothers Pepin and Grifo to compete for control of the Frankish lands. Grifo sought refuge amongst the Saxons until he was eventually driven out of Saxony in 747 CE by a Frankish-Thuringian army led by Pepin. Oddly enough, no battle seems to have actually taken place, and the face-off ended when Grifo sued for peace. By 748 CE Grifo ceased to be a threat to the dominion of his brother.

Until this time, the Frankish peoples had been ruled by the Merovingian family. Nevertheless, since the days of Charles Martel, the Merovingian kings had been little more than political front men, symbols behind which the Carolingians, the family of Charles Martel, unofficially ruled the Franks. This formality was dispensed with in 750 CE when Boniface, the Archbishop responsible for forcing Christianity upon the Frisians and for desecrating the Hessian oak held sacred to Þunar, presided over Pepin's coronation as king of the Franks. Nothing good would come of a king blessed by Boniface's hands. With the rise of the Carolingian family to the Frankish throne, a dark shadow was cast to the east over the land of the Saxons.

Unholy War

It was through King Pepin and Bishop Hildegar that Archbishop Boniface (whom the Christians call St. Boniface) turned the sword of Christ toward the Heathen Saxons. Since 716 CE Boniface had, by politics as much as by preaching, actively pursued the eradication of the Heathen religion of the Germanic peoples. In particular, he set his sights upon the Hessians, Frisians, and Thuringians, all tribes that the Christian Franks sought to subdue and assimilate into their expanding empire. His conflict with the Heathen Frisians led by King Radbod brought him into close association with Pepin's father, Charles Martel, but if Charles Martel's battles with the Saxons shared the same religious ambitions as Boniface's, those intentions do not seem to be clearly recorded by history.

King Pepin of the Franks was joined by Hildegar, a bishop under

Archbishop Boniface, in a military strike against the Saxons in 753 CE. Hildegar's presence marked the first clear indication that the conflict between the Franks and the Saxons had transcended the scope of inter-tribal territorial disputes. The Franks now made it their unholy cause to bring the Heathen Saxons under Christian subjugation. By their own blood, the Saxons would be baptized.

Pepin and Hildegar's army marched into Saxony and met an opposing army of Saxons at Iburg. Although the Franks won the battle which ensued, Hildegar was slain, earning in this life his reward for the unholy war he had waged.

Though outmanned by the superior military force of the Christian Carolingians, the Germanic Heathens would not lay down their ancestral belief without a bitter struggle. In 754 CE Archbishop Boniface – filled with arrogance now that Radbod had been defeated, the Hessian Þunar Oak had been felled, and the Saxons had felt the edge of Christendom's sword – sought to extend his mission in Frisia, believing the people sufficiently beaten down to submit to the cross. What awaited Boniface's arrival, however, were armed Frisian Heathens who defeated the small forces Boniface brought with him. On that fifth day of June, Archbishop Boniface joined Bishop Hildegar in the depths of *Nebalhel (ON: Nifilhel).[51]

While Boniface's death may have been a setback for the Christian unholy war, the war continued. In 758 CE Pepin once again invaded Saxony, reducing the Saxon Confederation to a tributary state within the Frankish Kingdom.

Charles the Christian

When Pepin died in 768 CE, the Frankish Kingdom was left in the hands of his sons, Charles and Carloman, who were both made kings. By 771 CE Carloman was also dead, leaving Charles as the sole king on the Frankish throne.

King Charles, later known as Charlemagne, wasted little time in advancing the Christian cause against the Heathen Saxons. Charles took the fortress of Eresburg in 772 CE. From there he marched on to the Irminsûl ("Great Pillar"), a wooden pillar of enormous size dedicated to Uuôden. Following the example of Boniface, who had desecrated and hewn down the Hessian Oak of Þunar, Charles set his army upon the Irminsûl until it was felled. Its temple was also razed, and its gold and silver plundered.

The Irminsûl along with its neighboring temple was the most holy site in the Saxon religion. Jormun (Irmin) is a byname of Óðinn (Uuôden), and in Nordic sources he is the chieftain and father of the gods. He is said to have hung himself from Yggdrasill, the world tree which stands at the center of the universe, to gain knowledge of the secret mysteries of the runes. Likewise, the Irminsûl was held to be the "universal column" which "sustained everything."[52] Thus, in destroying the Irminsûl, Charles sought to strike at the very heart of the Saxon religion. Surely the will of the Saxons would be broken if their most holy site was desecrated. Surely they would see the terrifying power of Christ and therefore convert.

The Saxons were indeed impressed by the terrifying power of Jesus, so impressed that in 773 CE near the time of Ôstara (OE: Éaster), the holy tide of the goddess of spring, the Saxons marched into Frankish lands burning homes, churches, fields, and any other structure in their path. The Franks, accustomed to having the military upper hand, were not prepared for the hordes of angry Saxons who stormed into their land. Charles had desecrated the temple at the Irminsûl; now the Franks would suffer the righteous vengeance of the Saxons.

In 774 CE Charles sent out four armies to drive the Saxons back into Saxony. Later, while wintering at Quierzy in 775 CE, Charles set forth his official policy toward the Saxons. Though quoted earlier, it is worth repeating again:

> While the king spent the winter at the villa Quierzy, he decided to attack the treacherous and treaty-breaking tribe of the Saxons and to persist in this war until they were either defeated and forced to accept the Christian religion or entirely exterminated.

Utter conversion or genocide were the only options that Charles would afford the Saxon Confederation. As Jesus had declared, "But those mine enemies, which would not that I should reign over them, bring hither, and slay them before me." This, Charles would do.

Saxon Resistance

That same year, Charles would lead three campaigns against the Saxons.[53] Hassi, *aldarman* of the Austreleudi,[54] surrendered, thereby offering Charles both hostages and his hold oath. Likewise, after a battle in the Buki *gâ*, Bruno, *aldarman* of the Angrivarii, was defeated. Again, Charles took hostages to ensure the submission of the *aldarman*.

Following these two defeats, the Saxons resorted to their trademark guile to strike a blow at the Frankish forces. At Lubbecke beside the Weser River, Saxon warriors in disguise mingled with Frankish foragers as they returned late in the day to the Frankish camp. As night settled, the Saxons attacked the sleeping Franks, nearly wiping out their army before the Saxons were driven out of the camp.

Charles was incensed by the Saxon counter-offensive and fell upon the Westfali Saxons until they too offered up hostages and plighted peace. And so, Saxony was once again under Frankish rule.

The Saxons were not subdued for long however, and in 776 CE they rebelled, regaining the fortresses of Eresburg and Syburg. Charles moved quickly to put down the rebellion, setting his army upon the Saxons until he had extracted more hostages. It was then that Charles began forcing the Saxons to be baptized upon pain of death.

Widukind Heritogo

Charles called for *Þing* to be held at Paderborn in 777 CE. All of the Saxon *aldarmen* were expected to attend. Absent, however, was Widukind, *aldarman* of the Westfali *gâ*, who was possibly the last Saxon war-king.[55] Widukind, who had most likely been the leader of the 776 CE rebellion, sought sanctuary in the court of Sigifrid, King of Denmark.

Widukind returned from his stay amongst the Heathen Danes to lead another revolt in 778 CE. Under his banner Widukind marched Saxon fighters into Francia as far as the Rhine, plundering and burning churches exactly as Charles had plundered the Irminsûl temple six years before.

Not to be thwarted, Charles launched another campaign against the Saxons. By 779 CE Charles had not only managed to drive the Saxons out of Francia but to take the war to the Westfali *gâ*. Before 780 CE was over, both the Bardongavenses and Nordliudi Saxons would be defeated and forced to submit to Christian baptism.

Once more Charles held *Þing* in 782 CE with the intent of organizing the Saxons under his rule. Yet, as with the previous *Þing* held in 777 CE, Widukind boycotted the gathering. Upon Charles' return to Francia, he set his armies after the Slavs, affording Widukind the opportunity to raise the Saxons to arms in revolt. Upon hearing of the Saxon uprising, Charles dispatched a number of his emissaries with armies to crush the Saxons.

The Saxons had set up camp in the Suntel Mountains where the Frankish forces rushed upon them. According to the *Frankish Royal Annals*, Christian boldness, however, did not pay off:

> They took up their arms and, as if he were chasing runaways and going after booty instead of facing an enemy lined up for battle, everybody dashed as fast as his horse would carry him for the place outside of the Saxon camp, where the Saxons were standing in battle array. The battle was as bad as the approach. As soon as the fighting began, they were surrounded by Saxons and slain almost to a man. . . . The losses of the Franks were greater than the number might reveal since two envoys, Adalgis and Gailo, four counts, and twenty other distinguished nobles had been killed.[56]

Charles then led his own army into Saxony and managed to quell the rebellion. At Verden where the Aller and Weser rivers join, Charles summoned all of the Saxon *aldarmen*, demanding that those responsible for the rebellion be handed over to him. Some 4,500 Saxons were either handed over or rounded up along the banks of the Weser, though Widukind managed to escape to Nordmannia (Denmark). Charles had all of the 4,500 Saxon nobles, thanes, and warriors taken captive, bound, and executed. This Massacre of Verden, as it has come to be known, stands alongside the desecration of the Irminsûl as a testament to the enormity of Christian atrocity.

To these atrocities Charles would add, in the early 780s, a set of laws known as the *Saxon Capitulary*. The intent of these laws was to forbid the practice of the Heathen religion on pain of death. The

Capitulary read that

> If any one of the race of the Saxons hereafter concealed among them shall have wished to hide himself unbaptized, and shall have scorned to come to baptism and shall have wished to remain a pagan, let him be punished by death.[57]

Though their losses were severe, the Saxons continued to resist the onslaught of Christianity. In 783 CE Widukind returned and regrouped the Saxons. Although the revolt was quelled, the Westfali Saxons were soon joined by a large number of Frisians in 784 CE. Meanwhile, Charles was joined by his son, also named Charles, in the war against the Westfali *gâ*.

The Saxons were on the brink of extermination by 785 CE. If they continued to hold out, they could fight for a few more years, but defeat was inevitable; the Christian armies were just too vast and too quickly re-supplied. The Saxons were wounded and weary.

At Bardengau, Charles met with Widukind and Abbi, *aldarman* of the Bardongavenses. There he put forth the terms of surrender. Widukind and Abbi would meet Charles in Francia, taking a number of Frankish hostages with them to ensure their safe passage. At the village of Attigny, Widukind would be baptized.

The weight of the entire future of the Saxon peoples was upon Widukind's shoulders. If he continued to resist, Charles would surely kill every last Saxon just as he had promised. On the other hand, if he converted, they would be Christians and the beauty of their ancestral religion, the gods they loved, and the customs they cherished would all pass away. Either choice would, in its own way, herald the end of the Saxons. That year, Widukind journeyed to Attigny, and Saxony was subjugated to the Christian kingdom of the Franks. The war that Pepin had begun was over. As Einhard stated,

> So war was declared against the Saxons and fought for thirty-three years continuously with great ferocity on both sides; at a greater loss to the Saxons, however, than to the Franks. It could, indeed, have ended sooner but for the faithlessness of the Saxons.[58]

Thirty-three years of fighting for their ancestral belief and the Saxons were summarized as faithless. This is why the adjective "godless" still often precedes "Heathen" in Christian usage. It is not enough to conquer. Humiliation must be heaped upon the slain as well.

Saxons Defiant

In the years that followed, the Saxon armies were merged with those of the Franks. In 789 CE Charles led this mingled army on a campaign against the Heathen Slavic tribes of the Sorbs and the Obodrites. The Saxons joined the Franks in fighting against the Avars in 791 CE.

Still, a people with such love for their gods and their ancestors could not remain subdued for long. The Saxons once more raised arms against their Christian oppressors in 793 CE. By 794 CE, however, they were surrounded with no chance of escape, so they surrendered once more. The following year, in 795 CE, the Saxons formally renounced Christianity and rose up again, this time slaying King Witzen of the Obodrites who had converted to Christianity after his defeat at the hands of the Franks. This slight against Charles did not go unnoticed, and Frankish forces were quickly sent to dispatch the Saxon uprising.

The Saxons once again moved to reassert their independence by 797 CE. As the *Royal Frankish Annals* recorded,

> A campaign was launched into Saxony and pursued beyond swamps and pathless places as far as the ocean. After their return from Hadeln – this is the name of the place where Saxony borders the sea – the king accepted the submission of the whole Saxon people by receiving hostages and returned across the Rhine to Gaul.[59]

To Hadeln – the very place to which the Saxons had originally migrated and the return port from their excursion into Britannia – were the Saxons pursued by the Christian armies. To Hadeln the Saxons always returned.

Charles spent the remainder of the year in Saxony, organizing the affairs of the Saxons and seeing to their subjugation firsthand. Yet, the Nordliudi *gâ* soon rebelled. Around Ôstara 798 CE, they took a number of royal envoys prisoner, executing some and holding the others for ransom. The Franks were aided by the Obodrites in defeating the Saxons. In 799 CE Charles returned to Saxony to formally receive the defeated Nordliudi back into the fold of his soon-to-be empire.

At Christmas in 801 CE, King Charles was in Rome, where he was crowned as the "great and peaceful emperor of the Romans" by Pope Leo.[60] Thus, the Holy Roman Empire was born. Charles was by then the antithesis of all that was Germanic. Both Roman and Christian, he represented everything the Germanic peoples had struggled against from the time of Arminius of the Cherusci to the time of Widukind of the Westfali. Though he had been victorious in subduing many tribes beneath him, though his folk were numerous, though his luck had not failed him, and though his fame was known wide and far, to call him the most deplorable figure in Heathen history may very well be an understatement.

Damned if they continued as a Christian and Roman people, the Saxons on the far side of the Elbe, probably the Nordliudi and the Wihmuodi, rose up once more in 802 CE. By then Charles did not even have to muster his Frankish forces to put down the rebellion. Instead, he sent a Saxon army after the rebels. So terrible was Charles's reign that he could now pit Saxon against Saxon. As Jesus had promised

> I came not to send peace, but a sword. For I am come to set a man at variance against his father, and the daughter against her mother, and the daughter-in-law against her mother-in-law. And a man's foes shall be they of his own household.[61]

And so it was, the undead Middle Eastern god had turned kinsmen against one another in war, destroying the social institutions of tribe, clan, and family to complete the process of Christian conversion.

The desecration of the Irminsûl, the massacre at Verden, the pitting of Saxon against Saxon – to this list of unspeakable war crimes Charles would add yet another in his lifetime. To ensure that the Heathen will of the Saxons was broken, in 804 CE Charles had some 10,000 Nordliudi and Wihmuodi Saxons, with their wives and children, deported to Frankland. Deprived of their homeland and cut off from their folk, these Saxons were resettled in Frankish territory much in the same way Native Americans were repatriated to reservations. Charles gave the homeland they were torn from to the Slavic Obodrites.

Here end the atrocities that Charles the Christian, King of the Franks and Emperor of the Holy Roman Empire, inflicted upon the Saxon peoples. For over half a century, from the time of Pepin until the repatriation of the Nordliudi and Wihmoudi, the Christians made war upon the Heathen Saxons. The outcome of this great struggle is recorded by Adam of Bremen:

> Let it be known, then, that those who hitherto refused to bear the yoke of our overlordship, but now, thanks be to God, overcome both by arms and by faith, are, rich and poor, legally bound to pay to our Lord and Savior Jesus Christ and to His priests tithes of all their beasts and fruits and of all their fields, and income.[62]

If only St. Boniface and Bishop Hildegar had lived another fifty years, they could have retired quite wealthy.

The Stellinga

In the years after his death, the empire Charles built was torn by factious rivalries amongst his heirs. By 842 CE Louis and Lothair, the grandsons of Charles, were at war.[63] Half of the Saxon nobility sided with King Louis whereas the other took up the cause of Lothair. The support of the Saxon nobles that sided with Lothair must have been insufficient for he appealed directly to the Saxon peoples for support. Nithard recorded,

> He also sent into Saxony to the immense number of *frilingi* and [*liti*],[64] promising them, if they should side with him, that he would let them have the same law in the future which their ancestors had observed when they were still worshipping idols. Since they desired this law above all, they adopted a new name "Stellinga," rallied a large host, almost drove their lords from the kingdom, and each lived as their ancestors had done according to the law of his choice.[65]

Nearly sixty years after the official "conversion" of the Saxon peoples to Christianity with the surrender of Widukind, the Saxons still longed for the Heathen customs and belief of their ancestors. A return to their ancestral law would have annulled the *Capitulary*'s prohibition against the Heathen religion. No longer would the Saxons have to submit to baptism on pain of death. They had not forgotten their gods; that much was obvious. It was so apparent that even Emperor Charles' own grandson could see it.

Unfortunately, the Stellinga, the Companions, would soon find Lothair's promise empty.[66] In June Lothair made peace with his brothers, leaving the Stellinga to fend for themselves. The support that they had provided him went unrequited. Lothair had forsaken the very forces that he had raised. In the months that followed, Louis marched on Saxony to lay waste to the Stellinga, cleaning up the mess that his brother had made.

Saxon Heathendom Endures

When Archbishop Unwan assumed the See of Bremen in 1013, he found the conversion of the Saxons still far from complete. Christianity had been forced upon the Saxons numerous times throughout the eighth century, culminating in Charlemagne finally bringing the spirited Saxons under Frankish dominion. Nevertheless, three centuries later, enough Saxons still clung to their Heathen belief that Unwan had to institute aggressive measures against its practice. Adam of Bremen stated,

> He ordered all pagan rites, of which superstition still flourished in this region, to be uprooted in such a manner that he had new churches built throughout the diocese in place of the sacred groves which our lowlanders frequented with foolish reverence.[67]

Unwan's assault upon the Heathen religion of the Saxons was a partial success. From this point forward there appear to be no further references to outright Heathen worship. Still, the veneer of Christianity remained very thin among the Saxons as late as the nineteenth century. Even then peasants would cry out to Uuôden at harvest and leave the last sheaf of grain unmown that his horse might feed upon it. As Grimm noted, it was in Lower Germany that

"Heathenism maintained itself the longest."[68]

Toward a Reawakening

Though Heathen traditions endured among the Saxons well into modern times, there came a point during the Middle Ages when the process of conversion took hold and the Saxons were Christianized. By the tenth century, Otto the Great, son of Mathilda, a Widukind-sprung noblewoman, and King Henry the Fowler, Duke of Saxony, was crowned Holy Roman Emperor. The Saxons, so downtrodden under Charlemagne just a few generations before, now sat upon his throne and ruled his empire.[69]

From the thirteenth to the seventeenth centuries, the Saxons dominated commerce and trade in Northern Europe and the Baltic lands with the rise of the Hanseatic League of merchants. A powerful political and cultural force, the League exported more than trade goods, spreading Saxon culture far and wide as well. During this time the Saxon Low German language became the standard trade tongue along the Baltic Sea, influencing the linguistic development of that region.[70]

By the time of the Reformation, the Saxons had become a people of power and influence. Yet, their mark upon European and world history was not yet a thing of the past. Within their Christianity there still stirred that fierce Saxon independence and propensity toward rebellion against foreign authority.

On October 31, 1517, a Saxon monk by the name of Martin Luther set in motion the Protestant Reformation when he nailed his *95 Theses* to the Castle Church door in Wittenburg. In so doing, Luther cast off the yoke of the Roman Catholic Church, essentially making the way for that institution's decline. Just as Charlemagne's crown had come to sit upon a Saxon head, the Church that Charlemagne served had been dealt the largest blow in its history by a Saxon. Never again would the Catholic Church hold the same measure of power in Europe that it had wielded since Constantine declared it the religion of the Roman Empire.

Though Luther was probably further from being a Heathen than the Pope he railed against, contemporary Heathens may owe him something of a debt. By first preparing the field for Christian denominationalism, he also sowed the seeds for the very notion of freedom of religion. Had he not assailed the power of the Catholic Church, the revival of Saxon Heathenry could never have been a reality. In his grave, Luther is rolling over.

By 1976 the Heathen religion of the Anglo-Saxons was revived in the land the Vikings called Vinland, an ocean away from its homeland. With the success of various witchcraft and Neo-Pagan movements in England and America in the 1950s and 1960s, the time had come for a more authentic form of Germanic Heathen belief. In the small, tucked away town of Watertown, New York, Gárman Lord founded the Witan Þéod, the first contemporary Heathen fellowship whose purpose was to authentically reconstruct the Anglo-Saxon Heathen religion. Over the years this Anglo-Saxon Heathenry came to be known as *Þéodisc Geléafa*, Théodish Belief. From Théodish Belief have sprung directly, or through inspiration, a myriad of other Anglo-Saxon reconstructionist efforts, each of which has further advanced the reawakening of the old Heathen trow and thew. Indeed, the rediscoveries made by Théodish Belief have influenced nearly all of contemporary Heathendom, in particular the Norse Heathen revival of Ásatru as it is practiced in America.

By the early part of this century, the Heathen religion of the Old Saxons joined this reawakening movement with the emergence of several Old Saxon Heathen fellowships. Of these, the Sahsisk Thiod, later known as the Marklosahson, was the most prominent. It was among the Marklosahson that the gods were, once again, given worship in the ancient Old Saxon language. For a time, their altars were reddened by blót. In a new land, far from the coast of the North Sea, the Saxon belief stirred again in the hearts of the far-flung children of Saxony. Though the Marklosahson has since disbanded, it is unlikely that a generation will go by before Old Saxon Heathendom re-emerges. To Hadeln the Saxons always return.

HÉAFODCWIDE/HEADQUIDE/CHAPTER II
SEARCHING FOR SAHSNÔT: COMPARATIVE MYTHOLOGY

Forward

Imagine, if you would, that long ago in the Saxon era there existed a bejeweled goblet of great worth. Its owner was beset upon by visitors from afar who wished to take his hall from him. In the midst of the ensuing battle, the goblet was shattered into so many pieces. Some of the jewels, those small and easily overlooked, mixed with the dust and rushes of the hall's floor and were sadly lost in the skirmish. Yet, when the hall's lord was laid low, the guests who had fallen upon him gathered up the glowing gems that remained and set them into their own chieftain's grail. By mingling the old king's royal jewels with his own, the new chieftain legitimized his claim to the old chieftain's hall. Such is the history of Christianity and its incursion into the lands and lives of the Saxons; the bejeweled goblet of great worth is a metaphor for the richness of their ancient Heathen religion.

Now imagine yourself as an archeologist, many centuries later, attempting to reconstruct that original bejeweled goblet with only the gems that the new chieftain saved for his own chalice. Without the gold vessel-form in which they were first set, you find yourself looking toward similar bejeweled goblets found among the other continental Teutonic tribes. These are helpful even though they are woefully damaged. So it is to the more perfectly preserved, albeit imperfect and chipped, goblets found in the grave goods of Norse jarls that you turn to find a familiar form upon which to re-graft the gems. Such a comparative approach lies at the very heart of contemporary Heathen reconstruction.

Sahsnôt, or Seaxnéat as he was known among the Anglo-Saxons, is among the gems an *eorcnanstán*, a "holy stone," of great worth. As the progenitor of the East Saxon kings and as one of the most revered gods among the Old Saxons, the goblet of Heathendom would be incomplete in its reconstruction without Sahsnôt's stone set into its proper place. Yet, of this god, little is recorded. Sahsnôt, whose cult was of apparent prominence during the Migration Era, is a god seemingly lost to time. Or so it would seem. It is the aim of this chapter to employ the very comparative mythological analysis discussed above for no lesser a purpose than the rediscovery of this ancient Saxon deity.

…Become the Devils of the New

> *But I say, that the things which the Gentiles sacrifice, they sacrifice to devils, and not to God: and I would not that ye should have fellowship with devils.*
>
> 1 Corinthians 10:20

Following his campaigns into the Saxon lands in 743 CE, Carloman, King of the Franks, issued a capitulary against the religion of the Saxons, prohibiting the worship of the Saxons' ancestral gods and forcing all within his reach to submit to Christian baptism. As part of the baptismal rite, the Saxons were forced to renounce the foremost of their gods, decreeing them to be unholy servants of the Christian Satan. Known as the *Abrenuntiatio*, this renunciation formula follows here in its original Old Frankish form, alongside the author's own translation:

> *Ec forsacho alum dioboles uuercum and uuordum thunaer ende uuoden ende saxnote ende allêm them unholdum the hira genotas sint.*

> I forsake all of the Devil's works and words, Þunar, Uuôden, and Saxnôt, and all of the hidden-ones that are their companions.[71]

Aside from serving as a lasting testament to the intolerance inherent in the Christian religion and to the atrocities that Christianity brought to the northern and western regions of Europe, the

Abrenuntiatio preserves the names of three of the Saxon gods. Of significance is the fact that the names of these gods are given as they were known to the Franks, rather than according to the Roman interpretation. It is not Mercury who is renounced but rather Uuôden. This is certainly a rather unusual break with medieval ecclesiastical tradition. The bishop that penned this formula knew very well that the worship of these particular gods was deeply rooted in the belief of the Saxons. Nothing short of renunciation of the gods by their Germanic names would suffice. There could be no confusion amongst the conquered as to which gods they were to forsake.

Of the gods listed in the *Abrenuntiatio,* Þunar and Uuôden are clearly the same gods the Norse knew as Þórr (NE: Thor) and Óðinn (NE: Odin). However, Saxnôt, or Sahsnôt as Grimm rendered his name in Old Saxon, does not appear by that name in any Nordic sources.[72] This has led to no small measure of debate over the identity of Sahsnôt. Outside of Carloman's capitulary, the name appears only once, across the North Sea in the genealogy of the East Saxon kings of Essex.

East Saxons

When the Saxons invaded Britannia in the fifth century, they brought with them the worship of the gods they had known in their homeland. Over time, the names of these gods changed as the Old Saxon language took on characteristics of the languages of other Germanic migrants to Britannia, eventually becoming the Anglo-Saxon language.

Setting aside the institution of temporary kingship necessary during times of war, the Saxons who migrated north across the sea soon adopted the more permanent form of kingship known to the Angles. Sacral kingship, as it is commonly called, required that the king trace his noble lineage back through the ages to one of the gods. Amongst the Swedes this line is traced to Yngvi-Freyr, whilst among the royal houses of the Anglo-Saxons this line is traced almost exclusively to Uuôden; the royal line of Essex though stands out as the exception since it traces its line to Sahsnôt, who is listed as the son of Uuôden in Florence of Worcester's twelfth century *Chronicon ex chronicis.*[73] Commenting on this in his work *Myth and Religion of the*

North, Turville-Petre claimed,

> Saxnot remains a riddle. Since he is together named with Thunaer and Woden, he must have been an important god. He must also have been known in England for the genealogies of the East Saxon kings are traced to Seaxnet. Seaxnet does not appear in the other royal genealogies, which shows that the kings of Essex were believed to descend from a divine ancestor who was not the parent of other dynasties.[74]

The meaning of "Sahsnôt"

That Sahsnôt was an important god among the Saxons is undisputed. Yet, as mentioned previously, the identity of this deity has remained controversial for some time. Regarding the etymology of his name, two leading theories have been proposed. The first would interpret Sahsnôt as "sword friend." This interpretation was favored by scholars of the nineteenth century although, since the mid twentieth century, it seems to have fallen out of favor. The second, and more preferred interpretation of "Sahsnôt," renders his name as "Saxon companion" or "friend of the Saxons."

The confusion began with the possible interpretations of the initial portion of his name: *sahs. *Sahs is the Old Saxon form of the Anglo-Saxon word *seax*, referring to a single-edged cleaving knife. The Saxons earned their name, "warriors of the *sahs," after they massacred a number of Thuringians at an inter-tribal Þing. The Saxons were able to utilize the *sahs against the Thuringians because the knife's small size allowed it to be concealed beneath a cloak. Interpreting *sahs as "sword," however, is quite a stretch. While some *sahs did indeed reach the size of the modern machete and were sometimes used as swords, most were much smaller. The vast majority of *sahs were utilitarian tools, quite useful for their cleaving ability. That is not to say that the *sahs was not carried into battle. All through Europe it was common for soldiers to carry a dagger or knife with them into battle as a weapon of last resort should they lose their spears or break their swords. Even as late as the Viking era, Scandinavian warriors were buried with *sahs along with their swords and spears.

That the Saxons would name one of their most important gods after a utilitarian tool, one to be carried into battle as a back-up weapon, seems rather odd. If that were the case, one might liberally interpret Sahsnôt to mean "The 'Oh-shit-occasions' friend of last resort weapon." It is doubtful that the Saxons would have bothered with worshiping such a god or that the Franks would have felt his cult a threat to the spread of Christianity.

Summarizing the thought of most modern scholars, Georges Dumézil put forth the following etymology of Sahsnôt in his *Gods of the Ancient Northmen*:

> The first two of these divine names are cognates for Thor and Odin. The third name, whose second element corresponds to modern Germanic *(Ge)noss* "companion," means nothing more than "companion of the Saxons."[75]

Though Sahsnôt may be taken to mean "companion of the Saxons," this still does very little to cast light on his identity. On this question there seem to be three popular proposals. The first is that Sahsnôt is a god unique to the Saxon peoples, entirely unknown to the Norse. The second connects him with Tiuu (ON: Týr). The third identifies him as Frô (ON: Freyr). In searching for Sahsnôt, each of these theories should be given due consideration.

Uniquely Saxon?

That Sahsnôt may be a god unique to the Saxons is an idea that has some appeal. Drawing such a conclusion from the start certainly spares the modern mythologist the need to invest any time and effort in examining the matter further. However, in such effortless agnosticism, the mythologist fails to utilize the various tools afforded him by comparative mythological studies, drawing his conclusion as soon as the tool of etymology has served its purpose. That is akin to attempting an archeological excavation using only a pick-axe when shovels, brushes, and a whole array of tools are needed to uncover what the passage of time has hidden.

That Sahsnôt was a god so revered by the Saxons that they called him their friend is hardly cause to assume he was known only to them. Uuôden and Þunar are both called by a number of bynames throughout Nordic literature. The same is the case with the goddess Frûa (ON: Freyja). Therefore, with such precedent already established, the possibility that Sahsnôt is an epithet for a god better known by another name should not be lightly dismissed.

The Sword of Sahsnôt

Writing over a hundred years ago when the serious study of Germanic lore was still in its infancy, Jacob Grimm wavered in his identification of Sahsnôt. Drawing from the popular etymology of the day which gave the meaning "sword companion" to Sahsnôt's name, Grimm focused heavily on those gods in mythology who were associated with the sword to draw his own conclusion, ultimately deciding upon Tiuu as the most likely candidate.

Aside from a single reference in the *Poetic Edda's* "Lay of Sigdrifa," wherein Sigurd is instructed to invoke Týr twice after carving victory runes on his sword,[76] there is nothing in the Nordic corpus that connects Tiuu to the sword. From this sole reference, it is a stretch to conclude that Tiuu was a sword god in particular, rather than a god of battle, which is how he is known in Snorri's *Prose Edda*.

To support the tenuous connection between Tiuu and the sword, Grimm made an attempt to connect the Teutonic deity with a "Mars" that had been worshipped among the Getae, Scythians, and Alans.[77] In the legends of these peoples, "Mars" is the god of war and is indeed associated with a divine sword, making him, in effect, a sword god. Aside from the confusion already presented by medieval writers, who seem to use "Mars" when referring to both Tiuu and Uuôden, a greater difficulty is presented by the fact that none of those tribes were Germanic peoples. The Getae were a tribe of Thracians whereas the Scythians and the Alans were largely of Iranian origin. That the Goths settled in Scythian lands and perhaps adopted the worship of the Scythian Mars does very little to identify that Iranian god with the Germanic Tiuu. Much less does it connect Tiuu to the Saxon Sahsnôt.

Later in his *Teutonic Mythology*, Grimm felt compelled to acknowledge that in many ways, even as a sword god, Frô may have been a much more suitable candidate for Sahsnôt.[78] In the *Eddas*, when Uuôden was given his famous spear and Þunar was given his mighty hammer, Frô was likewise gifted with a magical sword which was said to fight by itself. It is worth noting that these three gods alone received magical weapons from the dwarves. As Uuôden is considered a god of the spear and Þunar is considered a god of the hammer, it may very well have been that Frô was held to be a god of the sword. Thus, even if the etymology of the name Sahsnôt as "sword companion" held true, the body of lore would still point toward Frô as he, of all the gods, is the only one whose mythology is explicitly connected to the imagery of the sword.

In the end Grimm decided to identify Sahsnôt with Tiuu. This is not surprising since comparative mythologists of that era were hard at work trying to find in Tiuu some ancient supreme Indo-European sky-father based on the etymology of his name. Whether it was Irmin, Sahsnôt, Tuisco, or some other god whose identity was unclear, Tiuu was thrust forward as a likely candidate in an effort to give the popular theory of the day more weight.[79]

Nevertheless, there may be some merit in returning to Grimm's suggestion of a Tiuu-Sahsnôt association and examining it further. In discussing Frô's sword, Grimm wrote,

> There appear to have been other traditions also afloat about this sword; and it would not seem far-fetched, if on the strength of it we placed the well-known trilogy of 'Thunar, Wôdan, Saxnôt' beside Adam of Bremen's 'Wodan, Thor, and Fricco' and the Eddic 'Óðinn, Asabragr, Freyr,' that is to say, if we took Freyr, Fricco = Frô to be the same Sahsnôt the sword possessor. Add to this that the Edda never mentions the sword of Tyr. Nevertheless, there are stronger reasons in favor of Sahsnôt being Zio [Tiuu]: this for one, that he was a son of Wuotan, whereas Freyr comes of Niorðr, though some genealogies to be presently mentioned bring him into connection with Wôdan."[80]

Grimm may have been among the first mythologists to see a correlation between the worship at Uppsala of Óðinn, Þórr, and Freyr — a magico-religious formula which is repeated throughout Nordic poetry — and the parallel arrangement of Uuôden, Þunar, and Sahsnôt among the Saxons. As we shall soon see, he was by no means the last to see this association. However, before delving more deeply into this, we should examine further Grimm's argument for favoring Tiuu as Sahsnôt.

Gods and God-Sprung Kings

Since Grimm believed the sword connection to be a weak basis for drawing any conclusion about the identity of Sahsnôt, he was forced to look for a lineage with Uuôden to establish a connection with Tiuu. After all, Seaxnéat appears as a son of Wóden in Anglo-Saxon royal genealogy. It would follow then that the Norse counterpart to Sahsnôt would, likewise, be a son of Óðinn. It is upon this point that Grimm rejected Frô in favor of Tiuu. As mention in the previously quoted passage, Grimm held that his determination was based upon Tiuu being "a son of Wuotan whereas Freyr comes of Niorðr. . . . " Yet, in that very same sentence Grimm acknowledged that "some genealogies . . . bring him [Freyr] into connection with Wôdan."

Regarding Tiuu's Uuôden-sprung parentage, the Nordic corpus is anything but clear. In the *Poetic Edda*, the "Hymiskvida" names the Etin Hymnir as Tiuu's father.[81] However, in the *Prose Edda*'s "Skaldskaparmal" there is a reference to Tiuu being called the son of Uuôden:

> How shall Tyr be referred to? By calling him the one-handed As and feeder of the wolf, battle-god, son of Odin.[82]

It is upon this passage that Grimm seems to have established the familial relationship between Uuôden and Tiuu. Yet, in the very same book within the *Prose Edda*, Snorri counts Freyr to be among the sons of Óðinn as well:

> Odin's sons are Baldr and Meili, Vidar and Nep, Vali, Ali, Thor and Hildolf, Hermod, Sigi, Skiold, Yngvi-Freyr, and Itreksiod, Heimdal, Sæming.[83]

So, the case is not as clear as Grimm might have thought. There seem to be dual traditions regarding the lineage of both Tiuu and Frô. Whether this is an indication of evolution in the beliefs of the later Norse or is the result of the confusion caused by the onslaught of Christianity is uncertain. Of the two traditions, that relating Frô to Uuôden is actually attested to more than once.

In his work *From Myth to Fiction*, Georges Dumézil included a poem from the *Corpus Carminum Faeroensium,* a collection of traditional Faeroese ballads compiled in 1840. In the ballad, Frô is referred to as Veraldur, an Eddic byname which, as *veraldar goð*, meant "god of the world." As the poem unfolds, Veraldur goes to visit Zealand against his father's advice, a trip culminating in his untimely demise:

> Be welcome, Veraldur, Óðinn's son,
>
> You are a noble champion.
>
> Enter our stone hall,
>
> Drink mead and wine!"
>
> Veraldur entered the hall of stone
>
> That was full of deceit:
>
> It was open beneath his feet,
>
> He fell into the brewing vat.[84]

It would not be difficult to dismiss this as a late tradition if it were not echoed so closely in the *Ynglinga Saga*. There Fjölnir is the name given to Frô's son, who succeeds him as the king of Sweden. Like Veraldur, Fjölnir travels to Selund, (an older spelling for Zealand), where he manages to plummet into a vat of mead and drown:

> In the night he walked out into the passage to seek himself a certain place. He was then heavy with sleep and dead drunk. Then he went back to his sleeping-place. Then he walked along the passage to the door of another loft and went through it; there he slipped with his foot, and so fell into the mead vat and drowned.[85]

Thus, the tradition of Frô, or his son, drowning in a vat of mead seems to date back to Heathen times. In the *Ynglinga Saga*'s account, however, there is no mention made of Óðinn. This would seem to make the Faroese ballad an anomaly were it not for the fact that Fjölnir is also a name ascribed to Uuôden in the *Prose Edda*![86] In some way, shape, or form, the tendency in Nordic poetry is to connect Óðinn and Freyr, though perhaps unconsciously.

The weight of evidence clearly points to a stronger familial bond between Uuôden and Frô than it does to a bond between Uuôden and Tiuu. If there is a tradition linking Uuôden and Frô in a father-son relationship, it is probably because Uuôden was considered to be Frô's foster father after the Uuani [ON: Vanir] came to live with the Êse [ON: Æsir]. That Uuôden was obligated to give Frô a gift when the young Uuan cut his first tooth supports this conclusion. As a foster son of Uuôden, Frô fits well in the Essex royal genealogy as his son.[87]

Gods and Kingship

Among the scholars who have espoused a Sahsnôt–Frô correlation, Turville-Petre and Georges Dumézil are among the foremost and most respected. Alluding to the system of comparative mythology that Dumézil pioneered, Turville-Petre summarized this connection in his *Myth and Religion of the North* as follows:

> Saxnot has often been identified with Týr, but chiefly because he is named together with two other great Germanic gods. Probably he was conceived originally as the eponymous god of the Saxons, whether his name meant 'companion of the sword' or 'friend of the Saxons.' If Saxnot is to be fitted into the Indo-European tripartite system, he is better associated with Njord, or with Freyr, who under the name Yngvi-Freyr, was the ancestor of the ruling house of the Ynglingar, the ruling house of the Swedes.[88]

Before we examine further the concept of the Indo-European tripartite system, we should consider Turville-Petre's comment connecting Frô to kingship. As mentioned before, amongst the Anglo-Saxon royal houses, Uuôden is named as the progenitor of kings. Excluding the East Saxons of Essex, all Anglo-Saxon kings were able to trace their ancestry back to Uuôden. This mirrors the mythic-histories found in the *Prose Edda's* prologue, the *Ynglinga Saga*, and other Norse writings where Óðinn is depicted as being the first of the Germanic kings. These writings sought to bridge the gap between myth and history by explaining Norse mythology in the context of classical history. Though this hybridization does neither myth nor history much justice, it does cast light on a number of features of ancient Germanic and Norse belief, the most prominent of which is Uuôden's place in the lineage of kings.

That Uuôden was considered the divine ancestor of both Anglo-Saxon and Norse kings speaks of the prevalence of this belief in elder Heathen times. However, the belief among the Swedes is that Frô occupied this position. This is attested to numerous times throughout the sagas and histories of the Norsemen. There the royal house of the Swedes is referred to as the Ynglings, receiving its name from Yngvi-Freyr, its divine ancestor and first king. The medieval historian Saxo Grammaticus referred to the Ynglings as the "kinsmen of the divine Frø and faithful accessories of the gods."[89] This is clear testimony to the link between the sacral kingship of the Swedes and their most beloved god, Frô. Frô's line of noble descendants may have spread farther than Sweden. The Anglo-Saxon rune poem makes mention of Frô appearing among the East Danes, possibly to rule over them:

> *Ing wæs ærest   mid Éast-Denum*
> *gesewen secgun,   oþ hé siððan eft*
> *ofer wæg gewát;   wæn æfter ran*
> *Þus heardingas   þone hæle nemdon.*
>
> Ing was erst,   mid the East Danes
> seen by sedge-dwellers.   Then he went eft
> over the wave.   His wain ran after him.
> Thus the Heardings   named the hero.[90]

The concept of the divine descent of kings, known as "god-sprung descent," was an important feature of the tribal beliefs of the Germanic and Norse peoples. Commenting on this in his work *The Cult of Kingship in Anglo-Saxon England*, William Chaney recounted a story preserved in Procopius' *History of the Wars* which illustrated the great length to which the Herulians went to procure for themselves a god-sprung king after their own had been killed:

> A parallel of this familial inheritance of the royal *mana* [luck/main] is seen in Procopius' account of the Herulian embassy to their northern home, probably

near that of the Angles, to seek out a king. After slaying their own ruler, the Heruli who lived among the Romans sent a mission to their homeland of Thule to select a new king from the old *stirps regia* [royal line]. 'They found many there of the royal blood' and chose one, Procopius writes, and, when the latter died on the return journey, the embassy returned yet again and selected another. . . . Not only is there evidence here of the hold upon a folk of the tradition of the 'royal race' but also of the entire house as the potential source of kingly office. This relation of king and kin was founded upon common descent from an ancestor whose *mana* permeated the royal line. That ancestor was a god.[91]

That the Herulians would send for a king among a people they had left generations before, sending an embassy from Italy to Scandinavia, attests to the seriousness with which the ancient Heathens clung to their belief in god-sprung kingship. Because such importance was placed on this belief, it was vital that a king's line be clearly established. The entire "Lay of Hyndla" in the *Poetic Edda* was devoted to tracing the line of Ottar back to the gods so that his claim to a noble inheritance could be vouchsafed against a contender to his claim. That the East Saxons of Essex chose their king from those who could trace their line to a god was consistent with a Germanic tradition that was both longstanding and widespread.

It is important to note that no other god, save Uuôden and Frô, is listed as such a divine ancestor of kings. In the *Ynglinga Saga*, there is a passing reference to King Egil of Sweden as "the highly praised offspring of Týr,"[92] but as Egil is already an Yngling and Týr does not appear in the line of Egil nor in the line of any king listed in that saga, it is most likely that this was a poetic kenning. Egil had been battling a rebellion of "many evil men," runaway thralls lead by another thrall named Tunni. The established order of Scandinavian society was in danger of being destroyed in the chaos of revolt. As Tiuu was held to be the god of *Þing*, those institutions that govern and preserve the tribal society were believed to be under his jurisdiction. Therefore, "offspring of Týr" was an appropriate kenning for Egil whose role as the upholder of legitimate and lawful order was in contrast to the anarchy of Tunni's rebellion. Nowhere else in the lore is Tiuu ever alluded to as having some involvement in kingship.

Thus, if Sahsnôt as divine ancestor of the East Saxon kings was not Uuôden, as the *Abrenuntiatio* makes perfectly clear, there was only one other god from whom legitimate kings drew their line of the descent: Frô. It is worth noting that just as the Swedes took Yngvi-Freyr's name, calling themselves the Ynglings, people of Yng, the Saxons too bound the name of their god to their own, worshiping him as Sahsnôt, friend of the Saxons.

Formula and Functions

The mid-twentieth century saw a renaissance in comparative mythological studies with the publication of Georges Dumézil's studies of ancient Indo-European religion. He observed within Indo-European cultures a basic tripartite social structure based on the roles, or functions, of the nobles/priests, warriors, and farmers. Dumézil noted a correlation between the functions of the gods and the functions of those social groups. This was quite a revolutionary approach as comparative mythology had, until then, largely relied on etymology and the consideration of similarities between various myths. Dumézil's functional approach was revolutionary because it looked at the similarities between how gods related to the society of the people who paid them worship.

Dumézil argued that the gods were intrinsically associated with the castes their functions best aided. Gods of law, magic, and sovereignty were favored by nobles and priests who sought their divine favor. Gods of war were called upon by the warrior class which sought from them victory in battle and the embodiment of the warrior's ethic. Gods of fertility and fecundity were venerated by those whose lives depended upon the success of the fields.

Dumézil observed that, throughout Indo-European mythology, there appeared formulary groupings of the most representative of these gods. Amongst the pre-Vedic Indians this grouping manifested as Mitra-Varuna, the gods of sovereignty, Indra, the god of war, and the Nāsatya, twin gods of health and fertility. In the most archaic form of Roman mythology this formulation appears as Jupiter, Mars, and Quirinus. In the far north of Scandinavia it took the form of Óðinn, Þórr, and Freyr.[93]

To fully explore the trifunctional approach put forth by Dumézil would be beyond the scope of this work. The above summary should suffice for the average reader.[94] As this treatise concerns itself only with Norse-Germanic deities, the trifunctional approach will only be considered here in relation to those gods.

It should be noted that Dumézil's trifunctional approach to comparative mythology is but one tool among many. Like all tools it has its specific purpose and limitations. Gods of one function are by no means exclusively worshiped by the social class with whom they are most associated. Though Uuôden is foremost a god of kings, there are traditions preserved among the Saxons which connect him to the harvest as well. This connection is largely due to Uuôden's popularity among the Saxons, a topic which will be explored more fully in the next chapter as it pertains to the Irminsûl. Likewise, while Frô is largely a god of fertility, among some of the Germanic and Norse peoples we see him function as a god of kingship as well. And both gods are likewise known for their association with war and victory. The boar crests of Beowulf and the title "war-leader of the gods" that is given to Freyr in "Skirnir's Journey" certainly attest to his battle prowess. Thus, as Dumézil readily admitted, the trifunctional approach is one which looks for patterns and general rules. Gods are much too complex to fit neatly into categorizations. Yet, as with etymology and other mythological approaches, a tool should not simply be discarded because it is not an end-all. There is no end-all system or approach to myth and religion.

As promised earlier, the connection that Grimm drew between the common grouping of Óðinn, Þórr, and Freyr throughout the Nordic corpus and the Uuôden, Þunar, and Sahsnôt of the *Abrenuntiatio* can now be explored in light of Dumézil's findings. What follows here are various examples of the trifunctional formula that Dumézil cited in *Gods of the Ancient Northmen*. While we often see more than these three gods listed, when an additional god is mentioned it is always one of the Uuani, reflecting the same plurality of third function fertility gods seen in the pre-Vedic formulation.

Adam of Bremen's account of the temple at Uppsala states,

> In this temple, entirely decked out in gold, the people worship the statues of three gods in such that the mightiest of them **Thor**, occupies a throne in the

middle of the chamber; **Wotan** and **Frikko** have places on either side.[95]

While a curse in *Egil's Saga* declares,

> Let the gods banish the king,
>
> Pay him for stealing my wealth,
>
> Let him incur the wrath
>
> Of **Odin** and the gods.
>
> May the tyrant flee this land,
>
> **Freyr** and Njord; may **Thor**
>
> The land-god be angered at his foe,
>
> The defiler of this holy place.[96]

Skirnir curses Gerd in the "Skírnismál" by proclaiming,

> **Odin** is angry with you,
>
> **Thor** is angry with you,
>
> **Freyr** will hate you;
>
> Most wicked girl,
>
> you have brought down upon you
>
> the potent wrath of the gods.[97]

Finally, Hallfreðr Vandræðaskáld renounces the gods and states,

> Let **Freyr** and Freya rage,
>
> And **Thor** the thunderer too;
>
> Let wretches worship **Odin**:
>
> I forsook the folly of Njord.[98]

The prevalence of such a magico-religious formula among the Norse is evidenced by examples such as these. We find these three gods grouped together in Nordic art as well, appearing aside each other in the Skog Church tapestry, a twelfth century tapestry from Halsingland, Sweden. Whether in worship or in the working of magic, the purpose of this formula was to invoke the fullness of the divine society as embodied by the most representative gods of each function.

These examples certainly add weight to the argument that Grimm began and which Turville-Petre and Dumézil advanced, recognizing the Saxon Sahsnôt as the Norse Freyr.[99] Most telling, however, is the Hallfreðr example because, like the *Abrenuntiatio*, we find in it a formula of renunciation. Just as Olaf's poet renounced the fullness of the divine society, so too were the Saxons called upon to renounce the fullness of such holy company as well.

That Sahsnôt and Frô are the same god should be apparent at this point. Still, a question lingers. Why was Frô given the name *Friend of the Saxons*? This is not unusual in Indo-European mythology. The etymology of Quirinus, the ancient Roman god whose function was identical to Frô's, bears much in common with that of Sahsnôt. Akin to the word "*curia*," the foundational unit which comprised the early Roman tribes, the name Quirinus is that of "the god of the whole curiate organization, of the people as a whole."[100] That the Romans invoked their chief fertility god by a name which connected him directly to them as a people, and that the Saxons did the same with Frô, further attests to the common thread which runs throughout Indo-European myth. As the bulk of any ancient civilization is made up by those who cultivate the fields and raise livestock, the god most important to their survival truly becomes the "friend of the folk."

Sahsnôt Rediscovered

In this search for Sahsnôt, a variety of tools have been utilized to sort through the body of evidence available to us. The leading theories of Sahsnôt's identity have been considered, the strengths and weaknesses of each examined, and their sources sought out. This search has gone from Saxony, to Scandinavia, to India, to Rome, and to Saxony again, covering the breadth of Indo-European society and religion. In the end, Sahsnôt has been found, exactly where one might expect to find him, alongside Uuôden and Þunar in the myth, magic, and beliefs of the ancient Germans and Northmen.

HÉAFODCWIDE/HEADQUIDE/CHAPTER III
POLES, PILLARS, AND TREES

In modern Heathenry the Irminsûl is both a popular symbol and topic of discussion, though one largely misunderstood with little attention given to its place as a Saxon idol of old. In a chapter on the topic of sacred pillars, poles, and trees, it is only to be expected that the Irminsûl and its significance should be considered. This work, however, seeks to go beyond the Saxon veneration of the Irminsûl to explore its place within the beliefs of several Germanic tribes and among the Norse. This common symbol among the Heathens of old has often been overlooked but is worth restoring in the modern revival of Heathen belief. Before we can begin raising such poles, we must first consider what they were, to whom they were dedicated, and what purpose they served.

Irminsûl

> They worshiped, too, a stock of wood, of no small size, set up in the open. In native language, it was called Irminsûl, which in Latin means 'universal column,' as it sustained everything.[101]

The year was 851 CE when Rudolf of Fulda penned this account of the most famous of Saxon Heathen monuments, the Irminsûl at Eresberg, in his *Translatio Sancti Alexandri Wildeshusam*. From Adam of Bremen's eleventh century *Gesta Hammaburgensis Ecclesiae Pontificum* onward, this has become the most cited reference to the Irminsûl in Anglo-Germanic literature.

In the past century, the Irminsûl has reemerged as an important religious icon in the revival of ancient Germanic belief. Several Heathen organizations have attempted to incorporate it into their organizational emblems. A few have even made it central to their devotion. But what was the Saxon Irminsûl? How much is really known about this idol of old? In truth, most of what is popularly believed about the Irminsûl is apocryphal. To truly understand the Irminsûl we must deconstruct the myths. Not the ancient myths that we earnestly seek to revive, but modern myths based on political ideology, 20th century occultism, and a gaping void in original Heathen scholarship. Just as Fredrick Nietzsche set about deconstructing the philosophical assumptions of his day by "philosophizing with a hammer," so too must we critically deconstruct our assumptions in our search for authentic Heathen practice and belief. Let us stand before our concept of the Irminsûl with hammer raised high, ready to smash that which is false so that the true Irminsûl may be raised anew.

The Myth of the Externsteine

It has come into popular contemporary Heathen belief that the Irminsûl was located at a natural rock formation, called the Externsteine, located near Paderborn along the Teutoburg Wald. *The Royal Frankish Annals*, however, clearly place it in the proximity of Eresburg, some thirty to forty miles to the south:

> The most gracious Lord King Charlemagne then held an assembly at Worms. From Worms he marched into Saxony. Capturing the castle at Eresburg, he proceeded as far as the Irminsûl, destroyed this idol and carried away gold and silver which he found. A great drought occurred so that there was no water in the place where the Irminsûl stood. The glorious king wished to remain there two or three days in order to destroy the temple completely, but they had no water.[102]

The origin of the Externsteine-Irminsûl myth has its root in the late sixteenth century writings of a Lutheran theologian and historian, Hermann Hamelmann. In 1546 Hamelmann put forth the idea in the *Oldenburgisch Chronicon* that the Externsteine had been a Saxon holy site that was destroyed by Emperor Charlemagne in the eighth century during his Christian war against the Saxons.

During the late nineteenth century, interest was renewed in Hamelmann's theory that the Externsteine was a Germanic Heathen holy site. It was during this period that the Germans began to take great interest in their pre-Christian past. Jacob Grimm was publishing his *Teutonic Mythology*, Richard Wagner was composing his *Der Ring des Nibelungen,* and German romanticism, which anticipated the German nationalism of the next century, was in full bloom. The German peoples longed for their ancient and glorious past. To anyone who has researched the scholarship of that time, it is evident that the German peoples *wanted* to believe in these depictions of their past. This desire to believe led many to draw conclusions about their past that were often more fanciful that factual. The image of the horn-helmed Viking is but one of many such examples of this.

The identification of the Externsteine with the site of the Irminsûl came about in 1926 with Wilhelm Teudt's, publication of *Germanische Heiligtumer, Teutonic Sanctuaries*, a curious work replete with extraordinary claims. In 1933 Adolf Hitler became Prime Minister, ushering in the reign of the Nazi party in Germany, and the Ahnenerbe branch of the SS was formed in 1935 to explore Nazi interests in German archeology with a particular interest given to pre-Christian German holy sites. Teudt's theory concerning the Irminsûl's location at the Externsteine fit well with the propagandist aim of the Ahnenerbe, which existed to provide archeological support for the idea of an advanced ancient Germanic civilization. In 1934, Teudt, concerned that other researchers would influence current excavation's results turned to Heinrich Himmler, head of the SS, for support. According to Martin Schmidt and Uta Halle's work *On the Folklore of the Extersteine*, "Teudt's influence at the time was such that from 1935 control over the excavations, and indeed over the Extersteine itself, was seized by Himmler's SS."[103]

In 1934 and 1935, geologist and Nazi party member Professor Julius Andree began excavations of the Externsteine with the goal of uncovering evidence of pre-Christian use of the site. Much of what contemporary Heathens believe today about the Externsteine is actually based on Andree's unscientific attempt to force the archeological evidence to fit into the Nazi party's claim that the

Externsteine had been a Germanic Heathen sanctuary.

It is important to note that in 1093 CE the Externsteine was purchased by the Paderborner monastery of Abdinghof and a hermitage was erected at the site. It may have been that the caves within the Externsteine already existed at this point, making it an ideal location for such monastic purposes. Its chapel was constructed around 1115 CE, and a famous rock engraving depicting Jesus' crucifixion was carved somewhere between 1130 and 1150 CE.

Most of the archeological features that Andree focused on, such as a supposed altar he reconstructed in 1935, are quite traceable to the period of time when the Externsteine was used as a monastery or even to the late seventeenth century when Count Hermann Adolf had it briefly converted into a fortress. Even the Externsteine's much-discussed rock grave and upper chapel are nearly identical to Christian rock graves and chapels found in Jerusalem. It would seem then that the most remarkable features to be found at the Externsteine are of Christian rather than Heathen origin.

Fortunately, the ceramic and metal artifacts uncovered during the Nazi excavations survived and are stored at the Lippi state museum in Detmold. The oldest ceramic artifacts date to the eleventh century when the Externsteine housed the monastery. Of the metal artifacts, none could be dated earlier than the twelfth century. In the rock fields surrounding the Externsteine, flint points and other deposits have been found from the Paleolithic age, yet nothing conclusive has been found to indicate that the Externsteine was used by ancient Europeans as anything more than a shelter. Even if it is conceded that the Externsteine may, at one time, have served as a Paleolithic astronomical observatory, which is quite debatable, there is no archeological evidence that the Externsteine was ever used as holy site during the age of Germanic Heathenry.

The Image at the Externsteine

Since the rise of Nazi Germany, the most popular image of the Irminsûl has come from a sizable relief in the rock at the Externsteine which depicts the crucifixion of Jesus. The following illustrations show this depiction along with highlights of the "Irminsûl" as imagined by modern Heathens.[104]

Figure 1 The Crucifixion scene depicted at the Externsteine monastary

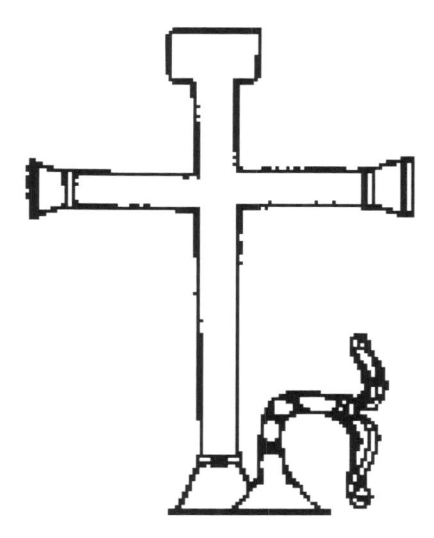

Figure 2 Cross and accompaying palm tree

Figure 3 Close-up of the palm tree

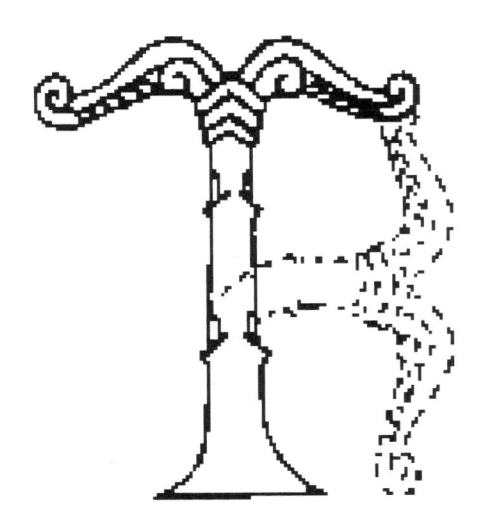

Figure 4 Palm tree reimagined as a pagan pillar

In this carving the removal of Christ's corpse from the cross is depicted. One of the figures, a man standing upon a bent object with his arm draped over the cross's T-beam, appears to be a Roman soldier charged with removing the body. Alternatively, the figure might have been intended to represent one of Jesus' disciples. What struck William Teudt's interest in this carving was the bent object upon which this figure is standing. Teudt theorized that this object was intended to represent the Irminsûl. Its position bent underfoot was thought to symbolize the defeat of the Germanic Heathen religion and the victory of the cross of Christ over the Irminsûl.

While a comparison between the Cross and the Irminsûl is no doubt tempting to ponder, it is an incredible leap to interpret this crucifixion scene as anything but just that, a depiction of Jesus' death in the first century, rather than King Charlemagne' felling of the Irminsûl in the seventh century.

Teudt was correct, however, in concluding that the object in question is indeed a tree. It is, in fact, a tree that has commonly been depicted on stone carvings and coins throughout the Mediterranean for thousands of years: the date palm. The following images all originate from the Mediterranean and Middle East, strongholds of Christianity at the time the Externsteine monastery was built.

Figure 5 Assyrian Relief from Kalhu/Nimrud 9th century BCE

Figure 6 Near Eastern cylinder seal, circa 2500 to 1000 BCE

Figure 7 Phoenician decorative plates

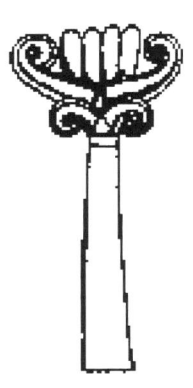

Figure 8 Assyrian sacred tree, Nineveh

The similarities between these carvings and that found on the Externsteine are rather remarkable. In his desire to find evidence of a

Heathen holy site at the Externsteine, Teudt saw in a Mediterranean date palm tree the Saxon Irminsûl. Not only does the object in the Externsteine wall relief match attested images of the date palm, it also fits well into the overall Christian character of the carving. When Jesus entered into Jerusalem, before his later arrest and crucifixion, it is said that palm branches were laid beneath his feet for him to ride and walk over. To this day, the date palm is venerated by Catholic and Anglican Christians in the observance of Palm Sunday, when crosses are woven from palm leaves. Come Ash Wednesday of the next year, those palm crosses are burned to ash which is then used to anoint the worshipers.

Bending the Bough

Of course, none of this explains why in the Externsteine's crucifixion carving the date palm is depicted as bent. The answer to this question may be found in an apocryphal tradition which was popular during the Middle Ages. According to what is commonly called the *Gospel of Pseudo-Matthew*, a work most likely penned in the early seventh century, the infant Christ, as the family fled to Egypt, commanded a date palm to bend so that his travel-weary mother, Mary, might partake of its fruit. As it appears in chapter 20 of the *Gospel of Pseudo-Matthew:*

> And it came to pass on the third day of their journey, while they were walking, that the blessed Mary was fatigued by the excessive heat of the sun in the desert; and seeing a palm tree, she said to Joseph: Let me rest a little under the shade of this tree. Joseph therefore made haste, and led her to the palm, and made her come down from her beast. And as the blessed Mary was sitting there, she looked up to the foliage of the palm, and saw it full of fruit, and said to Joseph: I wish it were possible to get some of the fruit of this palm. And Joseph said to her: I wonder that thou sayest this, when thou seest how high the palm tree is; and that thou thinkest of eating of its fruit. I am thinking more of the want of water, because the skins are now empty, and we have none wherewith to refresh ourselves and our cattle. **Then the child Jesus, with a joyful**

countenance, reposing in the bosom of His mother, said to the palm: O tree, bend thy branches, and refresh my mother with thy fruit. And immediately at these words the palm bent its top down to the very feet of the blessed Mary; and they gathered from it fruit, with which they were all refreshed.[105]

At some point in the Early Modern Age, shaped by Protestant puritanism as it was, this particular apocryphal tale fell out of favor in Christendom and has since largely been forgotten. Yet, while apocryphal to Christianity, the bending of the date-palm's bough became holy canon in Islam. According to the Qur'an, 19:22-25:

> Then she conceived him; and withdrew with him to a remote place. And the throes of childbirth drove her to the trunk of a palm-tree. She said: Oh, would that I had died before this, and had been a thing quite forgotten! So a voice came to her from beneath her: Grieve not, surely thy Lord has provided a stream beneath thee. **And shake towards thee the trunk of the palm-tree, it will drop on thee fresh ripe dates.**[106]

The differences between the two accounts — the Christian version taking place during Jesus' infancy with the tree bending upon the Christ-child's command and the Islamic version taking place during Jesus' birthing and in answer to Mary's prayer — are no doubt significant in Abrahamic theology. However, to the contemporary Heathen, these details matter little. What is clear for our purpose is that throughout the Middle Ages the bending of the date-palm was an important myth associated with both Jesus and Mary.

More to our purpose of understanding the image engraved at the Externsteine monastery, there exists a remarkably similar work of art which is contemporary to the Externsteine's own engraving. Sculpted in bronze and adorning the Pisa cathedral door, the panel below dates to 1150 C.E., approximately the very same time period in which the Externsteine's crucifixion scene was being carved.[107]

Figure 9 Bended palm tree upon the Pisa cathedral door

That the Externsteine's sculptor chose to allude to this myth on the eve of Christ's rebirth (resurrection) was masterfully poetic. Furthermore, a bearded figure standing behind the bent date-palm, with hand raised in a symbol of religious blessing, may very well have been intended to represent Nicodemus or Joseph of Arimathea, early Christian saints who were permitted by Pontius Pilate to remove Jesus' body from the cross and prepare it for burial. That one of them should be commanding the palm tree to aid them in their holy task keeps well with the Christian tradition of venerating Christ's body.

One might very well ask what an engraving of a Mediterranean date palm tree was doing in the heart of Germany. Surely such would seem out of place, yet Medieval European history was far more interconnected with that of far-off lands than our high-schooling has led us to imagine. During the eleventh century, a large number of Byzantine artists and architects were employed in Germany. The foreign influence of such imported artisans can be seen in the development of sculpture and architecture throughout the German Ottonian Empire during this era. Ottonian sculptural style of the tenth and eleventh centuries was characterized by massive size, distinct rounded forms, and distinct facial expressions. Thus, in all likelihood, the carver of the Externsteine was either such a Byzantine artist or some other sculptor trained in the Ottonian style.

Praying the Palm Tree

The connection between the date palm and Christ need not be restricted to iconographic representation during this period, however. Among the Anglo-Saxons, close cousins to the Old Saxons, there is preserved within their writings a particular veneration of the palm-tree, one which extends beyond the traditions of Palm Sunday and Ash Wednesday. For the Anglo-Saxon, the palm-tree was a representation of the *Pater Noster*, the very prayer that Christ taught to his disciples. More commonly known among Protestants as the Lord's Prayer or the Our Father, the *Pater Noster* represented, to the early convert, the most accessible method of communion through which an individual worshipper might hope to gain the *hél*, luck or grace, of the new god.

The religio-magical power and importance of the *Pater Noster* among medieval Saxons, as well as the palm-tree symbolism it was so steeped in, is best captured in the tenth century Anglo-Saxon poem, *Solomon and Saturn I*. As the poem reads,

> The **palm-twigged (*gepalmtwigede*) Pater Noster** opens up heaven, blesses the holy, makes the Lord merciful, strikes down murder, extinguishes the devil's fire, kindles the Lord's.[108]

As can be seen in the passage above, the "palm-twigged *Pater Noster*" was to Saxon Christians more than a mere prayer. Its words were believed to contain magical power comparable to the rune-spells recalled by Óðinn in the *Hávamal*. Such is not surprising. In the ninth century Old Saxon poetic text *Hêliand*, the gospel was presented in terms more readily accessible to the newly converted Saxons. As the poem progresses, Jesus's disciples ask him to "*gerihti ûs that gerûni,*" "righten for us the runes (mysteries)." [109] To this request, Jesus then teaches his assembled apostles the *Pater Noster*. In commenting on this verse, Ronald Murphy noted that "the Lord's Prayer thus becomes most specifically the replacement for Wóden's runic charms that were relied on in the north to give access to the divine."[110]

Yet, in *Solomon and Saturn I*, the Palm-tree *Pater Noster* acquired an additional attribute which originally belonged to the runic charms

– *gealdoring*, "singing":

> No man must draw out the weapon's edge without forethought, though its appearance be pleasing to him. But ever must he sing (*singan*), when he draws his sword, the *Pater Noster*, and **pray to that palm-tree (*palmtréow*)** with bliss, that it might give him both life and limb, when his enemy should come.[111]

In the aforementioned passage, the Saxon Christians were admonished to "sing . . . the *Pater Noster* . . . and pray to that palm-tree" as a battle-charm nonetheless. In doing so, the *Pater Noster* fulfilled the function of several rune-songs recorded within the *Hávamál*. Where Wóden had once hung upon the windswept ash tree to gain knowledge of the runes and their songs, such magic was now supplanted by a foreign palm tree and the prayer of the *Pater Noster*.

The Irminsûl: Early Modern Era and Prior to WWII

Whilst Hermann Hamelmann first introduced the idea that the Extersteine had been a Saxon Heathen holy site, it was not until William Teudt's publication of *Germanische Heiligtumer* in 1926 that the Irminsûl was associated with the Extersteine. Only thereafter would the sacred godpole of the Saxons be portrayed in popular literature as a Christian palm tree.

Within Hamelmann's own lifetime, Sebastian Münster published his most famous work *Cosmography* in several editions between 1550 and 1614. Unadulterated by Teudt's ideology, Münster's representation of the Saxon Irminsûl represents a raw, untampered with, representation of the Heathen idol as understood during the Early Modern Era.[112]

Figure 10 Münster's depiction of the Irminsûl

Rather than the stylized palm tree, Münster's Irminsûl resembled a *Jupitersäule*, "Jupiter Pillar," a type of Roman religious monument found throughout Roman occupied Germania during the second and third centuries. If the etymology of Irminsûl proves to be "the pillar of the god Irmin," then Münster's depiction of an idol aloft so small a pedestal is more than sufficient in its representation. Moreover, even if Irminsûl is rendered as "the pillar of the god Irmin," this does not necessarily preclude a reading of "the great (large) pillar" either. In fact, such a reading will be shown to bear fruit when Rudolf of Fulda's account is considered. As it so happens, there also existed within early Migration Era Germania what were known as *Jupitergigantensäule*, "giant Jupiter pillars," towering pillars upon which the image of a god was beheld.

Two and half centuries after Münster, yet still prior to Wilhelm Teudt's conflating of a Christian palm-tree with the Heathen Irminsûl, German artists of the Romantic era generally portrayed the Irminsûl as a large pillar with either the head or the full statue of the god Irmin at its top.

An excellent example of such portrayal is provided by Alfred Rethel who painted a series of frescos for the Aachen Rathaus in the 1840s commemorating the life of the Emperor Charlemagne. One such fresco shows Charlemagne standing over the toppled column of the Irminsûl as soldiers remove its head.

The following is a photograph of Rethel's portrayal of the Irminsûl.

Figure 11 Rethel's depiction of the Irminsûl

Although Rethel's Irminsûl has a flair to it that is unattested in actual Heathen god images yet discovered, the general form of his depiction, a column with a head at the top, is in keeping with early descriptions of both the Irminsûl and other such godpoles. The twelfth century German epic poem *Kaiserchronik* makes reference to such an Irminsûl. "Upon an yrmensûl stood an idol huge, him they called their merchant."[113] It is worth noting that the god Uuôden (ON: Óðinn) is often referred to in Nordic sources by the names Farmaguð and Farmatýr,[114] each of which mean "god of cargoes," an indication that Uuôden the Wanderer was worshipped by the seafaring Norse merchants.

A similar account of a godpole, also associated with a god worshipped by merchants, can be found in the tenth century writings of Ibn Fadlan, an Arabic traveler who had the opportunity to observe the Rûs Vikings firsthand. The following account details their veneration of a large wooden pole with the face of a merchant god carved upon it:

At the arrival of their ships at this anchorage, each of them came ashore with bread, meat, onions, mild and rank, and proceeded to a tall pillar of wood which has a man-like face carved into it, and around it are small figures, behind which long, tall wooden poles are erected. And (the Rûs) comes to the large figure and prostrates himself before it, and then he says: "O my lord (god), I have come from far-away land and I have with me so-and-so many sable pelts," until he has recounted all the trade-goods he has transported (then he goes on): "I have brought this gift for you." Then he lays down what he has with him in front of the pole . . . . If he has difficulties with what he hopes to accomplish, he will then bring a gift to all these small figures [godpoles] and ask them for intercession, and he says: "These are the wives, daughters and sons of our lord," and so he goes on and approaches each figure, one after the other, and requests intercession, imploring and humbly praying before it.[115]

Again, we have a god of cargoes and merchants, yet this time there can be little dispute that the god mentioned is Uuôden. Just as this god is surrounded by his wives, daughters, and sons, Uuôden is known to the Norse as the Alfaðir (All-Father), father of the Êse and chief among them.

The Týr Rune

Unfortunately, understanding of the Irminsûl did not cease to be obscured with the fall of the Third Reich. Drawing upon the palm tree image established by Wilhelm Teudt, some have sought to identify "Irmin" as the god Tiuu (ON: Týr), despite all the evidence contrary. Traceable to the discredited solar mythological theory which sought to find in Tiuu some supreme Indo-European god, this idea has only been sustainable by the poor scholarship rampant in contemporary Heathendom.[116] The argument in favor of the Irmin-Tiuu identification seems to largely rest on the supposed similarity in appearance between the Týr rune and the image of the "Irminsûl" found at the Externsteine. Yet, when one looks at them closely, it is more than apparent that the Týr rune and the palm-tree image found at the Externsteine are not, in any way, identical. Furthermore, it is a true stretch of even the modern Heathen imagination to conceive of a runic monument of such size. The runic monuments that do exist are mainly stones with runes carved upon them. Nowhere is there an indication that the ancient Germanic or Norse peoples built massive free-standing runic images.

Those who favor the Tiuu-Irmin association could very well cite Widukind of Corvey, whose tenth century history of the Saxons, *Res Gestae Saxonicae*, describes an Irminsûl pole erected by the Saxons during the early sixth century after their victory over the Thuringians as follows:

> In the morning they planted their eagle at the eastern gate and, piling up an altar of superstition of their fathers, representing by the name Mars, by the likeness of the pillars of Hercules, by position of the Sun, who is called Apollo by the Greeks. Hence the view of those who hold that the Saxons are descended from the Greeks has a certain probability, for Mars is called Hirmin or Hermes in Greek...[117]

According to the Roman interpretation which was used by the Christian church throughout the Middle Ages, the Germanic gods corresponded to the Roman gods. Thus, when monks wrote of the Germanic gods, they often used a Roman name instead. Generally speaking, Mercury corresponds to Uuôden, Mars corresponds to Tiuu, and Hercules and Jupiter both correspond to Þunar. Problematically, the name Mars is also sometimes applied to Uuôden, creating no small measure of confusion.

In looking at Widukind of Corvey's description of an Irmin pole, it becomes apparent that he too was confused. He mentions the names of four gods in his attempt to explain why Mars was called Hirmin (Irmin). In doing so, he equates Mars with Hermes, the Greek name for Mercury, who is exclusively understood to represent Uuôden. It is quite likely that Widukind was identifying Uuôden with Mars, similar to other medieval authors such as Adam of Bremen,[118] largely because of the victory over the Thuringians that was attributed to him.

In giving his worshipers victory in battle, Uuôden is preeminent among the gods. Known to the Norse as Sigðir (victory bringer),

Sigföðr (victory father), Siggautr (victory Gaut), Sigmundr (victory protection), Sigrhofundr (victory founder), Sigrúnnr (victory tree), Sigthror (victory success), Sigtryggr (victory true), and Sigtýr (victory god), Uuôden's place as granter of victory is unquestionable in Heathen lore.

Universal Column

With our hammer in hand, we have fractured modern myth, hammered out the identity of Irmin, and separated the image of the Irminsûl from Christian symbolism and Nazi propaganda. We can now turn our attention toward exploring the significance of the Irminsûl to the Saxon peoples.

Though quoted previously, Rudolf of Fulda's description of the Irminsûl is worth examining again:

> They worshiped, too, a stock of wood, of no small size, set up in the open. In native language, it was called Irminsûl, which in Latin means 'universal column,' as it sustained everything."[119]

Given the parallels we have seen so far between the religion of the Saxons and that of the Norse, there is no need to expect that this consistency should fail now. Just as the Saxons venerated a wooden "universal column" which held the world in place, the Nordic Heathens venerated a heavenly ash tree known as Yggdrasill which, like the Saxon Irminsûl, was believed to have "sustained everything." In his *Prose Edda*, the Icelandic poet and historian Snorri Sturluson depicted the Yggdrasill as follows,

> Then spoke Gangleri: 'Where is the chief centre or holy place of the gods?'
>
> High replied: 'It is the ash Yggdrasill. There the gods must hold their courts each day.'
>
> The spoke Gangleri: 'What is there to tell about that place?'
>
> Then said Just-as-high: 'The ash is of all trees the biggest and best. Its branches spread out over all the world and extend across the sky. Three of the tree's roots support it and extend very, very far. One is among the Æsir, the second among the frost giants,

where Ginnungagap once was. The third extends over Niflheim...'[120]

In Norse myth Yggdrasill is so associated with the god Uuôden (ON: Óðinn) that it even bears one of his many names, Ygg "terrible one." The name Yggdrasill means "steed of the terrible one." The idea of Uuôden riding the Yggdrasill as a steed is a poetic allusion to the myth of his hanging from this tree in order to gain magical knowledge of the runes.[121] As recorded in the Norse poem, the *Hávamál,* we find Uuôden recalling this occasion:

I know that I hung on a windy tree

nine long nights,

wounded with a spear, dedicated to Odin,

myself to myself,

on that tree of which no man knows

from where its roots run.

No bread did they give me nor a drink from a horn,

downward I peered;

I took up the runes, screaming I took them,

then I fell back from there.[122]

Just as the Yggdrasill bore one of Uuôden's many names, we find this to also be the case with the Irminsûl. The name Irminsûl is derived from the name Irmin, one of the chief gods mentioned by Tacitus in his first century work, *The Germania*. Irmin simply means "great" as in large or powerful. As a name it would mean "great one". Likewise, *sûl* is Old Saxon for "pole". The Irminsûl is thus Irmin's sûl, or the "pole of the great" (large, powerful) god. It should come as no surprise to learn that one of names ascribed to Uuôden by the Norse was Iormunr, the Norse cognate of Irmin.

Before moving on to other godpoles, it is worth summarizing what is actually known of the Irminsûl. The Irminsûl at Eresburg was probably but one of many Irmin poles erected at various times. The Eresburg pole was distinguished, however, by its immense size. Even the adjoining temple structure took three days for Charlemagne's army to pull down and and plunder in 772 CE. It was a large wooden pillar with, at least, the face of Uuôden, chief of all the gods, carved as its head. To the Saxons it was an earthly representation of the heavenly tree known to the Norse as Yggdrasill, which stood at the center of heaven and all the worlds. During the eighth century, it was the Saxons' most holy site, hence the first target of Charlemagne's unholy war against the Saxons to bring them to Christianity. This was the Irminsûl of old.

Godpoles and Þunar

Uuôden was not the only god to whom sacred poles were erected. We have already seen this in Ibn Fadlan's account of the Rûs Vikings. As early as the first century of the Common Era, Tacitus wrote in his *Germania* of "Pillars of Hercules" among the early Frisians, who neighbored the Saxons:

> . . . the Frisii, who comprise a larger section and a smaller section, called respectively Greater and Lesser Frisii. . . . We have even ventured upon the Northern Ocean itself, and rumor has it that there are Pillars of Hercules in the far north."[123]

In accordance with the classical and medieval tradition of *interpretatio romana*, Hercules and Jupiter are synonymous with the Germanic thunder god Þunar in Latin writings. Pillars to Þunar were quite popular amongst the Germanic tribes and their veneration lasted for centuries. In the eighth century, just years after the Frisian Heathens slew the despot Archbishop Boniface, the ecclesiastical historian Willibald wrote a history of the life of St. Boniface. Of the Archbishop's many crimes against the Heathen Germans, none matched the depravity of his desecration of the Hessian "Jupiter Oak," a tree held sacred to Þunar:

> Now many of the Hessians who at that time had acknowledged the Catholic faith were confirmed by the grace of the Holy Spirit and received the laying-on of hands. But others, not yet strong in the spirit, refused to accept the pure teachings of the church in their entirety. Moreover, some continued secretly, others openly, to offer sacrifices to trees and springs, to inspect the entrails of victims; some practiced

> divination, legerdemain, and incantations; some turned their attention to auguries, auspices, and other sacrificial rites; while others, of a more reasonable character, forsook all the profane practices of the Gentiles [i.e., pagans] and committed none of these crimes. With the counsel and advice of the latter persons, Boniface in their presence attempted to cut down, at a place called Gaesmere, a certain oak of extraordinary size called in the old tongue of the pagans the Oak of Jupiter.[124]

Though Archbishop Boniface may have brought down Þunar's holy oak among the Hessians, the Heathen veneration of oak trees continued for many centuries. In 1883 Jacob Grimm attested to their continued reverence among the North Germanic peoples in the first volume of his work *Teutonic Mythology*:

> Several districts in Lower Saxony and Westphalia have until quite recent times preserved vestiges of holy oaks, to which the people paid a half heathen half Christian homage. Thus in the principality of Minden, on Easter Sunday, the young people of both sexes used with loud cries of joy to dance a ring round an old oak. In a thicket near the village of Wormlen, Paderborn, stands a holy oak, to which the inhabitants of Wormlen and Calenburg still make a solemn procession every year.[125]

Through one thousand years of Christian subjugation, the reverence of the holy trees endured. That itself speaks volumes of our people and their reverence for their gods.

The practice of raising poles or venerating oaks as part of Þunar's worship was by no means confined to the continental Germans. Even among the Norse Vikings, the image of Þunar was often carved into pillars along the hall's high-seat. The Icelandic *Book of Settlements* refers to such pillars of Þunar when it records of the Viking Thorolf that

> . . . when he'd come west as far as Breidafjord, he threw his high-seat pillars overboard. They had an image of Thor carved on them. Thorolf declared that

Thor would come ashore where he wanted Thorolf to make his home.[126]

The idea of godpoles supporting a *symbel* hall bears a certain semblance to the idea that the Irminsûl held up the heavens. In the Anglo-Saxon poem "Cædmon's Hymn," we find heaven compared to a roof:

> *Hé ærest scóp,   eorþan bearnum*
>
> *Heofan tó hrófe.   Hálig Scieppend*
>
> He erst shaped   for the earth's bairns
>
> Heaven as a roof,   the Holy Shaper[127]

It may be that the Þunar poles set up within the symbel hall symbolized the sustaining power of Þunar or the gods upholding the roof of the hall which stood in place of Heaven. If such is the case, symbel inherits a new measure of magnificence.

Godpoles and Frô

As has already been explored in chapter II, "Searching for Sahsnôt," the cults of Uuôden, Þunar, and Sahsnôt/Frô were inextricably bound together in ancient Heathendom. Therefore, it should come as little surprise that common cultic thew was held between them. Of such a tri-woven thread of thew, the veneration of godpoles and holy pillars was no exception.

As was the case with Þunar, in the Icelandic *Vatnsdæla Saga* we find that Frô was likewise associated with high-seat poles. The account begins with the goði Ingmund, a devotee to Frô, receiving a prophecy from a Lapp seeress regarding his future move to Iceland:

> The Lapp woman answered, "What I am saying will come to pass and, as a sign of this an amulet is missing from your purse – the gift which King Harald gave you at Havsfjord – and now it lies in the wood where you will settle, and on this silver amulet the figure of Freyr is carved and when you establish a homestead there, then my prophecy will be fulfilled."[128]

Just as Thorolf believed the high-seat pillars bearing the image of

Þunar would guide him where it was best for him to settle, a sign was given to Ingmund that his silver amulet of Frô would likewise turn up at the place in which he was to settle. Ingmund was none too thrilled at the idea of leaving his home in Norway to settle in the wilderness of the newly discovered Iceland. He sought counsel with King Harald, who had given him the image of Frô:

> The king answered, 'I cannot deny that the prophecy may have some purpose, and that Freyr might wish his amulet to come to rest in the place where he wants his seat of honor to be established.[129]

Harold, Ingmund's friend and King, gave good *râd*, a holy counsel from the gods, by means of his sacral office. As what is doomed must be, Ingmund eventually set sail for Iceland:

> Ingmund chose a site for his home in a very beautiful vale and prepared to build his homestead. He built a great temple a hundred feet long, and when he dug holes for the high-seat pillars, then he found the amulet as prophesied.[130]

There are two remarkable features in this account. First, while the image of Frô may not have been carved upon the high-seat pillars, as was the case with Þunar's image on Thorolf's pillars or Uuôden's image on the Irminsûl, the image of Frô is nonetheless connected to the erecting of pillars in a holy place. A second remarkable feature is the massive size of the temple of Frô. The reader may recall that when Emperor Charlemagne felled the Irminsûl, its adjoining temple was of such size that it took three days to lay waste to it. Whereas in Tacitus' day the Germanic peoples seemed to have venerated trees or even outdoor pillars marked out for particular gods, the Saxons some centuries later erected temples alongside their sacred pillars. Later, in the Viking age, these pillars were moved completely indoors, quite possibly reflecting the colder climate of Scandinavia or even a development in Heathen worship.

Regarding the temple at Uppsala, where Uuôden, Þunar, and Frô were worshipped together, one might expect to find some reference to a godpole such as the Irminsûl. While there is no such reference to a pole, there is preserved in Adam of Bremen's account mention of a holy tree:

> Near this temple stands a very large tree with wide-spreading branches, always green winter and summer. What kind it is nobody knows.[131]

As the Heathen Norse conceived of the Irminsûl as Yggdrasill, the world tree, it is only fitting that a tree would be found beside the temple dedicated to the three most venerated gods. A sacred grove is also recorded in connection to the temple at Uppsala. Adam of Bremen tells of the hanging of sacrifices from the trees within this grove, a detail which resembles that of offerings being hung upon godpoles by Ibn Fadlan:

> The sacrifice is of this nature: of every living thing that is male, they offer nine heads, with the blood of which it is customary to placate the gods of this sort. The bodies they hang in the sacred grove that adjoins the temple.[132]

The Pillar-cult in Medieval Christianity

Although pillar worship would decline with the onslaught of Christianity, its demise was not immediate. Grimm related an account, originally written in the early seventeenth century, of how godpoles were erected as part of the Hildesheim cathedral's pre-Easter celebration of Laetare. Saxon children were encouraged to desecrate these representations of Heathen gods. Grimm preserved this account:

> Letzner[133] relates: The Saturday after Laetare, year by year, cometh to the little cathedral-close of Hildesheim a farmer thereunto specially appointed, and bringeth two logs of a fathom long, and therewith two lesser logs pointed in the manner of skittles. The two greater he planteth in the ground one against the other, and a-top of them the skittles. Soon there come hastily all manner of lads and youth of the meaner sort; and with stones or staves do pelt the skittles down from the logs; other do set the same up again, and the pelting beginneth a-new. By these skittles are to be understood the devilish gods of the heathen, that were thrown down by the Saxon-folk when they became

Christian.[134]

It is of particular significance that, as late as the seventeenth century, the Christian Saxons were still encouraged to annually renounce the gods of their Heathen forebears. This is reminiscent of the renunciation formula found at the end of the *Capitulary of Carloman* in 743, issued by Charlemagne's uncle against the Saxons when he attempted to bring them under Frankish reach. A modification of the standard baptismal vows that require the renunciation of Satan and his works, this vow called for the further renunciation of not just the Saxon gods, but of Uuôden, Þunar, and Sahsnôt specifically:

> *Ec forsacho alum dioboles uuercum and uuordum thunaer ende uuoden ende saxnote ende allêm them unholdum the hira genotas sint.*
>
> I forsake all of the Devil's works and words, Þunar, Uuôden, and Saxnôt, and all of the hidden-ones that are their companions.[135]

As baptism was generally preformed at Easter, it fits that Saxon children would be encouraged to desecrate the ancient gods in the days preceding this Christianized tide. The casting off of the old gods would naturally come before the embracing of the new god.

Conclusion

Over the course of this chapter's shaping, the metaphorical Nietzschean hammer has morphed its form into that of the more familiar fiery axe-hammer of Anglo-Saxon Heathen lore. Under the auspices of rediscovering a more authentic representation of elder Heathenry, the axe's edge was set against the trunk of the Christian palm-tree at Externsteine. With the foreign weed's falling, we have found ourselves free to rediscover the Irminsûl's ancient root buried beneath the great Heathen godpole at Eresburg.

In following that root's course, well buried by the centuries that have passed since conversion, we have found, to the far north, high-seat pillars and *wéoh* (idols) wrought of wood held holy to Þunar and Frô. What might we make then from the appearance of so many oak, ash, and yew around and within the holy temples of old?

In writing of the Suebi, Tacitus observed that "all tribes of the same stock gather in a grove hallowed by the auguries of their ancestors and by immemorial awe" and that "the grove is the centre of their whole religion."[136] It is only natural that, in a many-godded belief, a many-treed grove should come to represent the host of gods gathered about above the branches and beneath the roots in so holy a stead. That a single godpole, pillar, or tree should be worshipped as a *wéoh* flows from this proto-Germanic thew. Such *wéoh* were, after all, the wooden men adorned with gifts by Óðinn himself in the *Hávamál*.[137]

The godpole-pillar-holy-tree was, to the elder Heathen, the gods made manifest among mankind. Likewise, our fore-elders held that Óðinn and his brothers shaped the first of our kind from the ash and the elm. The heart of Heathendom, the wood-wrought *wéoh*, was a deep rune (mystery) of the old religion: gods wrought of wood, made by men, who were, from wood, first wrought by gods. For those souls so bold as to undertake the reconstruction of our old Heathen religion, an eldritch wisdom would bid you to begin by carving poles, setting pillars, and by worshiping trees. The boughs above, bark about, and roots below belong to both gods and men.

HÉAFODCWIDE/HEADQUIDE/CHAPTER IV

BETWIXT BLOOD BESPATTERED BENCHES: THE LORD-RETAINER RELATIONSHIP IN THE LIFE OF HENGEST[138]

History has been unkind to Hengest. Bede's *Historia Ecclesiastica Gentis Anglorum*, Nennius' *Historia Brittonum*, Ælfred the Great's commission – the *Anglo-Saxon Chronicle*, Geoffrey of Monmouth's *Historia Regum Britanniae*, and even *Beowulf* stand among the more prominent reckonings of his life. Yet, when chronicled, Hengest has, with only early and rare exception,[139] been exclusively portrayed as a villain. Moreover, beyond these early medieval works, Hengest has simply been left unsung or altogether forgotten. Caxton and his Arthur-worshipping[140] ilk penned no great works of praise to honor Hengest, the father of their nation, to whose guile they owed their very tongue.[141] Even in the dreamy and decayed morass of folk memory,[142] there are no ancient-old, handed-down, or even partly remembered pagan folk songs[143] sung in pubs and alehouses by Morris dancers, mummers, or other misfits to recall Hengest and his importance in English history.

In one of the earliest surviving Anglo-Saxon records which makes mention of Hengest, we are given a glimpse of his royal pedigree. As noted by William Chaney in his work, *The Cult of Kingship in Anglo-Saxon England*, "In each kingdom the royal race – the *stirps regia* – which sprang from its founder provided the source from which the individual rulers were chosen, and beyond the earthly founder was the god who was the divine ancestor of almost every Anglo-Saxon royal house, Wóden."[144] In true Teutonic fashion, Hengest's lineage was linked to Wóden, the unpredictable and sometimes treacherous god of kingship, war, and magic. According to England's oldest ecclesiastical history,

> These new-comers were from the three most formidable races of Germany, the Saxon, Angles, and Jutes. . . . Their first chieftains are said to have been the brothers Hengest and Horsa. . . . They were the sons of Wictgils, whose father was Witta, whose father was Wecta, the son of [the god] Wóden, from whose stock sprang the royal house of many provinces.[145]

With these words Bede, the eighth century Northumbrian monk, preserved for posterity one of the earliest records of the Anglo-Saxon invasion that befell the former Roman province of Britannia some three centuries prior.[146] Completed circa 731 C.E., Bede's *Historia* described the arrival of three longships filled to the brim, as we might romantically imagine them, with Teutonic[147] warriors armed to the tooth with sword, spear, and shield – each and every one of them ready to wage war as soon as the hull's underside struck sand. From these three ships, dragon-prowed sea serpents laden with Anglo-Saxon cargo, sprang forth the now famous nation of the English. It was under the leadership of Hengest, and for a time his brother Horsa, that world history was forever changed.

The supposed scion of a god, the conqueror of a kingdom, and the founder of a nation, it seems unlikely that Hengest would, as a historical leader, be relegated to an obscure villainy. However, for manifold reasons this is exactly what happened to Hengest. Religiously, Hengest was a Heathen and thus held to the beliefs that his ancestors had known since time immemorial. His arrival was tolerated and welcomed by the Briton king Vortigern, perhaps a Pelagian heretic, but a Christian monarch in a Christian kingdom nonetheless. This, as one might imagine, scandalized early historians who were, without exception, ecclesiastics of some form or fashion. Politically, Hengest's descendants displaced the Briton lords and conquered all of Britannia save what is now known as Wales and Scotland. This did little to endear him to Welsh historians who, as monks, already detested his Heathen belief. Even Anglo-Saxon historians like Bede, being good churchmen, would do little more than mention Hengest as a matter of fact. Likewise, the Normans, in conquering the English, were hardly interested in having a hero-cult build up around an Anglo-Saxon king. Even as late as the Early Modern Era, the Tudors found it both religiously and politically expedient in breaking with Rome to exaggerate their supposed Arthurian lineage at the expense of their far more historical Anglo-Saxon heritage.[148]

Beyond this, Hengest offends our modern sensibilities. During his life Hengest gave and broke his oath, coveted revenge, conquered another people, brought Heathen worship back to a Christian country, and massacred, on two different occasions, halls filled with unwitting or unarmed men. And yet, if Hengest offends our modern sensibilities, it is because we do not live in his world. Only in the most distant and diluted sense are we heirs to the *weltanschauung*[149] of the Migration Era. "The elder Heathenry, its ethic and thew," is largely lost on us.[150] In his work, *The Germanization of Early Medieval Christianity*, the theologian James C. Russell coined the useful acronym BAVB (Beliefs, Attitudes, Values, and Behavior) and applied it to understanding the substratum of a converted people's worldview.[151] While BAVB is slow to change and often survives the more ceremonial circumstances of conversion by centuries, the BAVB that informed Hengest's ethical decisions has largely been uprooted and, if it survives in our collective conscience at all, it does so only in fragmented form.

Rather than weigh the rights and wrongs of Hengest's actions by our modern standards, this chapter will look to find Hengest at home in the Migration Era mead-hall and to measure his deeds within the lord-retainer relationship of his own age. In particular, the two hall-slaughters for which Hengest was responsible, that which befell the Frisian hall of Finnesburh in 434 CE and the far more infamous hall-slaughter at Amesbury in 455 CE, will be examined from this perspective. In doing so, this chapter will attempt to examine Hengest's decisions and deeds as a leader by means of a psycho-historiographical analysis of his life, an approach described in Peter Northouse's *Leadership: Theory and Practice.*[152] Furthermore, his own transition from thane, to reluctant-leader, to decisive-leader will be explored in terms of Jungian archetypes as these play an important role in the psychodynamic approach to understanding leadership.[153] By putting Hengest's leadership in its proper cultural, religious, and historical perspective, what at first appears to be treachery can be better understood as a gut wrenching moral dilemma, the burden of reciprocal obligations intrinsic to the lord/retainer relationship.

Toward Finnesburh: The Prehistory of Hengest

According to the comparative mythologist Joseph Campbell, the most fundamental mythic archetype is that of "the hero's journey."[154] It should come as no surprise then that the story of Hengest begins with his journey to the Frisian hall of Finnesburh. A thane of Hnæf, a Danish lord, Hengest has come with his liege to the hall of Hnæf's brother-in-law, Finn. One may very well ask how Hengest, a Jute, found himself in the service of a Scylding (Danish) lord to begin with. According to Tacitus, "Many noble youths, if the land of their birth is stagnating in a long period of peace and inactivity, deliberately seek out other tribes which have some war in hand. For the Germans have no taste for peace; renown is more easily won among perils, and a large body of retainers cannot be kept together except by means of violence and war."[155] During Hengest's early life, the Cimbrian peninsula was inhabited by numerous Germanic tribes. The Danes named their kingdom Denmark, the "Dane March." The Jutes inhabited a portion of the peninsula thereafter named Jutland, and the Angles held the kingdom of Angeln. It is sufficient to say that these tribes sometimes fought, sometimes intermarried, and for the most part shared a common language, culture, and religious belief.

At some point during the mid to late fourth century, Offa, the legendary king of the Angles, defeated the invading Myrgings, a Saxon tribe that had aligned itself with the much more powerful Swæfe (Suebi) tribe, at Fifeldor. According to the Anglo-Saxon *scóp*[156] who composed the poem *Widsið*, "Ever since, the [Angles] and the Swabians have kept it [their border] as Offa won it."[157] From that day until Hengest's own, it is quite possible then that war, and thus the opportunity to earn a name, had been wanting in the lands that neighbored the Jutes. The glory of war that the young Hengest sought would have to be found in the company of another king. Therefore, Hengest left the hall of his father and sought a place in the retinue of Hnæf, a Scylding lord.

Another possibility, put forward in the posthumously published work *Finn and Hengest* by J. R. R. Tolkien, is that Hnæf, the son of Hoc Half-Dane, had conquered part of Jutland. Whereas some Jutes had fled, Hengest and the remaining Jutes sided with Hnæf, swearing hold-oaths of fealty to him and joining his war band.[158] If this is the case, it is possible that Hengest was sent by his father to Hnæf's court to guarantee peace between the Danes and the Jutes. Either way, the young Hengest would have been restless to enter into the service of a liege lord for whom he might fight. If he were ever to prove himself amongst his peers and win the renown that he would need to someday become a lord in his own right, Hengest could not afford peace. So stood Hengest, perhaps just eighteen years old, when he accompanied Hnæf and fifty-nine other thanes[159] to the marsh laden land of Frisia, to Finnesburh, the fortress of Finn. One may very well imagine Hengest, at this point in the archetypical "hero's journey," to be what the depth psychologist Carol Pearson referred to as the *orphan* archetype. Having begun his "hero's journey," Hengest traded the safety of his homeland for the opportunity afforded by adventure.[160]

Betrayal at Finnesburh – Revenge and the Lord-Retainer Relationship

Between the *Finnesburh Fragment* and the details preserved in *Beowulf*, it appears as if Hnæf, a Danish lord, was invited to visit the hall of his Frisian brother-in-law, Finn, the son of Folcwald.[161] Finn had married Hnæf's sister, Hildeburh, and together they had a son, Friðuwulf, who was himself probably close to Hengest's age and no less eager than the Jutish *æðeling*[162] to prove himself in battle-play.

What stands out in this story is not that Finn and Hnæf somehow fell out and a great battle thus ensued, but that it happened in a mead-hall, a sacred space in the old Heathen religion. Furthermore, as Finn's guests and by marriage Finn's kinsmen, Hnæf and his men should have been afforded *frið*, an Anglo-Saxon word usually translated as "peace" though perhaps better understood as "the privilege of special protection . . . that we would today call sanctuary."[163] That a lord would break the *frið* of his own mead-hall and fall upon his guests would have been nearly unfathomable.

Thinking outside of the box, Tolkien proposed a theory for why this tragedy came about. The genius of Tolkien's reconstruction is that, not only does it provide insight into the story's background, but it does so by solving a problem that has plagued more than a few translators: an over-abundant use of the word *eoten* (Jutes). *Eoten*, the Old English word for Jute, is deceptively close to *Éoten*, the Old English word for giants, the enemies of the gods. This, in and of itself, has led to some rather humorous, even if unintentionally so, renderings of the *Beowulf* portion of this story.[164] While most translators have avoided this seemingly[165] gigantic translation pitfall, many have not known what to make of the ambiguous use of *eoten*. Indeed, if one reads the texts through in Old English, one cannot help but be baffled by the presence of this third *þeod* (tribal group) in what, at first, appears to be a Scylding-Frisian feud. Tolkien proposed that the reason the *eoten* are so ambiguously prevalent in the tale was due to their being Jutish retainers among both Finn's and Hnæf's thanes. Indeed, the dispute may have, at its heart, been between Jute and Jute, with Scylding and Frisian factions being drawn into the fray by means of the hold-oath bond that existed between lord and thane.

As Tolkien forthput, just as there were Jutes in Hnæf's retinue who had sworn fealty to him following his conquest of Jutland, there were in Finn's retinue Jutes who had fled Hnæf's onslaught and who now wished to avenge their fallen kinsmen upon such "traitors" as Hengest. At some point during Hnæf's stay, perhaps even before the invitation was issued, Finn's Jutish thanes had persuaded him to ambush his brother-in-law in the hall. And so, the *Finnesburh Fragment* abruptly begins:

> "Are the gables burning on this hall?" Hnæf answered him, the young and warlike king: "No eastern dawn is this, no dragon flying, nor are the gables burning on this hall. But now starts war; the carrion-birds shall sing, the grey-cloaked wolf shall yell, the spear resound,[166] shield answer shaft. Now shines the wandering moon behind the clouds . . . wake yourselves my warriors now . . . be noble of heart."[167]

In the midst of the night as Hnæf and his men lay asleep in the hall, Finn and his thanes set upon them as Grendels against their own Heorot, intending to make short work of the slaughter-craft they had set their hands to undertake. However, Hnæf rallied his retainers, among whom Hengest, Ordláf,[168] and Guðláf stand out prominently, and held back the attack at the hall's doors for five days before finally succumbing to the Frisian onslaught. It was here, in the Frisian assault upon Hnæf, that Hengest entered into the next phase of "the hero's journey", becoming what Pearson called the archetype of the *martyr*, the hero dedicated to a greater cause, in this case his liege-lord.[169]

Alas, the details of how Hnæf was slain or of how many of his thanes fell at their liege lord's side are lost between the *Finnesburh Fragment's* abrupt ending and the story's continuation in *Beowulf*. Among the dead though are Hnæf and Friðuwulf,[170] Finn's own son and Hnæf's nephew, who Tolkien believed took the side of his uncle. It is also quite likely that Sigeferþ[171] and Eaha,[172] two of Hnæf's thanes who held the hall door, as well as two of Finn's own thanes, Gárulf[173] and Guðere,[174] fell in the fray since they are not mentioned in *Beowulf*.

Before addressing the attack's aftermath, it is worth observing that the fragment's *scóp* makes specific mention of mead-drinking among Hnæf's thanes and its significance in the lord-retainer relationship. According to the poet, "Never have I heard of sixty staunch warriors who bore themselves in battle more honorably, nor have retainers ever better repaid[175] their mead."[176] It is important to understand that as their lord Hnæf would have been expected not only to reward his followers with the spoils of war but also to feed them. According to Tacitus, "Their meals, for which plentiful if homely fare is provided, count in lieu of pay."[177]

By partaking of the lord's mead, the Teutonic thane obligated himself to repay the lord in battle, even with his own life.[178] As noted by Tacitus, "to leave the battle alive after their chief has fallen means lifelong infamy and shame."[179] This sentiment is echoed in the words of the old thane Byrhtwold in "The Battle of Maldon," who "lifting his shield and shaking his spear" rallied the Anglo-Saxon troops against the Viking invaders whilst crying out, "Courage shall be firmer, heart all the keener, spirit the greater, as our might grows less. Here lies our leader, fatally cut down, the good man in the dust. Forever shall that man mourn who now thinks to leave the battle! I am far advanced in my years and I shall not leave. I intend to lie by the side of my dear lord."[180] Likewise, in that same poem, the duty of the thane to repay the lord's mead by avenging his liege's death is made explicitly clear in the exhortation of "the son of Alfric, a warrior young in years," who cries out for this fellow thanes to

Remember all the vows we raised in the mead-hall when we often pledged to do our part in battle. Now it can be seen who is truly brave. . . . Never shall the thanes among my people have cause to revile me, saying that I wanted to desert this army and seek my home, now that our leader lies cut down in battle. That is, to me, the greatest of grief . . . .[181]

It is with this *scild*[182] — an Anglo-Saxon word that meant both "debt" and, by means of an unpaid debt, "guilt"[183] — sitting heavily on Hengest's heart that the story resumes in *Beowulf*. Hengest has not only outlived his liege lord but, as perhaps the only god-sprung *æðeling* among the Danes, become their spokesman by default. In truth, the hall-slaughter had been fought to a draw. Hengest had inflicted so many casualties upon Finn's own thanes that the Frisian lord proposed a *friðowær*, a pledge to restore the *frið*. The conditions of the pledge were that, in exchange for their lives, Hnæf's surviving thanes were to remain in Finn's hall under his command ". . . and that no man should break the agreement by word or deed, or even complain of it in malice, although they would be following the slayer of their leader – they had to do this since they were without a lord. Then if any one of the Frisians were to recall the feud in provocative speech, the sword's edge should settle it."[184]

It was a moral dilemma in the truest sense. To have died beside his fallen lord would have certainly been heroic, yet Hengest's position in the retinue had changed. Though they were not his sworn men, they were, in a manner, still his charge. Their lives, which they would have gladly given, would have been lost for little. Though they could have died trying, Hengest knew that they were not in a position to avenge Hnæf's murder. The deontological burden then weighed upon preserving the lives of his fellow thanes. Weary from five days of defending the hall while hopelessly trapped in a foreign and hostile land, Hengest reluctantly agreed to Finn's offer.

Following the funeral[185] of Hnæf and Friðuwulf, many of the thanes departed to their homes in Frisia while Hengest weathered out the winter with Finn in the memory-haunted hall. It is at this point in the hero's journey that Hengest and Hnæf's thanes enter into what Pearson called the *wanderer* archetype.[186] The *scóp*'s description of Hengest's inner turmoil during this time is strikingly similar to the depression described in the Anglo-Saxon poem *The Wanderer*. In fact, the term *wrecca*, literally a "wretch," a word which meant "an exile, a thane who had outlived yet failed to avenge his lord," is used in both poems, being applied to both the wanderer and to Hengest. One may well imagine Hengest's own tormented and restless nights, filled with frustration, shame, and the burden of unfulfilled *scild*, to have matched those of the wanderer who described his misery thus, "When sleep and sorrow together bind the lone man in his wretchedness, to his mind it often seems that he embraces his lord, laying hands and head on his knee in homage as he used to do in former days . . . but then the friendless man wakes up again and sees before him nothing . . . ."[187]

All winter long Hengest nursed in his heart hatred for Finn, regretting the *friðowǽr* to which he had sworn. As thralls mended, scrubbed, and sanded the broken and blood-bespattered benches, Hengest turned his mind toward the means by which he might escape his oath to Finn, avenge Hnæf, and redeem his own honor. That opportunity presented itself when, "Hunlafing put the Battleflame, best of swords, on his lap."[188] The implication of this passage in the poem is that Hunlafing, a Dane, presented the Jutish Hengest with Hnæf's sword, "a blade well known among the [Jutes]" with which Hnæf had initially defeated the Jutes and thereby won Hengest's loyalty and service. In doing so, Hunlafing and the other Danes would have then set their hands upon the sword's hilt, their heads upon Hengest's knee, and given him their hold oaths. What a remarkable inversion. At that moment, the Danish thanes were no longer lordless, and Hengest as their liege would, in the event that another conflict arose, have to choose between this paternalistic lord-retainer oath to them and the *friðowǽr* he had made with Finn. By winter's end and summer's *icumen in*[189] such a crisis conveniently presented itself.

One may imagine that with summer's arrival Finn sought to celebrate the holytide of Bældæg[190] with a *symbel*. *Symbel*, which was generally held on the holy tides, consisted of ritualized mead-drinking[191] wherein toasts were raised to the gods, memory-horns[192] were dedicated to the ancestors, brags were made of one's past deeds, and boasts were made of deeds yet to come. [193] It was upon this occasion with Frisians, Danes, and Jutes all assembled in the hall that Ordláf and Guðláf were said to have "complained of the grim attack" the year before. In all likelihood they couched this "complaint" in a memory-horn raised to their own fallen lord. Under the pretext of honoring Hnæf, the Danish thanes were able to cast blame upon Finn for betraying him. With the *friðowær* thus broken by the Danes, Hengest, as their lord, drew the blade Battleflame and cut down Finn beside whom he was undoubtedly seated. The opportunity that he had hoped for, perhaps even conspired to create, had come. Finnesburh ran red once more as Hengest repaid his late lord's mead. As the archetypical hero's journey so wends, Hengest thus emerged from this conflict a harm-hardened *warrior-leader*.[194]

Within a matter of moments, the hall floor was littered with the corpses of Finn's thanes. The Danes and Dane-sided Jutes repaid the personal *scild* they owed to Hnæf for not avenging him when he had fallen. Yet, Hengest and his thanes were not the only symbelers in Finnesburh who owed *scild*. Finn's Frisian thanes and the Jutes who had sided with them had broken the mead-hall's *frið* when they laid siege upon Hengest and his men the year before. Finn's thanes thus owed a *scild* to the Danes and Dane-sided Jutes, one which could not be repaid in horses, slaves, silver, or gold-arm rings. In the taking of Finn and his men's lives, Hengest and his thanes collected upon the great debt they were owed.

Amesbury Understood

If it appears as if an inordinate amount of attention has been paid in this chapter to the less (in)famous Finnesburh hall-slaughter, this is because, unless one understands what transpired at Finnesburh and why, the hall-slaughter of Amesbury that followed some twenty-one years later can be only partially understood at best. Yet, as the Finnesburh hall-slaughter is entirely unmentioned by Nennius, William of Malmesbury, and Geoffrey of Monmouth, it has largely been overlooked by more modern historians. To this author's knowledge, there has been no significant treatment of these two events in which they have been considered together. That medieval Briton and Norman chroniclers made no mention of Finnesburh is hardly surprising. Such ecclesiastics were not concerned with recording Heathen history. A story of Heathens killing other Heathens, even if it was known to them, would have, in their esteem, been a waste of costly vellum and ink. It is fortunate for modern historians that the *scóps* who composed and the scribes who copied the *Finnesburh Fragment* and *Beowulf* felt otherwise.

In the decades that had passed since Finnesburh, the Cimbrian peninsula had flourished. In fact, it had flourished a bit too fully, with an overabundance of population that eventually led to war and famine. According to a tradition handed down from the earliest migrations,[195] runes were cast to determine the doom of those who must leave their homeland and find their fortune elsewhere.[196] As Wyrd[197] would have it, the lots fell in such a way as to indicate that Hengest and Horsa should lead a number of Angles, Jutes, and Saxons over Garsecg's arm[198] to the land of Britannia. Still, these first Anglo-Saxons, "a race hateful to both God and men,"[199] did not arrive there by accident; Vortigern, the king of the Britons, had sent for them. Following the withdrawal of Roman troops in 410 CE, the Romano-Celts of Britannia were ever increasingly harried by the Pictish horde that overflowed through the now undefended Hadrian's Wall. Therefore, Vortigern invited the Anglo-Saxons into his service to aid in the defense of his kingdom.[200]

That Hengest, Horsa, and their thanes served the king well is something that even Geoffrey of Monmouth, despite his contempt for the English, could not ignore. According to Geoffrey, "Upon their engaging, the battle proved very fierce on both sides, though there was but little occasion for the Britons to exert themselves [against the Picts], for the Saxons fought so bravely, that the enemy, formerly so victorious, were speedily put to flight."[201] To reward the brothers, Vortigern granted them lands and, with the king's permission, Hengest and Horsa sent word to their homeland to invite more Jutes, Angles, and Saxons to join them in their service to the king. Eighteen ships of Anglo-Saxons soon sailed unto Britannia's shores.

According to Geoffrey, Vortigern was smitten by the beauty of Hengest's daughter, Rowena, and as a gift to her father for marrying her, Hengest was given the country of Kent.[202] Furthermore, with the king's blessing, three hundred ships of Angles, Saxons, and Jutes were sent for so that the kingdom of Britannia might never have need to fear their Pictish enemies again.

Once the Anglo-Saxons had fulfilled their purpose and secured the kingdom, however, the Briton lords, who had grown uneasy about the numbers of Anglo-Saxon Heathens who had settled in their land, rebelled against their king. As Geoffrey admits,

> By their assistance he [Vortigern] vanquished his enemies, and in every engagement proved victorious. Hengest in the meantime continued to invite over more and more ships, and to augment his numbers daily. Which when the Britons observed, they were afraid of being betrayed by them, and moved the king to banish them out of his coasts. For it was contrary to the rule of the gospel that Christians should hold fellowship, or have intercourse, with pagans. Besides which . . . pagans married the daughters and kinswomen of Christians.[203]

Led by Vortimer, Vortigern's son, the Britons assailed the Anglo-Saxons. Out of fear that they themselves might be betrayed, the Britons broke the *frið* that had existed between them and the Anglo-Saxons and, apparently, attacked the Anglo-Saxon lands. It is worth noting that this was an act of treason against the king. The Briton lords who sought to usurp Vortigern and drive out the Anglo-Saxons were breaking the very hold-oaths they had given to their king. The Anglo-Saxon term for such an oath-breaker is *wærloga*, "one who lies in swearing an oath," a word from which the modern English warlock is derived. Lest the significance of this be overlooked, it is important to understand that this was civil war in the truest sense. Vortimer and Hengest were both kinsmen of the king, the former being his son, the latter being his father-in-law. Likewise, this was a war between competing factions of thanes, as Hengest and Horsa would have sworn hold-oaths to Vortigern then they had entered into his service.

After four bloody battles, the betrayed Anglo-Saxons reluctantly returned to Germania. Alas, Horsa did not return with Hengest, as he had been hewn down in battle while defending the Anglo-Saxon stronghold. Worse yet, the Anglo-Saxons were forced to leave behind their wives, the aforementioned "daughters and kinswomen of Christians" that Geoffrey referred to. This sexual aspect to the civil war deserves more attention than it has hitherto been given.

The idea of Saxon Heathens bedding and wedding Christian Briton women vexed Geoffrey and his contemporaries. In Geoffrey's chaste and monkish mind, the marriage of Heathen men to Christian women represented an assault upon Christendom and the defilement of Christian purity. To borrow an analogy drawn from Gildas, "the vintage, once so fine, [had] degenerated and become bitter."[204] Thus, the Anglo-Saxons not only represented a religious threat to the Briton lords, but also a scourge of humiliation to their manhood.

In adding the detail that the Anglo-Saxons left "their wives and children behind them, [and] returned back to Germany,"[205] Geoffrey no doubt thought that he was being clever by underscoring what was surely an act of Anglo-Saxon cowardice. Yet, it is unlikely that the Anglo-Saxons would have left their wives and children behind out of choice. Tacitus is careful to note the importance of women in ancient Teutonic society. Far from the chattel they would become centuries after conversion, women were afforded special prominence in early Teutonic culture. According to Tacitus,

> It stands on record that armies already wavering on the point of collapse have been rallied by the women, pleading heroically with their men, thrusting forward their bared bosoms, and making them realize the imminent prospect of enslavement – a fact which the Germans fear more desperately for their women than for themselves. . . . They believe that there resides in women an element of holiness and a gift of prophecy; and so they do not scorn to ask their advice or regard their replies lightly.[206]

No, for Hengest and his men to have left their wives and children behind would have certainly meant they had no other choice, perhaps being entirely cut off from the camp where their families resided.

Following Vortimer's unexplained death, for which the Britons would later libel Lady Rowena's memory and accused her of poisoning him,[207] Hengest, accompanied by his son Æsc, returned to Britannia with their host to reclaim the Kentish lands that they had been given by King Vortigern. Though Vortimer was dead, the Briton lords cowed the king and persuaded him to meet his father-in-law with an army rather than with open arms. Surprised by this, Hengest decided to repay the king's treachery in kind. He sent word to Vortigern to stay his hand. He claimed that the Anglo-Saxons had merely returned to offer their service to the king once more and, if it was his wish, they would return to their homeland afterwards. They agreed to meet the king and his men at a monastery on the upcoming May Day to share one final *symbel* before they departed.

It had been twenty years since Hengest's experience at Finnesburh, yet that moment had made an indelible mark upon his life. With the mead-horn held out toward him, Hengest's heart turned toward the memory of his betrayed and slain brother, Horsa. Likewise, the Anglo-Saxons thanes who sat in the hall with him remembered the wives, daughters, and sons they had been forced to leave behind. Hengest and his thanes would, once more, lay claim to the *scild* owed to them. Taking the *symbel* horn in his hand, Hengest turned toward Vortigern, as if to wish him a *wes hál*.[208] However, words of well-wishing did not fall from the now seasoned Jute's tongue. According to Nennius,

> After [the Britons] had eaten and drunk, and were much intoxicated, Hengest suddenly vociferated, '*Nimed eure Saxes!*' [take out your knives] and instantly his adherents drew their knives, and rushing upon the Britons, each slew him that sat next to him, and there was slain three hundred of the nobles of Vortigern. The king being a captive purchased his redemption, by delivering up the three provinces of East, South, and Middle Seax, besides other districts at the option of his betrayers.[209]

Hengest then sat down, sipping his mead, accompanied by his thanes and the cooling corpses of some three hundred Briton dead. The honeyed wine was sweet to the taste. In that hall Hengest, felt satisfied, justified even.

The Dryhten's[210] Doom[211] - Leadership and Heroism Reconsidered

With this dreadful deed, Hengest was thenceforth branded a villain by Brittonic and English historians. Yet, when understood within the context of Germanic *þeaw*, legal custom,[212] Hengest acted not only within his own lawful right, but within the religio-socio-historical expectations and traditions of his day. With a breath, Hengest had avenged his brother's death and atoned for the forced abandonment of hundreds of women and children. As their lord, the *scild* for the harsh treatment that the wives and children of his men would have surely endured at the hands of hostile Christian Celts had, undoubtedly, pressed with unrelenting pain upon his breast when he sailed, hopelessly outnumbered, once more over cruel Garsecg's arm to an ill-wanted homecoming. Hengest had fulfilled the utmost obligation that the living might owe the dead: he had honored their memories. One may thus think of the blood that flowed in Amesbury that day as sweet mead, offered in propitiation to the spirits of so many loved ones who, every night, unfailingly, had haunted him. Meted and measured by the old belief, it would be hard to imagine a soul more sanctified by his deeds than Hengest.

It is difficult to say whether or not this moment marked Hengest's transition from the *warrior-leader* archetype to that of the *magician-leader*.[213] Pearson's envisioning of the *magician-leader* is quite agreeable in a bloodless and pleasingly sunny day sort of way – a "let's all work together for the common good" sort of chap. However, this is hardly the understanding that Hengest or his thanes would have had of a *magician-leader*. Like Pearson, Hengest and his contemporaries would have agreed that the ultimate archetype for leadership was that of the *magician-leader*, yet they would have drawn their understanding of that archetype from Wóden. A fickle god of kingship, war, and magic, Wóden was known in Germanic and Norse mythology for his extensive use of deception, even to deadly purposes. Hengest had not fallen far from Yggdrasill.[214]

The Hero's Journey Ends

Hengest's "hero's journey" begins and, for the purpose of this chapter, ends betwixt the blood bespattered benches of Finnesburh and Amesbury. In drawing upon Carol Pearson's ideas concerning the Jungian/Campbellian "hero's journey," Hengest's progression from follower to leader can be seen in terms of his passing through the archetypes of *Orphan*, *Martyr*, *Wanderer*, *Warrior Leader*, and, arguably, that of *Magician Leader*. Still, Hengest's bloody legacy is one that is not easily reconciled with our society's largely Judeo-Christian morality and *weltanschauung*. As such, Hengest's place in history has for centuries challenged both ecclesiastical chroniclers and modern scholars alike.

Hengest's use of deception should not be mistaken for mere consequentialism, however. Though the ends may very well have justified the means, lying to one's enemies was a perfectly acceptable practice according to Teutonic *þéaw*. Though composed centuries after Hengest joined his ancestors in the mound, the Norse *Hávamál*, a poem of gnomic verse, offered the following counsel: "If you've one whom you don't trust but from whom you want nothing but good, speak fairly to him but think falsely, and repay treachery with lies. . . . you should laugh with him and disguise your thoughts, a gift should be repaid with a like one."[215]

This notion of a gift being "repaid with a like one" hearkens back to the reciprocal nature of social obligation in Teutonic society. Just as a thane was obligated to repay his lord's mead, one who had committed a wrong was in debt and owed *scild* to the offended party. If the wrongdoer would not make proper restitution, it was expected that the wronged would settle the debt by "repaying" the wrongdoer in kind (treachery with lies). Thus, it was *þéaw*, rather than opportunism, that set Hengest's hand to hilt. More than consequentialism, Hengest was driven by a deep deontology, one that lay at the very foundation of Migration Era society: the lord-retainer relationship.

If this chapter has been overly sympathetic toward the Jutish *dryhten*, it has done so to counterbalance a long and honorable tradition of bias begun by Gildas and perfected by Geoffrey of Monmouth. As a psycho-historiographical analysis of Hengest's life, this work has drawn inspiration from John Gardner. Gardner, in his novel *Grendel*, gave cause to re-evaluate the motives of Heorot's monster by presenting the Anglo-Saxon epic from an entirely different perspective, that of Grendel.[216] It has been this chapter's aim to present Hengest's life and leadership within the cultural, religious, and historical context of the Migration Era society in which he lived. In doing so, it may be that Hengest emerges from the mead-hall, not as the monster we once imagined him to be, but rather as a bloodstained hero.

HÉAFODCWIDE/HEADQUIDE/CHAPTER V

DRAGONS AMONG THE DEAD: TRANSLATION AND COMPARATIVE ANALYSIS OF OLD ENGLISH, OLD NORSE, AND CONTINENTAL TEXTS AS THEY PERTAIN TO DEPICTIONS OF SHAPESHIFTERS, DRAGONS, AND THE DEAD IN ANGLO-SAXON HEATHEN RELIGION

Nay, this no eastern dawning, not here a drake flieth, nor here in this hall do the gable-horns burneth.[217]

Finnesburh Fragment

Dragons among the Gems

Calvert Watkins, in his monumental work *How to Kill A Dragon: Aspects of Indo-European Poetics*, described the poetic formula of the Indo-European dragon-slaying myth as "the central theme of a proto-text, a central part of the symbolic culture of the speakers of Proto-Indo-European."[218] In surveying the "cultic hymns and mythological narratives, epics and heroic legends, spells and incantations"[219] of the Vedic Indians, ancient Iranians, Hittites, Greeks, Slavs, Germanic tribes, and Scandinavians, Watkins was able to demonstrate the antiquity and enduring importance of the dragon-slaying myth in Indo-European religion and culture.[220]

One should not be surprised then to find the dragon-slaying myth also present among the Anglo-Saxons, themselves a Germanic people who, as the grave goods of the Sutton Hoo ship burial attest, were in close contact with their Nordic neighbors. What may be surprising, however, is just how often dragons appear in the fragmentary traces of the Anglo-Saxon Heathen religion that have survived. In appraising the treasures of the Anglo-Saxon corpus that relate to the old religion, it is difficult to find among its gems a myth, charm, or cultic practice that does not involve a dragon. In searching out *Beowulf*, the *Finnesburh Fragment*, *Solomon and Saturn* both *I* and *II*, the *Lacnunga*, or the *Anglo-Saxon Chronicles* – the bulk of the Anglo-Saxon corpus as it pertains to English paganism[221]– one is entirely unable to escape the dragon's eerie looming.

However, the association of dragons with the Anglo-Saxons is by no means limited to their own accounts. The Welsh chronicler Geoffrey of Monmouth, in *The History of the Kings of Britain*, preserved in his work a tradition known as the "Prophecies of Merlin," a curious blending of history and myth which pitted the red dragon of the Celts against the white dragon of the Angles in a battle for Britannia itself. Likewise, on the Bayeux Tapestry, which depicted the Norman victory at the Battle of Hastings, dragon banners are seen flying among the Anglo-Saxon host. In fact, it would be beneath the dragon banner that Harold Godpinson, the last Anglo-Saxon king, would fall in 1066. Thus, from the beginning of the Anglo-Saxon era to its end, the dragon remained a prominent religio-cultural motif.

It is the aim of this chapter to show that the near inescapable appearance of dragons in what remains of Anglo-Saxon Heathen lore is not accidental but rather a definable feature of the old religion. Furthermore, it will be established that the dragon, as an emblem of the sacral king, represented the ancient dead, interred within the earth, from which the king derived not only his claim to kingship but also the magical-divine luck upon which the bounty of the harvest and his victory in war were ultimately dependent. To conclude, this chapter will consider the significance of these details as they relate to Beowulf's own burial as it may have been understood by the saga's original Heathen audience.

Drakes and Wyrms: Dragons Defined

In his recently published article "Dragons in the Eddas and in Early Nordic Art," Paul Acker has, in great detail, chronicled the evolution of the medieval dragon from its originally envisioned slithering, venom-spewing, serpentine form to that of the more familiar winged, four-legged, fire-breathing terror of the sky. As the *wyrm* (ON: *ormr*), the dragon was nearly indistinguishable from an ordinary serpent, marked only by its enormous size. In fact, the words *wyrm* and *ormr* were regularly used to refer to serpents both mundane and mickle alike. In its winged, eventually-four legged, and fire-breaking form, the dragon was generally referred to as a drake (OE: *draka*, ON: *dreki*). Yet of the two terms, *wyrm* and drake, only the former belongs to Teutonic antiquity. As noted by Acker, "The *Poetic Edda* . . . never calls Fáfnir a *dreki*, only an *ormr*; the only *dreki* in the *Poetic Edda* is Níðhöggr, the winged dragon in hell that is likely a late, perhaps even Christian, addition to the otherwise pagan cosmology outlined in *Völuspá*."[222]

Whereas the imagery of the *wyrm* was indigenous to Germanic Heathendom, the imagery of the fire-drake, however, was an import. The Latin *draco* merged with the Teutonic traditions due to the influence of ecclesiastical hagiography and later French and German romances,[223] eventually emerging as the Anglo-Saxon *draca* and the Norse *dreki*. Over time, and particularly after conversion, the drake would win out over the *wyrm,* and the serpent would be largely reduced to a synonym employed for alliterative purposes.

Even so, the transition from *wyrm* to *draca* was not accomplished overnight. In *Beowulf* a dual imagery is employed with *wyrm* used some eighteen times to describe Beowulf's bane while *draca* is utilized eleven times in that same encounter.[224] And whereas the dragon that Beowulf battles is said to be a winged fire-breathing beast, it is its venomous bite which ultimately undoes the hero. This interchangeable use of *wyrm* and drake imagery is best seen in lines 2711b-2715a where the poet in depicting the bite of the earth-drake (*eorðdraca*) recounts the painful effects of its poison: "Then the wound began, that the earth-drake ere wrought him, to swelter and to swell. He soon found that, in his breast, bale-evil welled, the venom within."[225] The question should be asked then, does the distinction between the slithering *wyrm* and the flying drake matter when discussing the mythic significance of dragons in Heathen lore? To determine this, three *wyrm*-slaying myths will be briefly examined.

Unlike other parts of the world, Europe can only claim a few indigenous poisonous snake species, all of which fall under the category of adder. It is worth considering the significance that the creature, though uncommon, held in the old Heathen religion. In what is often called "The Nine Herbs Charm," the supreme-god of the Germanic religion, Wóden, is said to have slain such a serpent before granting mankind the gift of the nine healing herbs which "have main (power) against nine venoms." In this curious tale, which is only preserved in a single Anglo-Saxon text, a "*wyrm* came sneaking. It slit a man. Then took up Wóden nine glory-tines,[226] and slew with them the adder *(næddran)* so that she, into nine [pieces], flew. . . . that she never would bend-way (slither) into house."[227] Whilst the identification of the *wyrm* with the adder *(næddran)* is clearly made in this account, what may be more nebulous is the exact nature of the *næddran*. The detail, "that she would never bend-way into house," certainly favors an interpretation of a mundane snake. Nonetheless, it seems unlikely that Wóden would have troubled himself with the *wyrm* were it simply farmhouse vermin.

In the Norse *Völuspa* there is an account of the god Þórr (OE: Þunor, NE: Thor) battling the dragon Jǫrmungandr at *Ragnarǫk*, the Reckoning of the Gods, an end-of-days encounter between the *Æsir* (OE: *Ése*) and the *Jǫtnar* (OE: *Eotenas*). In the passage Jǫrmungandr is regarded as a *wyrm*, an adder, and even more surprisingly, a wolf. As it appears in the *Poetic Edda*,

> Yawning sky above   the Earth's Girdle,
>
> gapes its ugly jaws   the *wyrm* (*orms*) in the heights.
>
> Then shall Óðin's son   the *Wyrm* (*ormi*) meet.
>
> The death of the wolf (*vargs*)   is Viðar's kinsman.
>
> Then comes in the renowned   son of Hlóðyn.
>
> Óðin's son goes   to war against the *Wyrm* (*orm*) [alt. wolf (*ulf*)].
>
> Strikes him with mood[228]   Middle-Earth's warder.
>
> All men shall   their homesteads clear.
>
> Goes nine feet   Fjörgyn's bairn,
>
> barely from the adder (*naðri*)   not fearing scorn.
>
> Sun turns swart,   fold sinks into mere.

> From heaven turns   the bright stars.
>
> Rage both steam   and corpse-fire.
>
> Heat dances high   against heaven itself.[229]

The significance of the *wyrm* being described as a wolf (ON: *varg*, *ulf*) is a legal one. In Anglo-Saxon society the term *wearg* or *wulf* designated not only a wild beast of the woods but also an outlaw, one whose crimes had put them beyond the bounds of human society and the security (frith) afforded to those therein. More to the purpose at hand, we find a dragon described as both a *wyrm* and an adder (*naðri*). In this passage the dragon is described as an "earth girdler," a reference to the belief that Jǫrmungandr, having been tossed into the sea by Wóden, grew so enormous that it encircled the earth. And while the poem would seem to establish the dragon as a sea-serpent, it is also said to have "gaped its ugly jaws" in "the yawning sky above . . . in the heights," a depiction which would seem to ascribe the power of flight to the serpent, an attribute which characteristically belonged to the fire-drake. Thus, while Jǫrmungandr is never said to be a *dreki*, it would appear that, by the time of the *Edda*'s composing, the Teutonic *wyrm* had already begun to absorb the abilities of the Roman drake.

The mortally wounded dragon-slayer is a motif which re-emerges time and time again in Heathen belief, both in its original Heathen form and in its medieval Christian manifestation.[230] The similarity between Þórr and Beowulf, as noble wights[231] who defeat a dreadful dragon but who, nonetheless, succumb to its venom, is well-trodden terrain in the realm of Anglo-Saxon studies. Even so, it is worth mentioning that a nigh identical account appears in an Anglo-Saxon text, only slightly obscured by an unnecessary and awkward biblical allusion,[232] and the use of the *heiti*[233] "Wandering Wolf" to refer to Wóden's whelp[234] and his dragon-doom. As the account appears in the far-less-explored but, nonetheless, mythically rich *Solomon and Saturn II*,

> So was hight the mere's   seafarer
>
> Wandering Wolf (*weallende Wulf*),   couth among the men-tribes
>
> of the Philistines,   friend of Nimrod.

He on field slew   those twenty-five

drakes (*dracaena*) at daybreak,   and then death fell upon him.

For-then (therefore) that fold may not   any man,

that mark-stead,   [any] man seek,

bird fly-over,   no more the field's neat (cow or ox).

Thence the venom-kind (*átercynn*)   erst worthed (came to be),

widely awakened   that which now welling

through venom's breath   goes within, makes room.

Yet still his sword shineth   swith (exceedingly) it was sheened (polished),

and over the burial-mound   brightly its hilt.[235]

The thunder god's bittersweet encounter with the dragon is, although artificially multiplied, clearly captured in this account. In noting that it was through the slaying of the drake(s) that the "venom-kind (*átercynn*) erst worthed (came to be)," the author may have very well have alluded to the nine-venoms (*nygon attrum*) which sprang forth from the *wyrm* that Wóden had, in "The Nine Herb Charm," hewn into so many sections. Although it is certainly conjecture, it may be that the myth originally belong to the Wolf-god Wóden before becoming the cultural-cultic inheritance of Þunor, the Welling (raging, Wóden-ing) Wolf.

The question has been asked, did the distinction between the slithering *wyrm* and the flying drake matter when discussing the mythic significance of dragons in Heathen lore? Within the written record, the imagery of the *wyrm* and the drake is, even in the earliest sources, already hopelessly blurred. What would seem to matter more is the application of the dragon myth to sacred story-telling, the perseverance of which is well attested to even after conversion. As seen in the Old High German poem *Mûspelli*, the myth of the thunder-god mortally wounded by the defeated *wyrm* was easily translated into hagiography. In a clearly Christian interpretation of that religion's own *Ragnarǫk,* the battle between the Old Testament prophet Elias and the New Testament Antichrist echoes that of

Þunor/Beowulf/Wulf's own encounter with the dragon.

Lines 37-39 of the *Mûspelli* set the stage for the apocalyptic conflict revealing that

> This I heard reckoned   [by] the world-right-wise,
>
> that shall the Antichrist   with Elias battle.
>
> The wolf (*uuarch*) is weaponed,   then war begins to upheave between them.

Although the Antichrist is not referred to in this poem as a *wyrm* or drake, the imagery of the dragon-wolf-outlaw, as represented in the OHG term *uuarch*, has already been attested to in the Old Norse *vargs* and Anglo-Saxon *wearg*. That the Antichrist was imagined as a wolf by no means excludes a more draconic interpretation. As is seen in lines 44-55 of the *Mûspelli*, the eschatological aftermath of the thunder-god/wolf-hero's death was perfectly preserved in the otherwise Christian account:

> The Antichrist   standeth by the Old-fiend,
>
> standeth by Satan,   who shall forsench (forsake) him.
>
> Therefore shall he on the war-stead   wounded fall
>
> and in that way   victoryless become.
>
> But weeneth many that   [are] god-men (*gotmanno*)
>
> that Elias in the war   slaineth will be.
>
> So that Elias's blood (*pluot*) into Earth (*erda*) dripeth,
>
> so burneth the burgs   no beam standeth
>
> anywhere on Earth,   rivers drieth,
>
> the moor swalloweth itself,   flame sweltereth the heavens,
>
> Moon falleth,   burneth Middle-Earth.
>
> No stone standeth   when fareth strafe[236]-day in the land.

The imagery of the world poisoned and, thus, brought to utter ruin upon the death of the thunder-god/wolf-hero is clearly presented in the *Völuspa, Solomon and Saturn II,* the *Mûspelli*, and on a smaller and more localized scale, it is alluded to in *Beowulf* by means of the prophesied doom that would befall the Geats following the wolf-king's death. Yet, in the most Christianized of these accounts, the *Mûspelli*, an intriguingly archaic vestige of Heathen lore is preserved.

The *Mûspelli*'s reference to god-men (*gotmanno*) is one of the few non-Scandinavian surviving cognates to the Old Norse *góði*, a word which is oft translated as "heathen priest." Likewise, *pluot* is cognate with the Anglo-Saxon and Old Norse *blót*, a word which means "sacrifice." Furthermore, Earth (*Erda*) could, in ancient Germanic poetry, refer equally to the ground or to a goddess. In the *Völuspa*, Þórr is said to be the son of Hlóðyn (*mögr Hlóðynjar*), Fjörgyn's bairn (*Fjörgynjar burr*). Though the etymology of Hlóðyn and Fjörgyn have been dutifully disputed elsewhere, these *heiti* are generally agreed to refer to an earth-goddess elsewhere referred to as Jǫrð, a name which translates directly into English as "Earth" and which appears in Old High German as *Erda*. That the god-men, the Heathen priests, understood that thunder-god/wolf-hero's death was a *pluot in erda kitriufit*, "blood-sacrifice [that] into Earth dripeth" is then most certainly a borrowing from an older, pre-Christian, oral tradition regarding sacral kingship – a theme which will be extensively explored later in this chapter.

Based upon these three stories and that of *Beowulf*, which will be elaborated on in the pages to come, it would seem as if the distinction between the slithering *wyrm* (ON: *ormi*) and the flying drake (*dreka*) is, while a matter of historical interest, mythologically superficial. The particular form that the dragon happens to take is second to the religio-magical function that the dragon fulfills. Nevertheless, as will soon be seen, though the *wyrm*-drake distinction is not essential, the lich or "likeness" of the dragon is of tremendous importance in uncovering the vestiges of Heathen belief preserved by post-Conversion scribes.

Beneath the Hide: The Dragon as Shapeshifter

Of the Germanic dragons whose origins are recounted in Heathen lore, remarkably few are said to have been born as such.[237] In the Old Norse *Eddas* and sagas, only Jǫrmungandr[238] the *Midgarðsormr*[239] stands out prominently as having sprung from the womb as a *wyrm*. In the *Prose Edda* it is said that Jǫrmungandr was born to the giantess Angrboða and fathered by the god-giant Loki. And in late English legend, the Lambton Worm is said to have come to maturity sometime after being caught in a river and cast down a well.

Yet in several Norse sagas, dragons are depicted as mortal men who, through magical means, transformed themselves into such. In *Hálfdanar Saga Eysteinsson*, a battle is fought between the *víkingar* armies of Hárekr, king of Bjarmaland, and Earl Skúla. During the fray, the king suddenly shifted his shape. As it appears in the saga, "Then turned Hárekr into a flying-drake and struck Skúla with his tail."[240] In *Gǫngu-Hrólfs Saga*, an even more elaborate account of shapeshifting is recalled, wherein it is said of Grímr, a *berserkr*,[241] that "He had sometimes become a flying-drake, and sometimes a *wyrm*, a boar and bull, or other scathing monsters."[242] Another *berserkr*, Falr, is said to have "braided himself into a flying-drake's lich" in *Viktors Saga ok Blávus* while fighting the saga's namesake.[243] And in *Bærings Saga*, Skadevalldr is said to have changed into a "drake's lich"[244] (*drekaliki*) "so horrible that any of them which were on land dared not see it."[245]

Of even greater interest to Anglo-Saxon study is an episode which unfolded in the *Sörla Saga Sterka*. In a battle against Sörli, a Swedish atheling, a *berserkr* named Tófi transformed himself into a dragon. According to the saga, "Braided (*brást*) he then into a drake's likeness (*líking*), because he was a mickle skin-strong-man (*hamrammaðr*)."[246] While the means of this "braiding" into a dragon's likeness is not evident in a literal translation, *hamrammaðr* is often interpreted as meaning "wizard" or one who employs sorcery to shapeshift. It is this very idea of "braiding" ones "likeness" or lich by means of a magical "skin" that is preserved in the Anglo-Saxon poem *Solomon and Saturn I* and, quite possibly, in the story of Beowulf's battle with Grendel.

In lines 146-154 of the poem *Solomon and Saturn I*, "the word of God" is said to have the power to "bring to flight . . . the heap of the wicked . . . though they wondrously . . . braideth their blee (alter their appearance), and, about their bone-coves, feather-skins (*feðerhoman*) receive. Sometimes they wend in a *wyrm*'s lich (*wyrmes líc*)."[247] There are a number of noteworthy particulars in this passage that deserve special attention.

The first, while not pertaining directly to dragons, does describe a feature of shapeshifting that is attested to in Norse mythology – that being the donning of feather-skins. This phrase parallels line 3 of the Old Norse *Þrymskviða* where Loki asks the goddess Freyja if she would *jaðrhams léa*, "loan" him her feather-skin. In line 5 of the same poem, the feather-skin is referred to as *fjatrhamr*, which corresponds to the Anglo-Saxon *feðerhoman* mentioned here. To add to this, the word *onfóð* means "receive, accept." This is significant in that the feather-skin is, in both accounts, not the property of the wearer but rather something that is loaned or given by an external agency, most likely the goddess known to the Anglo-Saxons as Fríge whose Norse counterpart is Freyja.

This belief in donning the skins of an animal in order to assume its shape is by no means limited to feathered garments. In the *Völsunga Saga*, Sigmund and his son-nephew Sinfjötli (OE: Fitela) are said to discover a home with two men, surrounded by gold rings, sleeping therein, "with wolf-skins hanging (*úlfahamir hengu*) in the house over them."[248] In putting on the wolf-skins, Sigmund and Sinfjötli become werewolves in the truest sense. With the hides came an increased strength and a murderous savagery, the blinding rage of which culminated in Sigmund turning against Sinfjötli and nearly killing him. This idea of wearing hides to become wolves may be further preserved in the mentioning of the *úlfhéðnar* in the poem *Hrafnsmál*[249] as well as in the *Vatnsdæla Saga*.[250] The *úlfhéðnar* (singular: *úlfhéðinn*) were warriors who wore a type of sleeveless hooded shirt known as a *heðinn* (plural *héðnar*). As wolf-shirts, the term *úlfhéðnar* invites comparison to the bear-shirts of legendary berserkers (ON: *berserker*).[251]

As devotees of Óðinn (OE: Wóden), a god whose name springs from the Proto-Germanic *woþ-*, "madness," the *berserker* could enter into a frenzied state of battle-ecstasy known as the *berserksgangr*.[252] In this state a *berserker* possessed superhuman strength and stamina, bloodlust, and near invulnerability. While the Norse sagas do not explicitly make it clear that these warriors donned bear hides to summon the *berserksgangr*, their behavior indicates as much. As noted by Kris Kershaw, "From the literary and iconographic evidence it would seem that the *berserkr* and the *úlfhéðinn* are the same type of cultic warrior. . . . The warrior as wolf is Indo-European; the warrior as bear seems to be Germanic."[253] It would seem then that feather-skins (OE: *feðerhoman*, ON: *fjatrhamr*), wolf-skins (ON: *úlfahamir*), and bear-shirts (ON: *berserker*) each belong to the same magical tradition of shapeshifting. But what of dragons?

Before proceeding further with the passage from *Solomon and Saturn I*, another brief detour must be made. In *Beowulf* there is an unusual rendering of the hero's battle with Grendel that may allude to the skin-wearing shapeshifter motif. In his reckoning of the battle to Hygelác, king of the Geats, Beowulf offered a rather remarkable detail, one which is not mentioned elsewhere in the text. After describing Grendel as a "bloody-toothed bane" (*bona blódigtóð*), Beowulf then told his king of a glove (*glóf*) that the monster gripped into which it sought to stuff the hero.[254] According to Beowulf, the glove hung "wide and wondrously" (*síd ond syllíc*), "skillfully all adorned with devil's crafts and drake's fell" (*dracan fellum*).[255] From the account it is difficult to discern whether the glove is merely a poetic kenning intended to represent the monster's gaping maw, whether it refers to Grendel's outstretched hand, or whether it is a magical sack of some sort. Yet, if it does represent either Grendel's mouth or his hand, then the description of it being "adorned by devil's craft and dragon's fell" may indicate that Grendel was wearing a magical garment crafted out of dragon skin.

To return to *Solomon and Saturn I*, the phrase "wondrously . . . braideth their blee" is worth looking at twice. The use of the word *syllice*, here translated as "wondrously," is identical to the *syllíc* used to describe Grendel's dragon skin glove. Even more interesting is the use of the word *bregdað*, which is translated in this passage as "braideth." The Old English *bregdan* originally meant "to change, to move quickly, to move to and fro, or to weave" and survives in Modern English as "to braid." Likewise, its Old Norse cognate, *bregða*, also indicates a sudden change of appearance. The idea of braiding one's shape into that of a *wyrm* is invoked directly by Snorri Sturluson in the *Prose Edda*.

In the *Skáldskaparmál* portion of the *Edda*, the story is told of the god Óðinn venturing to the realm of the giants to retrieve the Mead of Poetry. The mead had been brewed by dwarves using the blood of the murdered god Kvasir. Through further misadventure, the magical mead came into the possession of the giant Suttungr. Óðinn, traveling in disguise under the name of Bölverkr, the bale-worker, struck a bargain with Suttungr's brother, Baugi, to help him steal the mead from the giant. It was decided that Baugi, using a magical auger, "should bore the mountain" under which Suttungr had hidden the mead. According to Snorri, once the interior chamber had been breached, "then braided (*brást/bregða*) Bale-worker into a *wyrm*'s lich (*ormslíki*) and slithered into the auger-rift."[256]

The braiding of oneself into a *wyrm*'s lich in both the Anglo-Saxon and Norse accounts is an important parallel, one which further underscores the idea that the Christian author of *Solomon and Saturn I* was working with a genuine pre-Christian tradition. That the Old English *wyrmes líc* and Old Norse *ormslíki* are linguistic twins, each being an exact cognate of the other, is certainly no accident of history. The textual analysis of these accounts in their original languages points toward an archaic *verbum receptus*,[257] an oral, poetic, and mythopoeic Proto-Germanic tradition from whence these separate accounts sprung. The antiquity of this tradition merits careful consideration, particularly as it pertains to the dragon as a shapeshifting wight. From these accounts there emerges a religio-poetic pattern in which the "wicked" or, as with Wóden, the "bale-workers," are able to shift their shape into that of a dragon by donning an enchanted skin. In the case of the shape-shifted dragon, this formula may be mapped out as follows:

Wicked One(s) → *Dons Skin* → *Braids Appearance* → *Wyrm's Lich*

Bearing this in mind, and with the promise to return to the motif of the shapeshifter-dragon but with new details, it is now necessary for this chapter to segue into a search of pagan sepulchers. Though it is not explicitly stated in the Old Norse text, the imagery found within the story of the Mead of Poetry is not far removed from that of the burial mound. The depiction of Baugi burrowing a narrow passage into the mountain where the treasure lays hidden and of Óðinn then crawling down through the passage to steal it may very well be intended to invoke the idea of grave-robbing. As it stands, Suttungr's "mountain," wherein he hid the mead that was guarded by his daughter Gunnlöð, is in Old Norse a *bjarg*, an elevation of earth, a word which could equally refer to a mountain, a hill, or a burial mound. In fact, its Old English cognate, *biorg*, is used in *Beowulf* to refer to both the dragon's barrow and to the Geatish king's own grave. With this in mind, and with a reminder that the topic will turn toward the shapeshifting dragon yet again, this chapter will now delve deeper into the mound to turn its attention toward the supernatural nature of the dead that dwell therein.

Ghosts in the Grave: The Norse Draugr and the Anglo-Saxon Gást

The author of "Maxims II" seems to have been aware of some of the same traditions from which the monsters of *Beowulf* sprung,[258] employing a line which may very well have been intended to allude to Grendel: "Thurse (*Þyrs*) shall in fen dwell, alone in the land."[259] In *Beowulf* we find a nearly identical poetic formula: "The grim ghost (*gæst*) was hight Grendel. Infamous march-stepper,[260] he held the moor, fen and fastness, monsterkind's earth. The wretched wight warded it for a while."[261]

Perhaps the most outstanding difference between these two accounts is the word by which Grendel is described, a detail that is not apparent in most translations. The Old English *þyrs* found in "Maxims II" is often rendered as "demon," "monster," "ogre," "troll," or even "enchanter." Its Norse counterpart *þurs* appears as an alternative term for *jǫtunn*. Much like *þurs*, the meaning of *jǫtunn* is often lost in (mis)translation. Etymologically, a *jǫtunn* (OE: *eoten*) is "an eater, a devourer," though it appears in English translations most frequently as "giant," regardless of the wight's true height. Ettin, an archaic English word which was reintroduced to the common parlance by Tolkien, would be the most linguistically accurate translation of the Old English *eoten*. Likewise, *Beowulf*'s *gæst/gást* is also frequently translated as "demon," as if the Anglo-Saxon Heathen religion was somehow anachronistically possessed by Christian devils. Yet, the Old English *gæst/gást* is no less than the direct linguistic ancestor of the Modern English "ghost."

One might very well ask what connection exists between *þyrs* and *gæst/gást*. In *Beowulf*, both terms are among several which are used interchangeably to refer to Grendel.[262] One may wonder then, what was a "ghost" to the Heathen? After all, in a tale strewn with torn corpses, one can hardly imagine the ghosts of *Beowulf* as the ethereal phantasms and will-o'-the-wisps that come to mind when the word is mentioned today.

Whilst the form of the ghost has changed over the centuries, its essential nature has not. Although it is occasionally used poetically to refer to a "spirit" or other supernatural being, such as is the case with the "Holy Ghost," "ghost" is, more often than not, a word associated with the dead. More importantly, "ghost" represents the dead that have been disturbed. In its most ancient, original, Proto-Indo-European form, *ǵʰeysd-, *ǵʰisd- ("anger, agitation"), the unsettled nature of the ghost becomes painfully apparent. That Grendel and the dragon are both said to be ghosts is significant.

The Proto-Germanic *gaistaz, the wellspring from which the Old English gæst/gást arose, does not seem to have survived in Old Norse. In its place we find the *draugr*, a lich, an animated yet altered corpse comparable to the continental *revenant* or Slavic-Serbian вампир.[263] Throughout Norse lore, *draugar* are depicted as monstrous beings, corporal wights armed with supernatural strength, talon-like claws, and terrifying, fiendish maws. In his lecture, "The Making of Beowulf," Smithers explained that the Heathen conception of the dead as a "living corpse" rather than as a phantom was "due to a view of the human being as having a single indivisible form and substance, and not a spirit or soul as distinct from, and separable from, a body: at death, he occupies the grave, and there is no question of a life of the spirit (as such) elsewhere."[264] To this point, the Norse *draugr* is identical to the Anglo-Saxon *gæst* as it refers to Grendel and his mother.

The objection could be raised that Grendel and his mother are never referred to as *draugar* and that the Old Norse *draugr* and the early Heathen use of the Anglo-Saxon *gást*, while similar, represent distinct traditions concerning the dead. This can be explained by natural linguistic divergence, however. Both Old Norse and Old English emerged from a common Proto-Germanic tongue during the Migration Era. That *gaistaz was lost to the Norse lexicon is not surprising. Of its daughter languages, there is no heiress to the entirety of the Proto-Germanic wordhoard. To some degree, each of the early Germanic languages failed to produce or preserve cognates for each word in the Proto-Germanic corpus. In the case of *draugaz*, which is well attested to in Old Norse, there does appear to be some philological evidence for an Anglo-Saxon *dréag*[265] having once existed, though its use was entirely eclipsed by *gást* in Old English literature. Thus, the Norse *draugr* and the Anglo-Saxon *gást*, as non-cognate synonyms, are equally applicable to the same ancient Germanic tradition of the mound-dwelling dead.

In *A Piece of Horse Liver: Myth, Ritual and Folklore in Old Icelandic Sources*, Jón Hnefill Aðalsteinsson cited several stories from the Norse sagas which may be used here to shed some light on the idea of the ghost as it appears in *Beowulf*. The first account presented by Aðalsteinsson is found in the mid-fourteenth century poem the *Griplur*, itself based upon an older, now lost saga. In the poem Hrómundr Grippson is said to have broken into the burial mound of the Gaulish king Þráinn with the intention of taking the treasure buried within. However, once inside the mound, Hrómundr was attacked by Þráinn's *draugr*. The *draugr*'s clawed hands dug into Hrómundr's hide as the two grappled, until Hrómundr was at last able to grasp Þráinn's own blade, Mistilteinn, and behead the ghost therewith.[266]

The next example provided by Aðalsteinsson is found in *Grettis Saga* where the saga's namesake is recorded as having broken into the barrow of Kárr the Old, a wealthy landowner. After grappling with the *haugbúa*, "howe-dweller," Grettir was able to decapitate Kárr's *draugr*. Yet unlike Þráinn, Kárr's ghost was not defeated by its own blade. Rather Grettir used his sword, Jǫkulsnaut, to accomplish the task. It is worth noting, however, that among the mound's treasures was an ancestral sword that had belonged to Kárr which Grettir took with him from the barrow.[267]

Aðalsteinsson carefully pointed out, however, that the *draugr*, though prevalent in Icelandic stories, was by no means exclusive to that island's literature, observing that "the oldest written source in which a living man struggles with the dead in the mound is Saxo's description (soon after 1200) of Ásmunder wrestling with the dead Ásviðr."[268] And, while Saxo Grammaticus' *Gesta Danorum* was penned in Latin, the description of Ásviðr mirrors that of the Norse *draugr*. Furthermore, Saxo's monster (*monstrifer*) with lacerating claws (*laceris unguibus*) and abominable canines (*infandoque canem*) very nearly matches the description of Grendel provided in Beowulf.[269]

In *Patterns of Folklore*, Hilda Davidson discussed a similar tale found in the *Flateyjarbók*.[270] Upon his death, the Norwegian king Ólafr Gudrødsson was placed in a howe alongside his treasure. As a sacral king, Ólafr's mound became a cult site with sacrifices being made to him to ensure continued good harvests. As was the case with several Yngling kings, Ólafr was regarded as a tribal god or *alfr*, "elf," and was given the name Geirstaðaálfr, the "Elf of Gierstað." Yet, a very different tradition also seems to have survived regarding Ólafr's existence within the mound as the same text described him as having become a *draugr*. In the story, Ólafr was eventually destroyed by a man named Hrani who, like Hrómundr, beheaded the *draugr* with its own sword.[271]

The pattern of the hero breaking into the barrow, wrestling with the dead, and either slaying the ghost therein with its own sword and/or taking the mound-dweller's sword from the grave is a motif that is repeated in *Beowulf*. Through Beowulf's battles with Grendel, Grendel's mother, and ultimately the dragon, we see this story told, albeit piecemeal and spread over three different encounters. In his fight with Grendel, Beowulf grappled with the ghost, tearing its arm from its body and mortally wounding the fiend. Later, when Beowulf entered the underwater lair to slay Grendel's mother, Beowulf's blade failed to bite. However, Beowulf was able to grasp, from among the items scattered in the hoard, a sword which had been wrought in ancient times by the Ettins. With the blade Beowulf was able to behead both the death-ghost (*wælgæst*)[272] and the lifeless corpse of her son Grendel. It was therefore by their own ancestral sword that Grendel and his mother were forever destroyed.

The objection might be raised that Grendel's lair is not described in the text as a barrow but rather a hall (*sele*) submerged beneath the marshy mere. Yet, the imagery of Grendel's corpse surrounded by a treasure hoard recalls the imagery of the Anglo-Saxon burial mound, which itself may be a reflection of the meadhall. In *Anglo-Saxon Burial Mounds*, Stephen Pollington, in discussing the grave-goods commonly found in barrows, noted that the "provision of drinking vessels, cauldrons, cups, harps, and gaming pieces all evoke the pleasures of the hall" and that "it seems natural that a transformed meadhall should have formed the backdrop against which [the dead's] worth continued to be displayed in death."[273] To further connect Grendel's hall with the imagery of the burial mound, we find Beowulf describing it to Hygelác as being an earthen hall (*grundsele*),[274] mirroring the earthen hall (*eorðsele*)[275] of the dragon. Even earlier in the poem, Grendel is referred to as a ground-dweller (*grundbúendra*),[276] a phrase that is strikingly similar to *haugbúa*, "howe-dweller," used in *Grettis Saga* to refer to the *draugr* of Kárr the Old. Finally, given the Anglo-Saxon and Norse tradition of barrow-ship-burials, the distinction between a watery hall and a burial mound is one that, in Germanic poetry, is certainly within the realm of reconciliation.[277]

So what do *draugr*, Grendel, and ghosts have to do with dragons? The purpose of this chapter is to discuss the role of the dragon in the Anglo-Saxon Heathen religion after all. The answer to that question is made abundantly clear in the Old English text of *Beowulf* where *gást* is used alongside both *wyrm* and *draca* to refer to the very dragon that Beowulf both slays and is slain by.[278] And, if the barrow is only alluded to in the battle with Grendel's mother, it is made far more explicit in Beowulf's encounter with the dragon. Thus, recalling this chapter's promise to return to the theme of the dragon as a shape-shifted wight, to the barrow's depths and the dragon's den, these pages now turn.

Within the Mound, Upon the Hoard: The Dragon as a Ghost

In the *Völsunga Saga* the dragon Fáfnir began his life as a *dvergr*, a dwarf. Whilst hunting, the gods Óðinn, Hœnir, and Loki mistakenly slew Fáfnir's brother, Ótr, who had changed his shape into that of an otter. After the gods had skinned and dined upon their game, they continued their journey until they came to the hall of Hreiðmarr, a *dvergr*. There they presented to Hreiðmarr the otter's pelt which, in horror, he recognized to be his own son's hide. The gods were then held hostage by the *dvergr* and made to pay Ótr's *wergild*, "man-price." However, the gold hoard that was given by the gods to Hreiðmarr as compensation soon became a source of enmity between Fáfnir and his father. According to the saga, "Thereafter struck, Fáfnir his father . . . and murdered him. . . . He became so ill-evil, that he laid out (*lagðist út*), and granted that none enjoy the fee (*fé*) he took, and became thereafter the worst *wyrm* (*ormi*) and lies now on that fee."[279]

The act of laying on the hoard and thereby or thereafter changing into a dragon also appears in *Gull-Þóris Saga*. Early in the saga, the following account appears: "A viking was hight Valr, who owned mickle gold. He bore the fee (*féið*) under one hill, north towards Dumbshaf, and laid upon (*lagðist á*) it thereafter, and his sons amid him, and all then became flying-drakes (*flugdrekum*)."[280] Later in the saga, a similar story is told of a *berserkr* named Þórir. Upon hearing the false report of his son's death, Þórir mysteriously disappears. His fate remains uncertain but, according to the saga's author, "men hold for sooth that he had become a drake (*dreka*) and had lain upon (*lagðist á*) his gold-chest. Much then and long thereafter, men saw a drake flying (*dreka fljúga*) . . . ."[281]

A magical formula emerges from these accounts, one by which a wight, eldritch or mortal, changes its shape into that of a dragon after having laid out across (*lagðist út*) or laid upon (*lagðist á*) a gold hoard. Yet, a key component to the formula should not be overlooked. In the case of Fáfnir, it is explicitly stated that his brother was killed and that he, thereafter, slew his father. In Þórir's account we find him grieving over the apparent loss of his son. In the story of Valr, there is no specific mention of his sons having died, yet the imagery of Valr beneath a hill, surrounding himself with his sons and with his treasure, calls to mind the imagery of a burial mound. Thus, it would seem as if the act of shapeshifting into a dragon is preceded by familial death and accomplished by withdrawing from the world by entering a hill, a mountain, or a mound and laying upon one's gold hoard. In this sense, it would seem as if shapeshifting into a dragon is accomplished in death. The pattern of this motif can be seen in the formula below:

Death of Kinsmen → Entering Mound → Laying upon Gold → Death → Becoming a Dragon

It is with this formula in mind that this chapter now turns its attention toward the dragon of *Beowulf*. After all, if Grendel and his mother as *gást* correspond with the Norse *draugr*, what does this say of Beowulf's other *gást*, the dragon? The implication would seem to be that the dragon is also an embodiment of the mound-dwelling dead.

In *More about the Fight with the Dragon,* an exhaustive analysis of lines 2208b-3182 in *Beowulf,* Raymond Tripp put forward an interesting theory regarding the identity and origin of the dragon in *Beowulf*. According to Tripp, the dragon that Beowulf battles was the original human occupant of the burial mound, the lone survivor "who became a dragon and later, for reasons of hateful greed, like Grendel before him, attacks a good king."[282] Tripp based his interpretation of the passage upon his own restoration of the badly damaged portion of the *Beowulf* manuscript, and, in doing so, he provided an alternative reading of the text.[283] Tripp's rendering of the passage is not without its critics, however. As noted by Christine Rauer in *Beowulf and the Dragon: Parallels and Analogues*, "Much of Tripp's argument is based on his radically altered text of the dragon episode . . . ."[284]

Yet, Tripp was not the first scholar to put forward the idea that the mound's mortal owner, in death, had transformed into a dragon. In the traditional rendering of the text, the mound's owner was the last of his kinsmen and tribe, an ancient nobleman who commended his wealth to the earth's keeping, raising a great burial mound for himself by the sea, wherein he entered to die at his life's end.[285] Thereafter, the dragon, seeking Heathen gold in the earth, discovered the barrow. For three hundred years the dragon warded the hoard until his rest was disturbed by a thief who took a gold adorned goblet from the grave. William Lawrence, in his article "The Dragon and His Lair in Beowulf" (1918), noted that, less than a decade earlier in 1910, the Danish folklorist Axel Olrik had "made the passage in *Beowulf* the basis for a new and very interesting suggestion, that in an earlier form of the tale, the dragon was the lamenting warrior himself, who, like Fáfnir, had been transformed from a man into a monster . . . ."[286] As Lawrence explained, "in the poem as it stands, the dragon is not connected at all with the aged warrior, but this separation was explained by Olrik as due to late Christian influence."[287] In her article, *"The Hill of the Dragon"* (1950), Hilda Davidson came to a largely identical conclusion, noting that "The account suggests that this is a rationalization of the idea (which would be repugnant to a Christian audience) that the dead man himself became a dragon."[288] Likewise, in his inaugural lecture, "The Making of Beowulf" (1961), G.V. Smithers remarked that, "One need only examine the Scandinavian tales of the grave-mound as a whole at first hand to see that the dragon in *Beowulf* must, at an earlier stage in the growth of the story in this work, have been identical with the nameless 'last survivor' – that is, that the last survivor must have entered the mound with his treasure while still alive and have turned into a dragon."[289] Thus, the association between the dragon and the dead need not depend on an alternate rendering or restoration of the surviving manuscript. Although it is a Christian text, *Beowulf* incorporates elements of an earlier Heathen oral tradition, the echoes of which can readily be perceived when compared with the pagan traditions of Scandinavia.

Yet, Beowulf's own battle with the dragon is not the only such encounter to be recalled in the poem. Much earlier in the saga as the folk gathered in Heorot to celebrate the hero's slaying of Grendel, Hroðgar's *scóp* recounted the story of Sigemund the Wælsing's slaying of a wyrm. Endless ink has been spilt on speculating whether or not this episode recalls Sigurðr's fight with Fáfnir, as found in the Icelandic *Völsunga Saga* or German *Nibelungenlied*, or whether the tale preserves a separate tradition concerning Sigemund, Sigurðr's father, slaying a different dragon entirely. To this point, Smithers has posited that Sigemund's defeat of the dragon represented an earlier tradition of the Volsung/Wælsing dragon-slaying myth in which the slaying of Fáfnir was "transferred from the father to his renowned son" over time.[290] If Tolkien was correct in his assertion that *Beowulf* belongs to the "age of Bede,"[291] the early 8th century, then *Beowulf* would indeed pre-date both the *Völsunga Saga* and *Nibelungenlied* by half a millennium, thus, lending credence to Smithers' theory.

That the poet paired the story of Sigemund's slaying of Fáfnir alongside Beowulf's defeat of Grendel is not accidental but rather an act of intentional foreshadowing. In the saga, Beowulf had just laid low[292] the first of three mound-dwelling *gást* that he would, in his lifetime, battle. He would soon thereafter take up arms against a *draugr* dame, perhaps echoing Þórr's own battles against the "bale-wise brides" of the Ettins.[293] Still, the poet knew that, like Þórr, Beowulf would ultimately perish, poisoned by the wyrm that he was doomed to die defeating. To draw a comparison between the *gást*s of Grendel and his mother and the *gást* of the dragon, the poet inserted the account of Sigemund's dragon-slaying fairly early into the *Beowulf* saga. In doing so he presented his audience with a motif already abundantly sown with very specific poetic phrases that he could, later, draw upon toward the epic's end as Beowulf himself dealt with a very similar dead-turned-dragon/*gást*.

The first of these scattered seeds is the poet's use of the word *áglæca* to not only refer to the sea-beast that Beowulf had battled *a prior* to the epic,[294] Grendel,[295] Grendel's mother,[296] the monsters in the mere,[297] and the dragon Beowulf fought,[298] but also to Sigemund[299] and Beowulf himself.[300] The Old English *áglæca* is, when applied to dragons and other such terrors, often translated simply as "monsters." However, when it is applied to Sigemund or Beowulf, it is more often rendered as "hero." This would seem like quite a contradiction, and indeed so it is. Such is the pox which plagues[301] the relentless work of the translator. This begs the question then, what is an *áglæca*? On this matter academia is unsurprisingly undecided. Yet, it would seem that *áglæca* consists of two distinct words combined, *ág* and *læca*, to make a compound word. Rather than delve into the din of carefully couched indecision that haunts present day Anglo-Saxon studies, this chapter's author would propose that *ág* owes its origin to the Gothic *aglo*, "trouble," and the Old Norse *agi*, "terror". Regarding *læca*, such a word survives not only in Old English but in archaic Modern English as "leech" – a physician, herbalist, or healer. Thus, *áglæca* may very well be rendered "wicked-leech" or even "un-healer," a turn of phrase that bears in it bosom a decidedly dark connotation. It must be asked then, why the poet would, in the careful weighing of his words, choose to brand Beowulf and Sigemund as *áglæca* along with the monsters they encounter? The implication to this would seem to be that he intended to insinuate that there was something unsettling, un-right, and monstrous about these heroes.

For any who have read the story of Sigemund in Old English, a particular passage is sure to stand out: *draca morðe swealt*,[302] the "drake sweltered in its murder." It may surprise the reader to learn that the Anglo-Saxon *morþor*, "murder," carried with it the exact same legal connotation that the word carries today, nearly a millennium and a half later. Murder, unlike *mannslaga*, "manslaughter," has always conferred with its use the idea of an unlawful slaying. That Sigemund, an *áglæca*, in breaking into Fáfnir's barrow and slaying the dragon therein, commits a crime is an important detail. As a sacral king, Beowulf would have embodied the law of his land. Yet, in addressing the unsettled dragon-dead that had, upon the despoiling of its own tomb, begun to harrow the kingdom, Beowulf is likewise referred to as an *áglæca*. Why? Of what crime could Beowulf be guilty?

In his work, *The Cult of Kingship in Anglo-Saxon England*, William Chaney described the socio-religious function of the pre-Christian pagan kings as follows:

> In northern heathenism [sic] the primary leader of the tribal religion was the ruler. The king's god was the people's god, and the king as *heilerfüllt* [luck-vessel] stood between his tribe and its gods, sacrificing for victory and plenty, 'making' the year. Tied into temporal and cosmic history by divine descent, he represented and indeed was the 'luck' of his people. Thus it was the king's relationships with the gods which 'saved' his folk as much as did the gods themselves.[303]

This then is the context in which the poet who shaped the *Beowulf* saga would have intended the Geatish king to have been understood by the poem's original audience. As a Wóden, Ing, and/or Sceaf-sprung scion, Beowulf in his traditional sacred king-priest function would have been far removed from the idea of the *áglæca*. Yet, though the term *áglæca* is applied to Beowulf while he was still alive in the story, it is not likely that, were he a historical king, he would have been referred to as such in his lifetime. After all, the Beowulf that is "alive" in the story is a Beowulf recalled from the past. He is a memory or legend of some distant king belonging to an earlier age. How then is it that Beowulf, in his grave, could later be thought of as a monster? In his use of *áglæca*, was the *scóp* foreshadowing a dreadful doom which befell the Geatish king, one that is not explicitly stated but rather implied?

That even good kings may, in their graves, become monsters is not entirely unknown in the Heathen corpus. In the case of the "lone survivor," there is nothing to condemn him in *Beowulf* aside from his love of treasure. Yet, it would seem as if the "lone survivor," in his barrow, became an undead beast nonetheless, the very dragon that Beowulf would battle. Likewise, Ólafr Geirstaðaálfr, the "Elf of Gierstað," was, after his death, seen as a both a benevolent deity toward which the folk might sacrifice for fecundity and, yet still, a terrible ghost in the grave. What can be said for certain is that the Heathen attitude toward the dead was nebulous. Whereas the dead might be hailed as great heroes, prayed to for good harvest, or be the beneficiaries of grains burned in their honor to speed the health of the living,[304] the dead were also, without contradiction in the Heathen mind, equally believed to be dangerous.

As a sacral king, Beowulf represented not only the gods, but also the generations of god-sprung kinsmen from which he had descended. A sacral king was thus not merely a conduit betwixt the folk and the gods but also a bridge between the folk and the ancient dead. As such the very legitimacy of his claim to kingship depended on his ability to maintain the *eald riht*, "old right, unbroken tradition."[305] In laying waste to Beowulf's own hall, the dragon had challenged Beowulf's worthiness to uphold that ancient tradition. That Beowulf's kingly claim was in question is made quite clear in the poem when it says that after inheriting the kingdom "he held it well for fifty winters, he was then an old king, the ancient ancestral land's warder, until that one began, in dark nights, the drake to rule (*rícsian*)."[306]

There are a few words in this passage that merit closer consideration. To keep with the point that Beowulf's sacral kingship had been challenged by the dragon, such is made clear in the use of the word *rícsian*.[307] A word related to the modern German *reich*, *rícsian* means "to rule," the implication being that the ancient dead within the barrow had, in the form of a dragon, usurped the reign of the living king as represented by Beowulf. What is then represented is a struggle between the whim of the living and what G.K. Chesterton might have called, "the democracy of the dead."[308]

Yet, the passage contains several other words and phrases which the poet employed to draw a comparison between Beowulf and the dragon. In fact, the poet's reckoning of their earlier reigns is remarkably similar, as seen in the illustration below:

Beowulf's reign prior to the dragon awakening	The dragon's reign prior to being awakened
Beowulf lines 2208b-2210	*Beowulf* lines 2277-2279
he held (ge**héold**) it well for fifty winters, he was then an old (**fród**) king, the ancient ancestral land's warder (éþel**weard**)	there he, Heathen gold, warded (**waráð**) old (**fród**) in winters....so the tribe-scather, for three hundred winters, held (**héold**) in the earth some hoard-hall.

It is important to realize that for fifty winters these two reigns overlapped. It was not until the frith[309] of the dragon's barrow, his hoard-hall, was broken by the act of grave robbery that the dragon, in turn, despoiled the frith of Beowulf's own hall, setting it asunder. It may be then that the poet's use of *áglæca*, to refer to Beowulf and the dragon alike, represented a subtle, yet scathing, criticism of the Geat's failure to uphold the *eald riht* and fulfill his function as sacral king.

Beowulf, as king, had allowed the desecration of the dead to go unpunished. In failing to uphold the law, he assumed the thief's own guilt. Furthermore, rather than appease the dead through offerings of livestock or through repayment of the robbed treasure, Beowulf sought to silence the dead by means of physical force. Beowulf, in his conflict with the ancient sacral dead, therefore, represents a break with tradition, a point which the chronicler no doubt intended to make. Thus, in the battle between Beowulf and the dragon, we find not a hero pitting himself against a monster but rather a far more profound recalling of a struggle between the *áglæca* of one age and the *áglæca* of a far more ancient era.

The poet's purposeful comparison between Beowulf and the dragon will be returned to, though for the moment, it is needful to address Sigemund's place among the *áglæca*. While it has been established in this chapter that Fáfnir in the *Völsunga Saga* represents a Heathen notion of the undead in which the lich of the once-living is braided into that of a *wyrm*, it should not be assumed that, half a millennium earlier, the poet who penned *Beowulf* would have shared this understanding. Yet, in this account a subtle hint is afforded which would seem to indicate that, even in the age of Bede, Fáfnir was counted among the dead-turned-dragon/*gást*. As observed by Smithers, "Moreover, Sigemund's dragon-fight in *Beowulf* and his winning of its treasure took place in what may have been a grave-mound, since it is described by the very same phrase as is applied to the mound in Beowulf's own dragon-fight, and that by no means an obvious or well-worn one - *under hárne stán*,"[310] "under hoary stone."

As is said of the Wælsing atheling, "Sigemund sprang after his death-day, of no little doom (reputation), since the war-hardened one quelled the *wyrm*, the hoard's herder, he under the hoary stone (*under hárne stán*)."[311] It is important to note in this episode that Sigemund in descending "beneath the hoary stone," does so alone without the benefit of Fitela, his *nýdgesteallan*, "need-stabled companion," and nephew-son. Likewise, when this phrase is employed yet again, it appears at the moment when Beowulf enters into the dragon's barrow, alone and, for the moment, without the companionship of his distant cousin Wiglaf. Of the old Geatish king the poet recalled that "When angered he was, the Weder Geat's man let from his breast a word fare forth. The stark-heated one stormed, his summons came in, roaring battle-clear, under hoary stone (*under hárne stán*)."[312]

In the imagery of Beowulf, as the present sacral king, entering the barrow of a far more ancient king, bellowing in rage, intent upon drawing the dead-turned-dragon's ire directly toward him, we find a sacral king attempting to re-assert his own rule. Yet, in doing so we also find a king in defiance of the inertia exerted by the dead upon the living, a concept known in the old Heathen religion as *wyrd,* in which the weight of the past gives rise to and defines the present. As we will soon see suggested, history repeats itself and the hero's effort to overcome *wyrd* amounts to little more than a fool's folly in the old religion. That which is doomed is damned and deemed to be so, not by a future fatalism but rather by the momentum of the past. This is a sentiment that is concisely captured in the Old Saxon *Hêliand*: *uui mid ûsun dâduin ni sculun uuit auuerdian*, "we, by our deeds, shall not ward against a whit."[313]

So what then is this hoary stone? Based upon what we know of Norse Heathenism, it would seem that this particular turn of phrase was intended to recall the practice of raising rune stones to commemorate the dead. As attested to in the *Ynglinga Saga*, Óðinn initiated the tradition in which "honorable men should howes yare (make ready) to their memory . . . [and] should raise slain-stones; and this custom was held for a long time."[314] The association between the living and the obligation thereof to honor the dead is made even more clear in the Norse *Hávamal* where it is said that "a son is better, though he is begotten after the going (death) of the man (father). Seldom a slain-stone stands nigh by the path lest a kinsmen to a kinsmen undertakes to raise it."[315] Furthermore, as Paul Acker observed in *Dragons in the Eddas and in Early Nordic Art*, the dragon motif figured prominently amongst the oldest rune-stones inscriptions.[316] It is beneath this hoary slaughter-stone, inscribed by runes, that we must then look to understand the fullness of Beowulf's relationship with the dragon.

The Cairn of the King: Beowulf the Dragon

In the *Carmen de Hastingae Prolio*, a poem penned by Bishop Guy of Amiens in 1067 to commemorate the Battle of Hastings, the body of Harold Godpinson, the last Anglo-Saxon king to sit upon the English throne, is said to have had a similar slaughter-stone raised over his grave. Yet, more surprising are the other details provided by the *Carmen*, details which are mirrored in the burials of both the "lone survivor" who became the dragon and in the burial of Beowulf himself. According to the *Carmen*, Duke Williame

> . . . ordered that the corpse to be entombed on the summit. Forthwith someone, part Norman and Angle, a companion of Harold, freely acted on the order. The corpse of the king he quickly took up and sepulchered; laying over it a stone, he inscribed the title: 'Per mandate of the Duke, here King Harold rest, as custodian, remain on the shore and sea.' The duke, along with his gens, plangently wailed over the sepulchered ossuary, distributed money to the paupers of Christ. The name of duke he postponed (put off), and the king interred, having adopted the royal name, he departed."[317]

In his history of the Battle of Hastings, David Howarth commented that "This strange ceremony was a purely pagan Viking rite."[318] In their commentary on the *Carmen*, Morton and Muntz noted that "the inscription, no prayer for the dead king's soul, but an injunction that he rest and keep his watch, savours of age-old magic."[319] As the descendants of the Danish Vikings lead by Hrólfr (Rollo) who invaded France and made the duchy of Normandy their home in 911 C.E., the Normans were comparative newcomers to Christianity. Even if Catholic saints had supplanted Heathen gods, many of the traditions and superstitions of the old religion were still alive in the eleventh century.

The *Carmen*'s account of Harold Godpinson's heathenish burial may very well offer a deeper insight into Beowulf's own internment. Mortally wounded by the dragon, Beowulf implored Wiglaf, his thane and distant kinsman, to raise a low (*hlǣw*) over his body upon the cliff overlooking the sea. As it appears in the poem, "A low work (make), bright after bale, at brim's nose (cliff). It shall be a reminder to my people, towering high on the whale's ness (headland), so that seafarers, who on ships over the flood's mists drifteth afar, sithence will hight it 'Beowulf's Barrow.'"[320] It would seem then that, rather than a mere monument, the mound was also intended to house the luck of the sacral king, so that even in death, Beowulf might be a guardian of the land.

That the grave mounds of deceased kings became important cult sites has already been made clear in the case of Ólafr Geirstaðaálfr. As with the Elf of Geirstað, the Yngling king Freyr is also said to have been interred in a mound whereupon his corpse was presented with offerings, so that the folk might continue to benefit from the late king's luck. As relayed by Snorri Sturluson in the *Ynglinga Saga*,

> Freyr took sick, but as he on the way to death, his men sought rede, and let few men come to him, but built a mickle howe, and there were three doors and three holes. When Freyr was dead, they bore him secretly to the howe, and said to the Swedes that he lived, and warded him there three winters. But all scot they hid in the howe, in one hole gold, in another silver, in the third copper pennies. Then there was bountiful harvest and frith.[321]

In the case of Freyr, Snorri has euhemerized a Germanic deity of great antiquity, known as Yngvi-Freyr in Scandinavia, Ing, Ingui, and Fréa among the Anglo-Saxons, and whose name is recalled by the 1st century Roman historian Tacitus in his *Germania*.[322] With Ólafr Geirstaðaálfr, however, a historical king had, within his howe, been demi-deified. It may be that Beowulf's followers, in an older more purely pagan version of the tale, intended a similar elfish-apotheosis. And, while it is doubtful that the Christian Normans had any mind toward venerating the vanquished Harold, it would appear as if Williame intended to enshrine within the land the sacral luck of the late king. As noted by Morton and Muntz, "The most remarkable pagan note, however, lies in William's assumption of the kingly name beside the howe. This, rather than the duke's coronation in the abbey housing Edward's tomb, fits P. E. Schramm's suggestion of an appeal to 'that pre-Christian magic by which a king took his stand on the tumulus of his predecessor.'"[323]

But what has this to do with dragons? In the *Cult of Kingship in Anglo-Saxon England*, William Chaney discussed the significance of the dragon as a royal emblem and battle banner of both the West Saxon and Mercian kings. By the time of the Battle of Hastings, the dragon banner had come to represent the kingship of England itself as, on the Bayeux tapestry, Harold is seen fighting the Normans beneath his dragon banner. As a royal cult-object, the dragon banner may have very well originated in the Anglo-Saxon homeland on the continent. Widukind of Corvey, in his *Res Gestae Saxonicae*, reported that Hagathat, an Old Saxon chieftain, upon entering into battle "took up a sign that they held sacred, ensigned with the effigy a lion and a dragon and an eagle flying above."[324] Likewise, the Welsh chronicler, Geoffrey of Monmouth, imagined the invading Anglo-Saxons as a white dragon.[325] And, if the *Vita Barbati Episcopi Beneventani* is to be believed, the image of the serpent, itself only distinguishable from the earliest representations of Germanic dragons by size, may have been revered by other continental tribes such as the Langobards. As the *Vita* reports, "In those days, though the sacred waters of baptism had abluted the Langobards, nevertheless they held to the former rites of the gentiles, as they continued with bestial mind, to a beast's simulacrum, which is vulgarly (commonly) named a viper, to flex their collars (bow their necks), the flexing of which is a debt they owe to the Creator."[326] Such an account would be easy to dismiss as monkish fantasy were it not for the recent discovery in Staffordshire of an Anglo-Saxon gold hoard. As it so happens, several small golden serpents were found among the artifacts, a discovery which has baffled archeologists. And, although the Staffordshire hoard was not buried alongside a body, its sheer size suggests that it belonged to an Anglo-Saxon king. In his presentation for the BBC Radio, historian Michael Wood has suggested that the hoard is the same hoard paid by the Northumbrian King Oswald to the pagan Mercian king Penda to end his siege of Stirling in 654 C.E.[327] If that is the case, then the presence of golden serpents in the hoard should come as no surprise, as where else might one expect to find dragons, the cult-emblems of kingship, but guarding a Heathen king's hoard?

What then did the dragon represent to the Anglo-Saxon kings? If dragons were believed to have been the dead, transformed among the treasure within the grave-mound, and if the imagery of the dragon was connected to the cult of kingship, then it may follow that dragons were thought to be the embodiments of the king's own luck-bearing ancestors, enshrined within the earth as its guardians. Indeed, in *The Annals of St. Neots* the Frankish duke Charles Martel is said to have become a dragon after his death.[328] According to the *Annals*, "they proceeded to the predicted monastery, where the corpse of Charles himself was interred, opened his sepulture and, seeing a dragon suddenly exit, found the interior of the sepulture totally denigrated (blacked) as if it had been burned up."[329] While not a king, Martel did become the progenitor of the Carolingian dynasty. It would seem then that the dragon, as an emblem of kingship, recalls the relationship between the sacral king and the holy dead. Just as the king would sacrifice to ensure that the gods favored him, so too would the king call upon the kings of old, the dragon guardians within the land, to give him luck and victory. Thus, in bearing the dragon-banner into battle, the king was making a religio-political statement: the dead, through him, defended the living, even against the dragons of foreign kings.

What is to be made of this? Did the Heathens of old believe that the corpses of their kings became luck-bearing elves, deadly *draugr*, or ghostly dragons? In all likelihood the answer to that question defies easy answer. The wights of the old religion escape ready categorization. Elves are, at times, seen as gods. In the case of cliffs and burial mounds, they may very well resemble the Roman *genius loci*. Yet, elsewhere, as dun-elves, mountain-elves, sea-elves, and wood-elves they appear to embody a more natural *numen*. Likewise the lines between *god, giant, elf, ancestor*, and *hero* are, at best, blurred and, quite often, nearly nonexistent. Take Weland the Smith for example. He is a prince of the elves, an apparent god of blacksmithing, depicted as a semi-divine yet semi-human hero, and is said to be the son of a giant. Likewise, Wóden, the king of the gods, is also said to have been an earthly king who sired noble lines that are with us still. Indeed the nebulous, dreamlike, terrain of Heathen myth is a landscape which can only be mapped by the most uncanny of cartographers – the *scóp*, the shaper, the pagan poet of old.

In its most archaic, oral, pagan form, did Beowulf as a king in a cairn, lain upon the treasure of the dragon he had just slain and set in a mound upon the very same cliff whereupon the beast's own barrow had centuries before been raised, so too in death become a dragon, a guardian overlooking the sea? The parallels between the two would seem to suggest as much, though it is a point which can never be proven. The text, as it presently survives, is a pagan tale retooled for a Christian audience. Yet, in the Geats' unceremonious dumping of the dragon's corpse off the cliff and the re-interment of the hoard in a new mound raised to the sacral king who had defeated the old, unsettled, ghost of the land, it would seem as if Beowulf's doom in death would have been to reign in the earth as the new ghost-dragon-king. *Le roi est mort, vive le roi.* The king is dead, long live the king.

Conclusion

Having set out on an adventure through the dreamlike, mythic landscape of the Anglo-Saxon Heathen, this work has encountered goddesses, gods, elves, berserkers, werewolves, giants, and ghosts – each of which is in some way pertinent to understanding the significance of the dragon in the old religion. As stated previously in this chapter, all that can be said for certain of the Heathen attitude toward the dead is that it was nebulous. This may, in part, be due to the damage done by conversion. Anglo-Saxon Heathen lore is a brittle and burnt parchment, barely decipherable after so many centuries. Yet, it may, equally, be due to the breadth of imagination or insight afforded by a worldview that was inherently pluralistic and whose transmission and preservation relied on the craft of the poet, the *scóp*, rather than the dominion of the theologian. In mirroring the uncertainty of life, the experiences which oft readily defy black and white interpretation, the Heathen's relationship with the dead was, likewise, naturally ambiguous. Such was the inherent thewy beauty of that now nigh forgotten *weltanschauung*.

As set forward in this chapter's introduction, the abundance of dragons in what remains of Anglo-Saxon lore is no mean accident of history but rather a definable feature of the old Heathen religion. More than mere monsters, the dragon was inextricably bound to the cult of kingship by the tethers of pagan magic and ancestor-worship. Inscribed upon rune-stones, the dragon slumbered beneath the barrow and among the royal ancestors. Awakened by war, the Heathen dragon flew over the battlefield, embroidered upon the king's banner. Yet, when disturbed by the desecration of the dead or the breaking of the *eald riht*, the dragon embodied the displeasure of the ancient god-sprung kings of old, upon whose luck the living king depended.

As the god of kingship, the dead, and magic – particularly the art of shapeshifting – Wóden stands alongside the dragon as the warp and weft upon which the weird (OE: *wyrd*) tapestry of Anglo-Saxon Heathendom was woven. Behind the bearskins of his *berserker*, within the wolf-hoods of his *úlfheðnar*, and beneath the barrows of Wóden's bairns, this chapter has sought the dragon's den and lair, the hall within which the Heathen treasures of yore awaited remembrance and discovery. Yet, forasmuch as the magic of the dragon owes its due to Wóden, the wolf-hero-king-dragon-slayer, as embodied by Þunor, the Wandering Wolf, and Beowulf, the importance of the Earth goddess in the dragon-slayer myth – be she named Nerthus, Erda, Hlóðyn or Fjörgyn – should not be overlooked. It is into her regenerative bosom, after all, that the poets of old commended the wolf-hero-dragon-slayer to undergo chrysalis. High overhead and deep beneath runs the dragon's significance in the old Heathen religion. Inescapable. We, by our deeds, shall not ward against a whit, much less against dragons.

ÞÓRBEORHT LÍNLÉAH

HÉAFODCWIDE/HEADQUIDE/CHAPTER VI
LORE AND LANDSCAPE: ENVIROMENTAL CHANGE AND ITS IMPACT UPON TEUTONIC MIGRATION AND HEATHEN BELIEF

The sacred grove of the Suebic tribes and the holy grove at Uppsala, wights within rocks and waterfalls worshipped, the holy isle and lake of Nerthus the Hidden and the sacred isle and spring of Fosite, mountains and ancestor-laden burial mounds – the sacrality of landscape abounded in Heathen belief from its earliest accounts until its eventual eclipse. 'Twas through the land itself, oft beheld as a goddess, that the bairns of Tuisto, the earth-born god, encountered the therewithness of their gods.

Tethered to this was the Teutonic king, himself an heir to an ancient Indo-European thew which bound him to the tribe's ancestral land, which may have been envisioned as his bride.[330] The devotion of the late Heathen Norwegian jarl Hákon Sigurðarson to the goddess Þorgerðr Hǫlgabrúðr (Thunder-Earth Hålogaland's[331] Bride), his subsequent procession through the land, and his bedding the wives and daughters of his bondsmen may allude to the marriage between the sacral head and the sovereign goddess or goddesses of the land.[332] This connection is made much more explicitly clear in Gerald of Wales' twelfth century *Topographia Hibernica*, wherein Irish kings, even in Christian times, were said to have married a mare, which may have originally represented the goddess Macha. Thereafter, the king ritually copulated with the mare before the assembled moot. The folk then slaughtered the beast and, from its corpse, prepared a feast.[333] This, in turn, echoes the Vedic coronation rite found within the seventhy century BCE *Śatapatha Brāhmaṇa* wherein a stallion sacrifice and accompanying intercourse betwixt queen and the beast's corpse was followed by a sacred feast.[334]

As the head of the tribe, the king was believed to descend from the divine-ancestor. The sacral king, coupled with the sacred landscape, served as the basis for communion with the gods. Nonetheless the history of Heathen belief is a story that is, more often than not, an unsettled tale of uprooting, moving, invasion, and migration. In a religion in which holy groves, islands, lakes, springs, mountains, and mounds were woven by Wyrd into its very fabric and whose holy-tides hung upon the wending of the agricultural year, what might be made of an environmental disaster? What might be made of orchards which "blossomed but the fruit [of which] withered and died on the bough?"[335] What might be made of acres which could not be remedied?[336] How might the god-sprung king of the kindred reconcile himself and his folk to the Earth when she withheld her blessing? As will be seen in the course of this chapter, the answers to such questions outline the very history of our people.

The First Migration – The Becoming of the Teutons

Insight into the earliest origins of the Teutons is dependent almost entirely upon the field of archeology. That said, environmental scientists - studying tree rings, pollen sediments, and other such evidences of drought, deforestation, and agricultural expansion - have begun to contribute to the ever broadening and deepening discourse on Teutonic pre-history.

Though no written records exist from this time period, it is believed that the ancestors of the Teutons, like the Balts and Slavs, were at least culturally, if not linguistically, connected to the archeological horizon of the Corded-Ware culture,[337] in particular the subgroup known as the Swedish-Norwegian Battle-Axe culture. The Corded-Ware culture was a settlement of Indo-European peoples who occupied the German lowlands and the North Sea's continental coastline during the Neolithic Era (circa 2900-2450 BCE). As evidenced by Scandinavian rock carvings,[338] a mass migration from this region into Scandinavia occurred circa 1800 BCE, beginning the era often referred to as the Nordic Bonze Age. In his article "Human

Impact and Climate Changes," Björn Berglund, Professor Emeritus in Quaternary Geology at Lund University, noted that "expanding agricultural settlement, particularly pastures in Scotland and Scandinavian, resulted in increased deforestation, especially along the western Scandinavian coast."[339] As explained by Manx archeologist Peter Gelling, "the population of southern Scandinavia at this time had arisen from a fusion between groups which had lived there since at least early in the Neolithic period and a body of immigrants – the 'Battle-axe people.'"[340] The proto-Teutons had arrived in Scandinavia.

From a linguistic anthropological perspective, it is important to designate these peoples as proto-Teutons since the first truly Teutonic language, Proto-Germanic – the etymological ancestor of English, German, Dutch, Swedish, Norwegian, and Icelandic – did not arise until circa 500 BCE. Yet by 500 BCE, not only had the Teutonic "mother tongue" distinguished itself from its Proto-Indo-European parentage,[341] but the Nordic Bronze Age ended, giving rise to the period in history known as the Nordic Iron Age.

The Second Migration – The Coming of the Teutons

On the centurial eve of the Nordic Bronze Age, Scandinavia began to experience significant climate change. As noted in a study in Scandinavian prehistory produced by the National Museum of Denmark, "Around 600 B.C. a climactic change occurred. Summers became colder and the weather in general more wet, reflected in a pronounced increase of peat formations in high moors and an extension of humid areas."[342] Prior to this period, the climate of Scandinavia was comparable to that of modern northern Germany or France. There is even archeological evidence that grapes and wine were produced in the region. As noted in the aforementioned study the "cumulative effects of settlement clustering, climactic change, and shrinking supplies of bronze were likely to trigger off a severe economic and political change,"[343] which of course is exactly what happened, ushering in the Nordic Iron Age.

It is quite possible, however, that this climate change impacted Heathen belief as well. Whereas the Scandinavian rock carving and metal art of the Nordic Bronze Age was replete with solar-god imagery, sun iconography waned from this period forward in Heathen belief. Throughout later periods, the sunwheel, a prevalent religious symbol of the Nordic Bronze Age, was utterly eclipsed by the swastika as the symbol of the thunder god, *Þunraz (OE: Þunor, ON: Þórr).[344] Though the Roman historian Tacitus wrote of a flourishing sun-god cult along the Baltic Sea in 98 CE,[345] there is no significant evidence of a sun-cult in later Teutonic periods.

By the time Viking Era mythology was recorded in written form, the sun-god had become a sun-goddess about whom very little is said. Her primary myth, recalled almost in passing, expresses an ancient religious anxiety regarding solar eclipses. As noted in the *Prose Edda*, the Sun goddess rides upon a wain, drawn by two horses across the sky. All the while she is chased by a wolf which, at the end of days, will overtake and devour her.

Though the sun-cult only diminished from the Iron Age forward, it is worth noting that the sole mythic reference that survived conforms to what we know of Heathen belief as it was practiced in the Nordic Bronze Age. Though the significance of the sun-god declined in cultic practice, the sacred wain motif, attested to in the Trundholm Sun Chariot, remained an important aspect of Heathen belief until the end of the Viking Age.

It may very well be that the sun-god's warmth was withdrawn from the North in 600 BCE when the climate grew cold and wet. Nonetheless, the Teutons seem to have successfully managed the climate change for four centuries. But, by 200 CE, environmental disaster was upon the Teutonic tribes. Though Teutonic etiology, the oral mythological narrative of tribal origins, was not written down until centuries afterward, histories from the sixth century CE forward all record variants of the same mythic-migration motif. As reported by Jordanes,

> Now from this island of Scandza, as from a hive of races or a womb of nations, the Goths are said to have come forth long ago. . . . But when the number of the people increased greatly and Filimer . . . reigned as king . . . he decided that the army of the Goths with their families should move from that region. In search of suitable homes and pleasant places they came to the land of Scythia.[346]

In some accounts, the problem of overpopulation and subsequent famine had grown so great that it was initially decided that vast portions of the populace should be put to death. In such stories, there was inevitably a character counted among those doomed to die who proffered a different solution. In an appeal to the whim of the gods, lots were then cast or drawn to determine who would remain in Scandinavia and who would, by divine decree, migrate southward.[347] And while the determination of such important political events may seem, to the modern mind, a decision that would not likely be left to lot-casting, one must remember that divination by such drawings was always an essential feature of the Teutonic religio-political paradigm. From matters of the state in the first century CE[348] to the conversion of Sweden at the end of the Viking Era,[349] all such important decisions were determined through divination.

Sparked by an inevitable environmental disaster in the form of overpopulation and famine — itself an outcome of detrimental climate changes some four centuries in the making — and guided by religious convention, the Teutons began to pour out of Scandinavia in 200 BCE. Some, such as the Goths, migrated south-eastward toward the Black Sea. Others, such as the Angles and Langobards, moved south-westward into northern Germany where they displaced through conquest the native Celtic populace. In time the Proto-Germanic language of the Teutons divided into the North Germanic, East Germanic, and West Germanic linguistic groups based upon which tribes remained in Scandinavia and which tribes migrated. Yet, in oral tradition and in later written etiology, Scandinavian descent remained an essential aspect of Teutonic identity. As noted by the Danish archeologist Lotte Hedeager, "the Scandinavian origin myth among the Germanic royal families/peoples, expressed in contemporaneous written sources, is supported by archaeological evidence, notably weapons, jewelry, and, not least, art and iconography."[350]

The Third Migration - *Furor Teutonicus*

From their re-arrival in 200 BCE until 400 CE, the Teutons were perpetually in conflict with the Celts, Balts, and Slavs, who they displaced, and the Romans, whose borders they continually threatened. But, for the most part, these six centuries were relatively stable. Religiously, the most significant development that occurred during this time was the appropriation of the sun-god's sacred wain iconography to the interrelated cults of the earth-goddess and the cult of kingship. As noted by the first century historian and ethnographer Tacitus in his account of the Angles and other tribes that inhabited northern Germany and Denmark,

> There is nothing noteworthy about these tribes individually, but they share a common worship of Nerthus, or Mother Earth. They believe that she takes part in human affairs, riding in a chariot among her people . . . . The priest can feel her presence in this holy of holies, and attends her with the deepest reverence as her chariot is drawn by cows. Then follow days of rejoicing and merrymaking in every place that she condescends to visit and sojourn in. . . . After that, the chariot, vestments, and (believe it if you will) the goddess herself, are cleansed in a secluded lake. This service is performed by slaves who are immediately afterward drowned in the lake.[351]

As previously mentioned, 200BCE to 400CE was a period of relative stability for the Teutons — and then the wind changed. As noted in a recent article on European climate change over the past 2,500 years, "increased climate variability from ~AD 250-600 coincided with the demise of the Western Roman Empire and the turmoil of the Migration Period."[352] By comparing oak ring width chronologies from Central Europe with historical accounts contemporary to the period, it can be shown that "distinct drying in the 3rd century" followed by "hemispheric-scale cooling that has been linked with an explosive, near equatorial volcanic eruption in AD 536, followed by the first pandemic of Justinian plague that spread from the Eastern Mediterranean in AD 542/543" produced environmental stresses which set the Teutonic tribes to march, this time successfully pushing not just into Roman provinces but into Italy itself.[353]

By the final decades of the third century, the Migration Era, or the *Völkerwanderung*[354] as it is sometimes called, had begun. This period would span nearly four centuries (circa 400 CE to 800 CE) and end with the onset of the Viking Age (circa 800 CE). Though tribes such as the Vandals would migrate as far south as North Africa and though other nations such as those of the Angles, Jutes, and Saxons would set sail to Britannia intent on invasion, such mass migrations were only possible because the strength of Rome had already been sapped by the Goths.

Though the Romans had been in sporadic conflict with the Goths — an eastern Teutonic tribe that had settled along the Black Sea — for much of the early to mid fourth century, in 376 CE the Goths crossed the Danube River to seek Roman protection. What brought them to Rome's borders, and ultimately changed the course of European and world history, was another invasion — that of the Huns, who were themselves migrating in response to climate change induced political upheaval in the far off land of China. As noted in a recent article published by several prominent Chinese ecologists,

> Historical records indicate that from 300 A.D until after 530 A.D., the Rouran tribe may have been at the initial states of founding a dynasty that governed or controlled neighboring tribes. However, during this period, a significant reversal of desertification in northern China resulted in frequent competition among dynasties for control of northern China and a high frequency of dynastic changes in Central China.[355]

According to the late Irish historian and Trinity College professor, John Bury, the Rouran (Zhu-Zhu) empire extended from the coast of the North Pacific to the borders of Europe. Their rise is believed by historians to have pushed the nomadic Huns westward into Europe – pushing the Goths into the Roman Empire.[356] Thus, pressed by the drought and famine rampant throughout Europe and by environmental changes occurring thousands of miles away, the Teutons began their third series of mass migrations, Germanizing much of Western Europe before the era drew to an end.

Climate and Kingship – Environmental Change and Heathen Belief

In his doctoral thesis, which explored the impact of climate change on the Teutonic migrations, David Holt, perhaps incidentally, offered an invaluable insight into the religious response to climate change during this period. Holt briefly examined the following passage from

Sozomen's *Ecclesiastical History* (composed early in the fifth century)[357] which pertains to events that occurred among the Goths during the 370s:

> Athanaric[358] was annoyed that those under his power also had been persuaded by Ulphilas to become Christians, and subjected many of them to many forms of punishment because the ancestral religion was threatened by innovation. . . . It is said that a wooden image [likely that of Ingwi, known to the Anglo-Saxons as Ing and the Norse as Yngvi] was placed on a wagon, and that those instructed by Athanaric to undertake this task wheeled it round to the tent of any of those who were denounced as Christians and ordered them to do homage and sacrifice to it; and the tents of those who refused were burned, with the people inside it.[359]

Whereas Sozomen, as a church historian, was interested in Teutonic orthopraxy only within the context of conflict between Christianity and Heathen belief, Holt was able to offer a more complete context for the event by drawing upon drought records. Noting that this event coincided with "the fourteenth year of a twenty-year poor period evident in the tree ring record,"[360] Holt's insight allows for a deeper understanding of Athanaric's actions. The worship of the gods, upon whom the tribe depended for luck in harvest and war, had been abandoned by Ulphilas' followers. And, in the wake of such apostasy, a deadly drought had come upon the land. As the sacral king, Athanaric's own life would have been forfeit had famine continued. Therefore, in following the thew of his Heathen belief, Athanaric sought to restore the worship of the gods to the Goths through sacrifice. Those who would not sacrifice to the gods would, themselves, be sacrificed.

As previously mentioned, during the Nordic Iron Age an important theological shift occurred within Heathen belief. The cult of the sun-god waned and the iconography of the sacred wain was appropriated by the cults of the fertility gods and the cult of kingship. As exemplified in the account of Athanaric,[361] the connection between kingship, abundant harvest, and the yearly procession of the chief fertility god(s)'s sacred wain was an essential element of Heathen belief.

As the Teutonic Migrations have not been adequately explored in regard to the role of kingship in Heathen belief and the response of such sacral kings to climate change, it may be worth examining the institution of sacral kingship further. As noted by the English mythologist William Chaney, "the king's god was the people's god, and the king as heilerfüllt[362] stood between his tribe and the tribal gods, sacrificing for victory and plenty, 'making' the year. Tied into temporal and cosmic history by divine descent, he represented and indeed was the 'luck' of his people."[363] From the time of Tacitus to the late post-Conversion histories of the thirteenth century, the king, as a descendant of the gods, was held to be the high priest of the tribe, upon whose regular intermediary sacrifices of livestock the "luck," victories, and successful harvests of the tribe depended.

Though in later ages the chief god from whom kings would draw their sacral pedigree was most predominantly Wóden/Óðinn, the god known variously as Ing, Ingui-Fréa, Ingvi-Freyr, Lýtir, Sceaf, Sahsnôt, and Seaxnéat remained the "king's god" among many of the Teutonic tribes. Such nations and royal dynasties included the Ingaevones (people of Ing) mentioned by Tacitus in the first century CE, the Continental Saxons, the Anglo-Saxon kings of Essex, and the Ynglings (Ing's descendants) of Viking Age Sweden. Of more direct interest to the deities already discussed, Ingvi-Freyr is said, in Viking Era sources, to be the son of Njörðr, a harvest and sea god whose name is a direct cognate, though a millennium removed, to that of the goddess Nerthus. Throughout both the Migration Era and the Viking Age, Ing was associated with both sacral kingship and with the seasonal procession of a harvest wain. As recalled in the Anglo-Saxon Rune Poem (circa eighth century): *Ing wæs ærest mid Eastdenum gesewen secgun, oþ hé siððan eft ofer wæg gewát, wæn æfter ran. Þus heardingas þone hæle nemdon.*[364] As obscure as this one Anglo-Saxon reference may be, the story of Gunnar Helming as relayed in the *Flateyjarbók,* concerning events that transpired in Sweden circa 940 CE, offers further evidence of a persistant belief in the annual procession of a wain borne Ing idol.[365]

Within the pages of the *Flateyjarbók*, there is preserved another account of the fertility-god/wain motif that clearly connects it to the cult of kingship. According to Cambridge mythologist Hilda

Davidson, "King Eric of Sweden is said to have led the god's wagon to a certain place, and waited until it became heavy, the sign that the god was present within. Then the wagon was drawn to the king's hall, and Eric greeted the god [here named Lýtir[366]], drank a horn in his honour and put various questions to him." Ornate wains found among sacrificial bog deposits in Dejbjerg, Denmark (circa 200 CE) and the majestically crafted wain found in the Oseberg ship burial (circa 850 CE) offer further archeological evidence of the wain's enduring significance in Heathen belief throughout the Migration Era.

Though an essential aspect of kingship within the theological framework of Heathen belief, medieval histories clearly indicate that the association of king and sacred wain did not end with baptism. Regarding Childeric III, the last Frankish king of the Merovingian dynasty (circa 743-753 CE), the Carolingian chronicler, Einhard, wrote that "when he had to go abroad, he used to ride in a cart, drawn by a yoke of oxen driven, peasant-fashion, by a ploughman; he rode in this way to the palace and to the general assembly of the people, that met once a year for the welfare of the kingdom, and he returned him in like manner."[367] So ingrained was the association between sacral and sacred wain that among the Franks, one of the first Teutonic tribes to embrace the new religion, such yearly processions continued for three centuries following their conversion.

Though lengthy, the above digression into the ritual practices of Heathen belief and the sacral nature of kingship was necessary to capture the *weltanschauung* of the ancient Teutons. Such insight is essential into understanding why the Teutons migrated *en masse* during this period of climate change. As noted by Holt in his thesis,

> There are long below means [rainfall] periods in the 3rd and 4th centuries, but probably never extreme enough to completely halt all food production. However, the productivity would have surely been reduced to a degree that is related to the extent and severity of the droughts. This reduction of productivity did not necessarily cross a migration-threshold but allowed for a conscious decision to be made by the chieftain to look for other areas of settlement or alternate means of nourishment.[368]

It was the role of the king, as *heilerfüllt,* to intercede on behalf of the tribe by sacrificing to the gods for good harvest. For the Teutonic kings, the failure of their offerings to obtain the *heil*[369] of the gods required to ensure an adequate, if not bountiful harvest, could prove fatal. The *Heimskringla*, a medieval history of the Norse kings, preserves two clear accounts in which sacral kings were sacrificed during periods of famine. Regarding King Dómaldi, the Icelandic historian Snorri Sturluson wrote,

> For the first harvest they [the Swedes] sacrificed oxen, but the crop was not bettered by it; for the next harvest they sacrificed men, but the crop was the same or even worse. The chiefs took counsel and held to a man that Dómaldi their king must be the cause of the bad seasons and also that they should have to sacrifice him in order to have a good season.[370]

As the reign of Dómaldi's son and successor, Dómar, was marked by "good seasons," the Swedes would have had every reason to believe that the sacrifice of Dómaldi had proven efficacious. Some generations later, Óláfr Trételgja,[371] whose byname may allude to a compounding issue of deforestation, met a fate akin to that of Dómaldi when the population of Vätmland exceeded the land's ability to support it. According to Snorri, "they gave their king the blame for it, just as the Swedes were wont to give the king blame both for good and bad years. . . . They gathered an army, went against king Olav, surrounded the house and burned him in it; they gave him to Odin . . . in order to have a good season."[372] This aspect of Teutonic kingship not only casts light on the actions of the Gothic king Athanaric, as previously described, but provides invaluable insight into why the Teutonic kings reacted to climate change by mobilizing their entire tribes to invade other lands. If the gods did not favor the king with a good harvest, then the king's only viable option was to go to war and hope that the "luck" won by his offerings would serve him better in securing military victory.

Concluding the Teutonic Religious Response to Climate Change

According to Holt, Teutonic movements in the third and fourth centuries can be "attributed to climate change 81.4% of the time."[373] As he summarizes,

The nineteen-year poor period (AD 364 to 383) may have been a contributing external factor, among the multitude of other reasons, to the welling attacks against the Roman Empire. . . . This is a very active period with many different tribes repeatedly attacking Rome. The fact that these incursions all occur in a below mean period as evident in the tree ring record at least merits consideration.[374]

Whereas the correlation between climate change and the Teutonic invasions is well evidenced by tree ring records, pollen samples, archaeology, and surviving historical accounts, these alone do not afford the reader much in the way of insight into the *weltanschauung*[375] of the Teutonic mind. To understand the migrations from the perspective of the fifth century Teuton, these *en masse* movements must also be seen, as least in part, as a religious response to environmental change.

The mythic motif of the luck-bearing god-sprung king, the deity of abundance, and the procession of the sacred wain of the fertility god and/or king wed to the sovereign goddess of the land remained a central tenet of Heathen belief for at least a millennium. In response to the questions of how might a religion so rooted in the agricultural cycle responded to environmental disaster and how the king might reconcile himself to the Earth when she withheld her blessings, the answer was, more often than not, migration, which brought with it war.

The sacral kings of the Teutons could, if harvests failed, themselves be sacrificed by tribal priests to regain the favor of the gods. As the highest intercessor of the tribe, the king's "luck" was also believed to provide for victory in battle. With climate fluctuations in Europe contributing to long periods of drought, and with climate changes in China setting into motion Asiatic political upheavals that ultimately pushed the Huns into Europe, for the fifth century Teutonic king only one viable option remained. As holy *heilerfüllt* the Teutonic king could wage war, and therein please the gods of battle while providing for his people.

It is during this period of history that the cult of *Wōdanaz (OE: Wóden, ON: Óðinn), whose cult came to embody *furor Teutonicus,* is thought by some scholars to have risen to its greatest prominence. If the early Iron Age earth-goddess and harvest god had inherited the holy wain of the Bronze Age solar-god(dess) then, in the age of folkwandering, the cult of the wandering war god was in position to, at least partially, eclipse that of Ing as the traditional god of kings.[376] From the folkwandering forward, Wóden was the divine ancestor from which rulers would, more often than not, thenceforth claim descent. A dry wind blew across China and a kingdom fell. The Huns were unleashed upon Europe. The Goths moved. Rome faltered. The Saxons sailed. Wóden became the foremost god of kings. [377] Wyrd goeth ever as she shall.[378]

HÓHINGA/HANGINGS/APPENDICES

APPENDICE I: BETWIXT BLOOD BESPATTERED BENCHES, RECKONING THE DRYHTEN

It is no easy feat to nail down dates for much of Hengest's life. The various histories that preserve the story of his life or even that of the Anglo-Saxon conquest are incomplete and, on occasion, contradictory. Neither Gildas, Bede, nor the *Anglo-Saxon Chronicle*, for example, mention Vortimer, his four victories against the Saxons, or even the Amesbury hall-slaughter. Nennius and Geoffrey of Monmouth provide and flesh out those encounters without necessarily providing dates. Still, to understand Hengest and who he was as a leader, it is imperative to have some insight into where he was, age-wise, in his life when each event unfolded.

According to the *Anglo-Saxon Chronicle*, when Horsa was slain at the battle of Aegelesthrep in 455 CE, Hengest shared the Kentish throne with his son, Æsc. The very next year, Æsc joined his father at Crecganford where they crushed the Briton armies, slaying some 4,000 men and forcing the Britons to flee to London. For Æsc to have ascended to kingship and military command in 455 CE would indicate that he had already reached adulthood by that time. Unlike the later monarchies of the Middle Ages, there were no boy kings such as Edward V, Henry VI, or Edward VI amongst the Migration Era tribes. As noted by the first century Roman historian Tacitus, "they choose their kings for their noble birth, their commanders for their valor" and that "hearing is given to the king or state-chief as his age, rank, military distinction, or eloquence can secure."[379] Furthermore, Tacitus observed that "The young men are slow to mate, and thus they reach manhood with vigour unimpaired. The girls, too, are not hurried into marriage. As old and full-grown as men, they match their mates in age and strength."[380] It follows then that, barring Æsc having been born a bastard, Hengest would have been "old and full-grown" when he fathered him and that Æsc, to have stood as king and military commander, would likewise have been in the prime of his manhood by 455 CE. This would have put Æsc somewhere around twenty and his father Hengest in the neighborhood of forty years old by the time Horsa was laid low.[381] With this date and age more or less secured, we can now examine the events of Hengest's life with the insight of knowing his approximate age at the time each unfolded.

One cannot say with certainty when it was that Hengest visited Finnesburh. As both Bede and the *Anglo-Saxon Chronicle* ascribe the year 449 CE to his arrival at Ipwinesfleet, Kent, the hall-slaughters that befell Finnesburh must have taken place sometime before then. Yet, based upon what has already been discussed concerning the age at which Germanic men married, it is quite likely that Hengest was just under twenty, perhaps eighteen or nineteen, when he followed his lord Hnæf to Finn's hall in Frisia. This would date the Finnesburh hall-slaughters to roughly 433 and 434 CE.

APPENDICE II: BETWIXT BLOOD BESPATTERED BENCHES, TIMELINE OF HENGEST'S LIFE

I have done my best to reconcile the dates provided by the *Anglo Saxon Chronicle*[382] with Geoffrey of Monmouth's history to form a timeline. The proposed date of the Finnesburh hall-slaughter was derived by means of the material covered in Appendice I. Fitting the Briton accounts of Hengest's return to Germany and of the hall-slaughter of Amesbury into the timeline proved difficult. As the *Chronicle* dates 455 CE as when Hengest and Æsc rule Kent together, I have determined that the Briton accounts must have lead up to this date.

Year	Event	Hengest's Approximate Age
415	Hengest and Horsa[383] are born.	Newborn
433-434	The Finnesburh hall-slaughters take place.	18-19

449	Hengest and Horsa arrive at Ipwinesfleet, Kent, with three ships of Anglo-Saxons. Hengest and Horsa enter into the service of the Briton king, Vortigern.	34
452	Voritgern is usurped by his son, Vortimer, who wages war on the Anglo-Saxons. Four battles are fought between the Britons and the Anglo-Saxons with the Britons being victorious. Horsa is slain.	37
453-455	The Anglo-Saxons are forced to flee to Germany and regroup. Vortimer dies, possibly poisoned by his step-mother, Hengest's daughter, Rowena.	38-39
455	Hengest decides to return to reclaim Kent. The Amesbury/Ambrius hall-slaughter takes place. Hengest and Æsc rule Kent together.	40
456	The battle of Crecganford is fought. Hengest and Æsc defeat a force of 4,000 Britons, forcing the Britons them to flee to London.	41

465	The battle of Wippedesfleot is fought. Hengest and Æsc are victorious. Twelve Briton ealdormen are slain.	46
473	Hengest and Æsc are again victorious against the Britons.	54
488	The battle of Cunungeburg is fought. The Anglo-Saxons are defeated. Hengest is captured and executed.	73

ÞÓRBEORHT LÍNLÉAH

APPENDICE III: BETWIXT BLOOD BESPATTERED BENCHES, RECKONING THE LORE

Work	Author(s) & Ethnic Perspective	Year	Depiction of Hengest
De Excidio et Conquestu Britanniae (On the Ruin and Conquest of Britannia)	Gildas – Briton clergyman	6th century	This work does not mention Hengest by name, but it does provide the earliest written account of the Anglo-Saxon arrival. It is a decidedly negative depiction.

Historia ecclesiastica gentis Anglorum (The Ecclesiastical History of the English People)	Bede – A Northumbrian (Anglo-Saxon) monk	731 CE (completed)	This work describes the arrival of Hengest and Horsa in Britannia. It is a largely neutral account. Neither hall-slaughter is mentioned.
Finnesburh Fragment	Unknown *scóp* (Anglo-Saxon)	Unknown, though the extensive use of Heathen imagery argues for an early date of composition, perhaps even predating Bede's work.	This work recounts an event from Hengest's life prior to his arrival in Britannia. Its portrayal is heroic.

Beowulf	This poem is the work of at least two unknown Christian *scóps* (Anglo-Saxon) working with a pre-Christian oral tradition.	The date of its original composition is disputed. Dates range from the 7th to 11th centuries. J. R. R. Tolkien, Dorothy Whitlock, C.L. Wrenn and Tom Shippey have all proposed an 8th century composition.	This work recounts an event from Hengest's life prior to his arrival in Britannia. Its portrayal is heroic.
Historia Brittonum (The History of the Britons)	Nennius – A Welsh (Brittonic) monk	828 CE (completed)	This work is decidedly negative in its portrayal of Hengest. It is the earliest surviving account of the Amesbury hall-slaughter.
Anglo-Saxon Chronicle	Various monks- Possibly commissioned	Late 9th century (begun)	This work records the arrival of Hengest and

	by Ælfred the Great, King of Wessex (Anglo-Saxon)		Horsa in Britannia. It is a largely neutral account. Neither hall-slaughter is mentioned. It also provides dates for some of Hengest's battles.
Gesta regum Anglorum (Deeds of the English Kings)	William of Malmesbury – A monk of Norman descent.	1125 CE	This work's portrayal of Hengest is decidedly negative with emphasis placed on the Amesbury hall-slaughter.

Historia Regum Britanniae (The History of the Kings of Britain)	Geoffrey of Monmouth – A Welsh (British) monk, Church canon, and teacher	1136 CE	This work's portrayal of Hengest is decidedly negative with emphasis placed on the Amesbury hall-slaughter.
The Prose Edda	Snorri Sturluson – Icelandic (Norse) politician, poet, and mythographer	Early 13th century	This work provides a genealogical account of kings whose lines sprang from Óðinn/Wóden. Regarding Hengest it is of neutral bias.

ÞÓRBEORHT LÍNLÉAH

APPENDICE IV: BETWIXT BLOOD BESPATTERED BENCHES, FINNESBURH IN ANGLO-SAXON POETRY: THE MEAD-HALL, THE POET'S STAGE

The tales of the twin hall-slaughters that befell Finnesburh are preserved in two Anglo-Saxon texts. Chronologically, the first of these texts, known as the *Finnesburh Fragment*, gives us, at least in part, the first half of this tragic story. The text itself, a work of Anglo-Saxon poetic verse, is particularly difficult to penetrate. One need only glance at three or four translations of this partially preserved poem to realize that even those well versed and affluent in that old and ancient language are often uncertain of its author's intentions. The difficulty in discerning certain portions of the poem arises not simply from its incomplete preservation or from the less rigid nature of Old English grammar[384] but from the very nature of Anglo-Saxon, and even Norse, *scópcræft*.[385]

Heroic poems were composed for public performance rather than mere literary review.[386] The theater for such performances was the mead-hall, itself often the centralized meeting place of any settlement. It was in the mead-hall[387] that the lord or king sat amidst his thanes – retainers whose loyalty was sworn to him by means of a hold-oath[388] taken upon the hilt of his sword – to hold the sacred rite of *symbel*. Together, these two rites, the swearing of the hold-oath and the seasonal celebration of *symbel*, both sanctified by the drinking of mead, exemplified the initiation and ongoing profession of the retainer-thane to the service of his liege lord.

As with any profession, the validity of words, accompanied by raised horn, was attested to by its public hearing. Likewise, *scópcræft*, which formed an important and essential part of *symbel*, was itself a public performance. Those upon whose ears befell the song of any particular *scóp*, accompanied by his strumming of the *hearp*,[389] were expected to have some measure of familiarity with the tale to which his song thus spoke. It is for this reason, because we are not privy to details of the story with which the intended audience was already acquainted, that we now find ourselves confused and confounded when we translate tales utterly unfamiliar to us, yet known more fully to those to whom they were originally told. However, if we are to make anything of Hengest's life, if we are to grasp the significance of the Finnesburh hall-slaughters, how they shaped Hengest as a leader and how they re-manifested decades later in the Amesbury hall-slaughter, it is imperative that we accept some reconstruction and agreed upon understanding of what unfolded in that Frisian hall some sixteen hundred years ago.

APPENDICE V: DRAGONS AMONG THE DEAD, OLD ENGLISH TRANSLATIONS

Finnesburh Fragment lines 3, 4

Né ðis ne dagað éastan   né hér draca ne fléogeð

Nay, this no eastern dawning.   Not here a drake flieth.

né hér ðisse healle   hornas ne byrnað.

Nor here in this hall   do the gable-horns burneth.

Anglo-Saxon Chronicle *(*Manuscript D: Cotton Tiberius B.iv)

793 A.D. - Hér wæron réðe forebécna cumene ofer Norðhymbra land, 7 þæt folc earmlic brégdon. Þæt wæron ormete þodenas 7 lígrescas, 7 fýrenne dracan wæron gesewene on þám lifte fléogende. Þám tácnum sóna fyligde mycel hungor, 7 litel æfter þám, þæs ilcan géares on VI. Idus Ianuarii, earmlice Hæþenra manna hergunc adilegode Godes cyrican in Lindisfarnae þurh hréaflác 7 manslihт.

793 A.D. - *Here were fierce fore-beacons come over Northumbria's land and sorely vexed the folk. There were whirlwinds without-mete and lightening-showers, and fiery drakes were seen in the loft flying. These tokens [were] soon followed [by] mickle hunger, and little after then, the ilken (same) year on the sixth day before the Ides of January (January 8th), vexing Heathen men harried God's church in Lindisfarne through robbery and manslaughter.*

Wóden and the Wyrm (*The Nine Herbs Charm* lines 30-35)

Þas VIIII magon   wið nygon attrum.

These nine have main   against nine venoms.

Wyrm cóm snícan   tóslát hé man

Wyrm came sneaking.   It slit a man.

ðá genóm Wóden   VIIII wuldortánas,

Then took up Wóden   nine glory-tines (tines of Wuldor),

slóh ðá þá næddran,   þæt héo on VIIII tófléah.

slew with them the adder   that she into nine flew.

Þær geændade   æppel and attor,

There earned   apple and venom

þæt héo næfre ne wolde   on hús búgan.

that she never would   bend-way (slither) into house.

Maxims II 26b-27a

         Draca sceal on hlæwe

         Drake shall [dwell] in the low (mound),

fród, frætwum[390] wlanc

ancient, of treasures proud.

Maxims II 42b-43a

         Þyrs sceal on fenne gewunian

         Thurse shall in fen dwell

ána innan lande

alone in the land.

Solomon and Saturn I lines 146-154

Mæg simle se godes cwide   gumena gehwylcum

The word of God may always   for every man

ealra féonda gehwáne   fléondne gebrengan

all [and] every fiend   bring to flight

ðurh mannes múð   mánfulra héap

through man's mouth,   [the] heap of the wicked

sweartne geswencan   næfre híe ðæs syllice

the swarthy to trouble,   never [though] they wondrously

bléoum bregdað   æfter báncofan

braideth (alter) their blee (appearance),   [and] about [their] bone-coves

feðerhoman onfóð   hwílum flotan gripað

feather-skins receive.   Sometimes they grip floating-ships.

hwílum híe gewendað   in wyrmes líc

Sometimes they wend   in a wyrm's lich (body),

stronges and sticoles   stingeð nieten

strong and stake-sharp   sting the neat (cows, oxen)

feldgongende   feoh gestrúdeð

[and the] field-going   fee-cattle[they] plunder.

Wandering Wolf and the Wyrm (*Solomon and Saturn II* 33-46)

Saturnus cuæð:

Saturn quoth:

Se mæra wæs háten   sælidende

So was hight the mere's   seafarer

weallende Wulf   werðeodum cuð

Wandering Wolf,   couth among the men-tribes

Filistina freond Nebrondes
of the Philistines, friend of Nimrod.
he on ðám felda ofslóg XXV
He on field slew those twenty-five
dracena on dægred and hine ða deað offeoll
drakes at daybreak, and then death fell upon him.
forðan ðá foldan ne mæg fira ænig
For-then (therefore) that fold may not any man,
ðone mercstede mon gesecan
that mark-stead, [any] man seek,
fugol gefléogan ne ðon má foldan neat
bird fly-over, no more the field's neat (cow or ox).
ðanon átercynn ærest gewurdon
Thence the venom-kind erst worthed (came to be)
wíde onwæcned ðá ðe nu weallende
widely awakened that which now welling
ðurh attres oroð ingang rýmað
through venom's breath goes within, makes room.
git his sweord scíneð swiðe gescæned
Yet still his sword shineth swith (exceedingly) it was sheened (polished),
and ofer ðá byrgenna blícað ðá hieltas
and over the burial-mound brightly it's hilt.

Sigemund and the Wyrm (*Beowulf* 875-900)

    wélhwylc gecwæð
     well-all he quoth
þæt hé fram Sigemunde secgan hyrde

OF GHOSTS AND GODPOLES

that he of Sigemund   heard spoke
ellendaédum   uncúþes fela
bold-deeds   many uncouth[391]
Wælsinges gewin   wíde síðas
the Wælsing's[392] *wars   wide wanderings*
þára þe gumena bearn   gearwe ne wiston
thereof which the bairns of men   yare not wist[393]
fǽhðe ond fyrena   búton Fitela mid hine
feuds and foul deeds[394]   *but Fitela, with him,*
þonne hé swulces hwæt   secgan wolde
then of such things   he would speak
éam his nefan   swá híe á waeron
[as an] uncle [to] his nephew   as they ever were
æt níða gehwám   nýdgesteallan
against every evil   need-stabled companions
hæfdon ealfela   eotena cynnes
had all-many   of the kindreds of Eaters (Devourers, Giants)
sweordum gesaeged   Sigemunde gesprong
with swords laid low.   Sigemund sprang
æfter déaðdæge   dóm unlýtel
after his death-day   [of] no little doom
syþðan wíges heard   wyrm ácwealde
since the war-hardened one[395]   *quelled the Wyrm,*
hoards hyrde   hé under hárne stán
hoard's hearder,   he under hoary stone,
æþelinges bearn   ána genéðde
atheling's bairn   alone dared
frécne daéde   ne waes him Fitela mid

151

the fierce deed.   Not with him was Fitela.
hwæþre him gesaelde   ðæt þæt swurd þurhwód
It befell him however   that the sword through-waded
wrætlícne wyrm   þæt hit on wealle ætstód
wondrously-bejeweled[396] Wyrm   that it a-stood[397] on the wall
dryhtlíc íren   draca morðre swealt
drightlike[398] iron   [the]Drake sweltered[399] in its murder
hæfde áglæca   elne gegongen
the wicked-leech[400] had   by boldness overcame
þæt hé béahhoard   brúcan móste
that, of the ring-hoard, he   might brook
selfes dome   sæbát gehléod
self's doom.   Sea-boat loaded
bær on bearm scipes   beorhte frætwa
bore on ship's bosom   bright treasures,
Wælses eafera   Wyrm hát gemealt
Wæls' heir.   The hot Wyrm melted.
se wæs wreccena   wíde mærost
That wretch was   widely renown
ofer werþéode   wígendra hléo
over the tribes of men   the lee[401] of warriors
ellendaédum   hé þæs ær onðáh
for bold-deeds.   He thus ere throve.

Beowulf 102-105

wæs se grimma gæst   Grendel háten
The grim ghost was   hight Grendel
mǽre mearcstapa   sé þe móras héold

infamous march-stepper he the moors held,
fen ond fæsten fífelcynnes eard
fen and fastness, monsterkind's earth,
wonsælí wer weardode hwíle
the wretched wight[402] warded [it for] a while.

Beowulf battles Grendel 2082-2090
bona blódigtóð bealewa gemyndig
The bloody-toothed bane, bales (evils) minded
of ðám goldsele gongan wolde
from the gold-hall would go
ac hé mægnes róf mín costode
but he, renown of main, tested mine.
Grápode gearofolm glóf hangode
Ready-hand gripped a glove [that] hung
síd ond syllíc searobendum fæst
wide and wondrously, cunning-bonds fast,
sío wæs orðoncum eall gegyrwed
it was skillfully all adorned
déofles cræftum ond dracan fellum
[with] devil's crafts and drake's fell (skin).
Hé mec þaér on innan unsynnigne
Me, he there in, without sin-shame,
díor dædfruma gedón wolde
the dire deed-one would (wanted to) put.

The Dragon and the Thief II (Beowulf 2270b-2279)

Hordwynne fond
Hoard-joy found
eald úhtsceaða   opene standan
[the] old twilight-scather   standing open
sé ðe byrnende   biorgas séceð
he who, burning,   barrows seeketh:
nacod níðdraca   nihtes fléogeð
[the] naked hate-drake   [who by] night flieth,
fýre befangen   hyne foldbúend
encompassed in fire;   him the fold-dwellers
swiðe ondrǽdað   hé gesécean sceall
swith dread.   He shall seek
hord on hrúsan   þaér hé Haéðen gold
the hoard in the earth.   There he, Heathen gold,
waráð wintrum fród   ne byð him wihte ðý sél
wardeth, old in winters. Beeth him not a whit better for that.
Swá se ðéodsceaða   þréo hund wintra
So the tribe-scather   for three hundred winters
héold on hrúsan   hordærna sum
held in the earth   some hoard-hall.

Beowulf 2208b-2211

              hé gehéold tela
              He held well
fiftig wintra   wæs ðá fród cyning
for fifty winters.   He was then an old king,
eald éþelweard   oð ðæt ón ongan
the ancient ancestral-land's warder,   until that one began
deorcum nihtum   draca rícsian
in dark nights,   the drake, to rule.

Beowulf Enters the Barrow (*Beowulf* 2550-2560a)

Lét ðá of bréostum   ðá hé gebolgen wæs
Let then from breast,   when he angered was,
Weder-Géata léod   word út faran
the Weder-Geat's man,   a word fare out.
stearcheort styrmde   stefn in becóm
[The] stark-hearted [one] stormed,   his summons came in
heaðotorht hlynnan   under hárne stán
roaring battle-clear   under hoary stone.
hete wæs onhréred   hordweard oncníow
Hate was stirred,   [the] hoard-warder knew
mannes reorde   næs ðǽr mára fyrst
the speech of man.   There [was] no more time
fréode tó friclan   from aérest cwóm
to seek frith.   Erst came forth
oruð áglǽcean   út of stáne
[the] breath of [the] wicked-leech   out of the stone,
hát hildeswát   hrúse dynede

hot battle-sweltering, [the] earth dinned.

biorn[403] under beorge   bordrand onswáf

[The] bear-warrior under barrow   [his] board-shield swung

wið ðám gryregieste

against the horror-ghost.

Beowulf's Death (*Beowulf* 2711b-2715a)

Þá sío wund ongon

Then the wound began,

þé him se eorðdraca   aér geworhte

that [which] the earth-drake   ere wrought him,

swelan ond swellan   Hé þæt sóna onfand

to swelter and to swell.   He soon found

þæt him on bréostum   bealoníð wéoll

that in his breast   bale-evil welled

attor on innan.

the venom within.

Beowulf's burial instructions to Wiglaf: 2802b-2808

hlǽw gewyrcean

A low (barrow) work (make),

beorhtne æfter bǽle   æt brimes nósan

bright after bale,   at brim's nose.

sé scel tó gemyndum   mínum léodum

It shall be a reminder to   my people,

héah hlífian   on hrones næsse

towering high   on whale's ness (headland)

þæt hit sǽlíðend   syððan hátan

so that it, seafarers   sithence will hight
Bíowulfes Biorh   ðá ðe brentingas
Beowulf's Barrow,   who the ships
ofer flóda genipu   feorran drífað.
over flood's mists   drifteth afar.

Beowulf 2813-2816
Þú eart endeláf   ússes cynnes
Thou art the end-leavings   of our kin,
Wǽgmundinga   ealle wyrd forswéop
of the Wǽgmundings. Wyrd swept-away all
Míne mágas   tó metodsceafte
of my kinsman   to the One-who-mete's shaping,
eorlas on elne   ic him æfter sceal.
earls in strength;   I shall go after them.

APPENDICE VI: DRAGONS AMONG THE DEAD, OLD NORSE TRANSLATIONS

Gull-Þóris Saga 3, Kafli (Chapter 3)

Valur hét víkingur er átti gull mikið. Hann bar féið undir helli einn norður við Dumbshaf og lagðist á síðan og synir hans með honum og urðu allir að flugdrekum.

A viking was hight Valr, who owned mickle gold. He bore the fee under one hill, north towards Dumbshaf, and laid upon it thereafter, and his sons amid him, and all then became flying-drakes.

Gull-Þóris Saga 20, Kafli (Chapter 20) – The Beserker Þórir's fate, who went missing when he heard that his sons were dead.

...en það hafa menn fyrir satt að hann hafi að dreka orðið og hafi lagðist á gullkistur sínar. Hélst það og lengi síðan að menn sáu dreka fljúga

...but that men hold for sooth that he had become a drake and had lain upon his gold-chest. Much then and long thereafter, men saw drake flying...

Völsunga Saga (chapter 14)

Síðan drap Fáfnir föður sinn," segir Reginn, "ok myrði hann. . . . Hann gerðist svá illr, at hann lagðist út ok unni engum at njóta fjárins nema sér ok varð síðan at inum versta ormi ok liggr nú á því fé."

"Thereafter struck, Fáfnir his father," said Reginn, "and murdered him. . . . He became so ill (evil), that he laid out, and granted that none enjoy the fee he took, and became thereafter the worst wyrm and lies now on that fee."

Skáldskaparmál 6

Baugi skal bora bjargit...

Baugi should bore the mountain . . .

Þá brást (**bregða**) Bölverkr í ormslíki ok skreið inn í nafarsraufina....

Then braided Bale-worker into a wyrm's lich and slithered into the auger-rift.

Ynglinga Saga Chapter 8

En eptir göfga menn skyldi haug gera til minningar; en eptir alla þá menn, er nökkut mannsmót var at, skyldi reisa bautasteina; ok hélzt sjá siðr lengi síðan.

How afterward, honorable men should howes yare (make ready) to their memory; how all honorable men then, who measured in manliness, should raise slain-stones; and this custom was held for a long time.

Hávamal verse 72

Sonr er betri

A son is better

þótt sé síð of alinn

though he is begotten

eftir genginn guma

after the going (death) of the man (father);

sjaldan bautarsteinar

Seldom slain-stones

standa brautu nær

stand nigh by the path

nema reisi niðr at nið

lest a kinsmen to a kinsmen undertakes to raise [them].

Ynglinga Saga Chapter 12

Freyr tók sótt; en er at honum leið sóttin, leituðu menn sér ráðs, ok létu fá menn til hans koma, en bjoggu haug mikinn, ok létu dyrr á ok 3 glugga. En er Freyr var dauðr, báru þeir hann leyniliga í hauginn, ok sögðu Svíum at hann lifði, ok varðveittu hann þar 3 vetr. En skatt öllum heltu þeir í hauginn, í einn glugg gullinu, en í annan silfrinu, í hinn þriðja eirpenningum. Þá hélzt ár ok friðr.

Freyr took sick; as he was on the way to death, his men sought rede, and let few men come to him, but built a mickle howe, and there were three doors and three holes. When Freyr was dead, they bore him secretly to the howe, and said to the Swedes that he lived, and warded him there three winters. But all scot they hid in the howe, in one hole gold, in another silver, in the third copper pennies. Then there was bountiful harvest and frith.

Þórr and the Wyrm (*Völuspa* 55-57)

Ginn lopt yfir   lindi jarðar
Yawning sky above   the earth's girdle,

gapa ýgs kjaptar   orms í hæðom
gapes its ugly jaws   the wyrm in the heights.

mun Óðins sonr   ormi [eitri] æeta
Then shall Óðin's son   the Wyrm [venom] meet.

vargs at dauða   Viðard niðia
The death of the wolf   [is] Viðar's kinsman.

Þá kemr inn mœri[404]   mögr Hlóðynjar
Then comes in the renowned   son of Hlóðyn.

gengr Óðins sonr   við orm [ulf] vega
Óðin's son goes   to war against the Wyrm [wolf].

drepr hann af móði   Miðgarðs véurr
Strikes him with mood,[405]   Middle-Earth's warder.

munu halir allir   heimstöð ryðja
All men shall   their homesteads clear.

gengr fet níu   Fjörgynjar burr
Goes nine feet   Fjörgyn's bairn,

neppr frá naðri   níðs ókvíðnum
barely from the adder   not fearing scorn.

Sól tér sortna   sígr fold í mar
Sun turns swart.   Fold sinks into mere.
hverfa af himni   heiðar stjörnur
From heaven turns   the bright stars.
geisar eimi   ok aldrnari.[406]
Rage [both] steam   and corpse-fire.
leikr hár hiti   við himin sjálfan
Heat dances high   against heaven itself.

ÞÓRBEORHT LÍNLÉAH

APPENDICE VII: DRAGONS AMONG THE DEAD, OLD HIGH GERMAN TRANSLATION

Elias and the Antichrist (*Mûspelli* 37-39 and 44-55)

(37-39)

Daz hôrtih rahhôn   dia uueroltrehtuuîson

This I heard reckoned   [by] the world-right-wise,

daz sculi der antichristo   mit Eliase pâgan

that shall the Antichrist   with Elias battle.

der uuarch ist kiuuâfanit   denne uuirdit untar in uuîc arhapan.

The wolf is weaponed,   then war begins to upheave between them.

(44-55)

der antichristo   stêt pî demo altfîant

The Antichrist   standeth by the Old-fiend,

stêt pî demo Satanase   der inan uarsenkan scal

standeth by Satan,   who shall forsench (forsake) him.

pidiu scal er in deru uuîcsteti   uunt piuallan

Therefore shall he on the war-stead   wounded fall

enti in demo sinde   sigalôs uuerdan

and in that way   victoryless become.

doh uuânit des uilo   ... gotmanno

ÞÓRBEORHT LÍNLÉAH

But weeneth many that [are] god-men (priest, ON: góði)

daz Elias in demo uuîge   aruuartit uuerde

that Elias, in the war,   slaineth will be.

sô daz Eliases pluot   in erda kitriufit

So that Elias's blood (OE: blót, sacrifice)   into Earth dripeth,

sô inprinnant die perga   poum ni kistentit

so burneth the burgs,   no beam standeth

ênîhc in erdu   aha artruknent

anywhere on Earth,   rivers drieth,

muor varsuuilhit sih   suilizôt lougiu der himil

the moor swalloweth itself,   flame sweltereth the heavens,

mâno uallit   prinnit mittilagart

Moon falleth,   burneth Middle-Earth.

stên ni kistentit   uerit denne stûatago in lant

No stone standeth   when fareth strafe[107]-day in the land.

APPENDICE VIII: DRAGONS AMONG THE DEAD, LATIN TRANSLATIONS

Vita Barbati Episcopi Beneventani: Life of Barbatus, Bishop of Benevento (p 557)

His quoque diebus quamvis sacri baptismatis unda Langobardi abluerentur, tamen priscum gentilitatis ritum tenentes, sicut bestiali mente degebant, bestiae simulacro, quae vulgo vipera nominatur, flectebant colla, quae debite suo debebant flectere Creatori.

In those days, though the sacred waters of baptism had abluted the Langobards, nevertheless they held to the former rites of the gentiles, as they continued with bestial mind, to a beast's simulacrum, which is vulgarly (commonly) named a viper, to flex their collars (bow their necks), the flexing of which is a debt (duty) they owe to the Creator.

Res Gestae Saxonicae: Libre I, 11 (p44)

Hic arripiens signum, quod apud eos habebatur sacrum, leonis atque draconis et desuper aquilae volantis insignitum effigie

He [Hathegat] took up a sign (banner), that they held sacred, ensigned with the effigy a lion and a dragon and an eagle flying above.

The Annals of St Neots *(based upon the Visio Eucherii, a vision that Hincmar of Reims attributed to Saint Eucherius of Orléans, concerning the afterlife of Charles Martel)*

Ipsi autem pergentes ad predictum monasterium, ubi corpus ipsius Karoli humatum fuerat, sepulchrum que ipsius aperientes, visis est subito draco exisse et totum illud sepulchrum inventum est interius denigratum ac si fuisset exustum

But they proceeded to the predicted monastery, where the corpse of Charles himself was interred, opened his sepulture and, seeing a dragon suddenly exit, found the interior of the sepulture totally denigrated (blacked) as if it had been burned up.

The Carmen De Hastingae Prolio of Guy, Bishop of Amiens (585-596)

Ergo uelut fuerat testatus, rupis in alto

Ergo as he had testified, in the cliff on high

precepit claudi uertice corpus humi.

he ordered that the corpse to be entombed on the summit.

Extimplo quidam, partim Normannus et Anglus,

Forthwith someone, part Norman and Angle,

compater Heraldi, iussa libenter agit.

a companion of Harold, freely acted on the order.

Corpus enim regis cito sustulit et sepeliuit;

The corpse of the king he quickly took up and sepulchered;

imponens lapidem, scripsit et in titulo:

laying over it a stone, he inscribed the title:

'Per mandata ducis rex hic Heralde quiescis,

'Per mandate of the duke, here king Harold rest,

vt custos maneas littoris et pelagi.'

as the custodian, remain on the shore and sea.'

Dux, cum genta sua, plangens super ossa sepulta,

The duke, along with his gens, plangently wailed over the sepulchered ossuary, pauperibus Cristi munera distribuit.

distributed money to the paupers of Christ.

Nomine postposito ducis, et sic rege locato,

The name of duke he postponed (put off), and the king interred,

hinc regale sibi nomen adeptus abit.

having adopted the royal name, he departed.

ÞÓRBEORHT LÍNLÉAH

APPENDICE IX: LORE AND LANDSCAPE, THE FIMBULVETR OF RAGNARǪK AND THE DUST VEIL OF 536 C.E. AS THEY PERTAIN TO SAXON HEATHENDOM

Hvat lifir manna, þá er inn mæra líðr

Fimbulvetr með firum?

What shall live of mankind when at last there comes,

the mighty winter to men?[408]

It has been over a millennium since an anonymous Norse *skald* set this question, attributed to Óðinn, chief god of the old Teutonic Religion, to verse in a poem known as the "Vafþrúðnismál." The *Fimbulvetr,* or the Mighty-Winter as it translates into Modern English, is an eschatological event in Norse mythology which heralds the beginning of *Ragnarǫk,* the "reckoning of the gods." As elaborated on by the Icelandic mythologist and law-speaker, Snorri Sturiuson in his work, the *Poetic Edda,*

> Mikil tíðendi eru þaðan at segja ok mörg. Þau in fyrstu, at vetr sá kemr, er kallaðr er fimbulvetr. Þá drífr snær ór öllum áttum. Frost eru þá mikil ok vindar hvassir. Ekki nýtr sólar. Þeir vetr fara þrír saman ok ekki sumar milli.
>
> *Mickle and many tidings are there to say of it [Ragnarǫk]. The first is that a winter will come which*

will be called the Mighty Winter. Then drifts of snow from all directions, then frost will be mickle and wind piercing. No use will be the sun. Three winters will fare the same and amid them not a summer.[409]

Whilst the term *Ragnarǫk* is to be found only within the Old Norse lexicon, this by no means indicates that Germanic eschatology was unique to Scandinavia. Rather, for a more archaic synonym, one might well look to the Old Norse *Múspell,* a curious word of uncertain etymology, which appears both as a component of creation in the form of *Múspellsheimr* and again at *Ragnarǫk* in the form of *Múspellssynir,* the "son of *Múspell,*" the fire ettins who fare forth to fight the gods.[410] Unlike *Ragnarǫk, Múspell* is indeed attested to in other Germanic languages as a gloss for the Christian apocalypse. The Old High German *Mûspelli,* the Heathen significance of which has already been elaborated upon in "Dragons among the Dead," and the appearance of *mûtspelli* in the Old Saxon *Hêliand* provide internal evidence for a continental Heathen eschatology. Moreover, on a broader Indo-European scale, Mallory and Adams have already, through comparative analysis between ancient Roman, Scandinavian, Iranian, and Indian mythologies, illustrated the existence of an archaic proto-myth concerning a final battle between the gods and their enemies.[411] As such, in pursuing a reconstruction of Saxon Heathen belief, the interest is not whether or not the Saxons, both Old and Anglo, held to a belief comparable to the Norse *Ragnarǫk,* but rather how many of the details preserved in the Eddas concerning *Ragnarǫk* were part of the pre-Viking, continental *Mûtspelli* narrative. It is upon this point that the *Fimbulvetr* will be considered in light of what the Saxon may have believed concerning the *Mûtspelli.*

In their article "Twilight of the Gods? The 'Dust Veil Event' of AD 536 in Critical Perspective," Gräslund and Price explored the religious implications that the dust veil of 536 CE had upon the Norse Heathen religion. Regarding the dust veil event itself, it is known through both soil samples and contemporary historical accounts that, beginning in 536 CE and lasting for three or four years thereafter, the world experienced the equivalent of a nuclear winter as dust, either from volcanic eruption or even extraterrestrial objects colliding with the earth, blocked out the sun.[412] In examining the archeological evidence for settlement collapse during this period, Gräslund and Price have summarized the dust veil's impact upon Scandinavia as such:

> Ruined harvest and grazing for two years in a row, combined with several cold summers and shorter growing seasons for a further decade, would have led unavoidably to serious famine in archaic agricultural societies. It seems reasonable to suggest that the populations of Scandinavia in the mid sixth century may have been halved.[413]

Gräslund and Price went on to propose that "the Old Norse traditions of the Fimbulwinter and Ragnarök may collectively remember terrifying experiences of starvation and collapse as a result of extreme weather phenomena during the years AD 536-550."[414] It is a fascinating proposal. After all, Old Norse lore is replete with accounts of historical details pertaining to the fifth century. The onslaught of Attila and the Huns and the deeds of Gothic kings are all preserved in Nordic verse. It therefore seems only reasonable then that a sixth century catastrophe of such proportion would have likewise found its way into the mythic memory of the Northern folk.

Of course, it is impossible to say with any certainty that the Old Norse *Fimbulvetr* arose from a deep dread brought about by such devastation. Yet, if Gräslund and Price's proposal is to be believed, then what might this tell us of the *Mûtspelli* as it would have been understood by Saxon Heathens prior to the dust veil's appearance? After all, the Anglo-Saxons arrived in Britannia in the year 449 CE, almost a century prior to the historical *Fimbulvetr*. That their Heathen belief had to it an eschatological component is understood as a matter of their Indo-European mythic inheritance. Nonetheless, if we are to take the dust veil to be the icy well from whence the Norse *Fimbulvetr* sprang, then it is quite likely that the *Fimbulvetr* would not have formed a part of the original *Mûtspelli* myth. The question remains then, would Saxon Heathen belief, in the years following the dust veil, have incorporated the *Fimbulvetr* into its eschatological lore?

Among the Anglo-Saxons, Heathendom officially ended in 686 CE with the death of Arwald, king of the Isle of Wight, and the massacre of that island's Heathen inhabitants.[415] Likewise, Heathendom, as an official religion, ended among the Old Saxons in 785 CE with the defeat of the Westfali and Bardongavenses and the baptism of

Widukind, their war-chieftain.[416] A century and a half of Heathenry among the Anglo-Saxons and two and a half centuries of Heathenry among the Old Saxons following the dust veil would seem ample time for the *Fimbulvetr* to find its way into Saxon myth. This is particularly the case given the abundance of archeological evidence attesting to interaction between the Saxons and Scandinavians during this time period. However, if the *Fimbulvetr*, as Gräslund and Price have proposed, entered into Teutonic eschatology as a memory of the dust veil, there is no way to measure its transformation over time from folk-memory to foretoken of the final battle. There is therefore no way, barring future findings, to discern how far along the dust veil was in its mythologization before Saxon Heathen belief was interrupted. Alas, only the *scóps* and *skalds* of old could say for certain and, for the moment, they are all at rest beneath their barrows awaiting *Ragnarǫk*.

BÓCHORD/BOOKHOARD/BIBLIOGRAPHY

Acker, Paul. "Dragons in the Eddas and in Early Nordic Art." In *Revisiting the Poetic Edda: Essays on Old Norse Heroic Legend*, 53-75. Edited by Carolyne Larrington. New York: Routledge, 2013.

Adam of Bremen. *History of the Archbishops of Hamburg-Bremen*. New York, NY: Columbia University Press, 2002.

Anderson, Carl E. "Formation and Resolution of Ideological Contrast in the Early History of Scandinavia." PhD diss., University of Cambridge, 1999. Accessed January 9, 2007. http://www.carlaz.com/phd/AndersonCE_1999_PhD.pdf.

Anlezark, Daniel, trans. *The Old English Dialogues of Solomon and Saturn*. Woodbridge, Suffolk: D.S. Brewer, 2009.

Aðalsteinsson, Jón Hnefill. *A Piece of Horse Liver: Myth, Ritual and Folklore in Old Icelandic Sources*. Translated by Terry Gunnell and Joan Turville-Petre. Reykjavík: Háskólaútgáfan, 1998.

---. *Under the Cloak: A Pagan Ritual Turning Point in the Conversion of Iceland*. Reykjavík: Háskólaútgáfan, Félagsvísindastofnun, 1999.

Anthony, David W. *The Horse, the Wheel, and Language: How Bronze-Age Riders from the Eurasian Steppes Shaped the Modern World*. Princeton, NJ: Princeton University Press, 2007.

Asser. *Annals of the Reign of Alfred the Great, From A. D. 849 to A.*

D. 887. In Giles, 41-56.

"The Battle of Finnsburh." Georgetown University. Accessed April 6, 2014. http://web.archive.org/web/20131029210649/http://www8.georgetown.edu/departments/medieval/labyrinth/library/oe/texts/a7.html.

"The Battle of Maldon." In Hieatt, 109-116.

Bauschatz, Paul C. *The Well and the Tree: World and Time in Early Germanic Culture*. Amherst: University of Massachusetts Press, 1982.

Bede. *Ecclesiastical History of the English People: With Bede's Letter to Egbert and Cuthbert's Letter on the Death of Bede*. Translated by Leo Sherley-Price. Harmondsworth: Penguin, 1990.

Beowulf. In Hieatt, 1-84.

"Beowulf in Anglo-Saxon." Internet Sacred Texts Archive. Accessed March 30, 2014. http://www.sacred-texts.com/neu/asbeo.htm.

Berglund, Björn E. "Human Impact and Climate Changes—synchronous Events and a Causal Link?" *Quaternary International* 105, no. 1 (2003): 7-12. Accessed April 3, 2012. doi:10.1016/S1040-6182(02)00144-1.

Bosworth, Joseph, and T. Northcote Toller. *An Anglo-Saxon Dictionary, Based on the Manuscript Collections of the Late Joseph Bosworth*. Oxford: Clarendon Press, 1898. Accessed January 18, 2014. http://lexicon.ff.cuni.cz/texts/oe_bosworthtoller_about.html.

Bugge, Sophus, ed. "Völuspá." In *Sæmundar Edda*. 1867. Accessed January 18, 2014.

http://etext.old.no/Bugge/.

Büntgen, U., W. Tegel, K. Nicolussi, M. Mccormick, D. Frank, V. Trouet, J. O. Kaplan, F. Herzig, K.-U. Heussner, H. Wanner, J. Luterbacher, and J. Esper. "2500 Years of European Climate Variability and Human Susceptibility." *Science* 331, no. 6017 (2011): 578-82. Accessed April 3, 2012. doi:10.1126/science.1197175.

Bury, J. B. *The Invasion of Europe by the Barbarians*. New York: Russell & Russell, 1963.

Cathey, James E., ed. *Hêliand: Text and Commentary*. Morgantown: West Virginia University Press, 2002.

Cederschiöld, Gustaf. *Baerings Saga*. In *Magus Saga Jarls, Konras Saga, Baerings Saga, Flovents Saga, Bevers Saga*. Lund: F. Berlings Boktryckeri, 1884. Accessed March 13, 2014. http://books.google.com/books.

Chadwick, H. Munro. *Origin of the English Nation*. Washington: The Clivedon Press, 1983.

Chaney, William A. "Paganism to Christianity in Anglo-Saxon England." *Harvard Theological Review* 53, no. 03 (1960): 197-217. Accessed April 3, 2012. doi:10.1017/S0017816000027012.

---. *The Cult of Kingship in Anglo-Saxon England: The Transition from Paganism to Christianity*. Manchester: Manchester University Press, 1970.

Charlemagne. *Capitulary for Saxony*. In *Translations and Reprints from the Original Sources of European History*. Vol. VI, Chapter 5. Translated by D. C. Munro. Philadelphia: University of Pennsylvania Press, 1900. Reprinted in Fordham University Internet Medieval Sourcebook. January 1996. Accessed January 9, 2007.

http://www.fordham.edu/Halsall/source/carol-saxony.asp.

Chesterton, G. K. "The Ethics of Elfland." In *Orthodoxy*. Chicago: Moody Publishers, 2009.

Cleasby, Richard, and Gudbrand Vigfusson. *An Icelandic-English Dictionary*. Oxford: Clarendon Press, 1874. Accessed January 18, 2014.
http://lexicon.ff.cuni.cz/texts/oi_cleasbyvigfusson_about.html.

Davidson, Hilda R. Ellis. "The Hill of the Dragon." *Folklore* 61, no. 4 (December 1950): 169-85.
doi:10.1080/0015587X.1950.9718012.

---. *Gods and Myths of Northern Europe*. Baltimore, MD: Penguin, 1964.

Davidson, H. R. Ellis. *Gods and Myths of the Viking Age*. New York, NY: Barnes & Noble Publishing, 2006.

---. *Patterns of Folklore*. Ipswich: D. S. Brewer, 1978.

Dörfler, Walter. "Rural Economy of the Continental Saxons from the Migration Period to the Tenth Century." In Green and Siegmund, 133-147.

Duerinck, Kevin. "Germanic Tribes." Germanic Tribes Portal. February 3, 2007. Accessed February 9, 2007. http://www.duerinck.com/tribes1.htm.

Dumézil, Georges. *Archaic Roman Religion*. Vol. 1. Translated by Philip Krapp. Baltimore, MD: John Hopkins University Press, 1996.

---. *From Myth to Fiction: The Saga of Hadingus*. Translated by Derek Coltman. Chicago, IL: The University of Chicago Press, 1973.

---. *Gods of the Ancient Northmen*. Translated by The Regents of the University of California. Berkeley, CA: University of California Press, 1973.

Dumville, David, Simon Keynes, and Michael Lapidge, eds. *The Anglo-Saxon Chronicle: The Annals of St. Neots with Vita Prima Sancti Neoti*. Cambridge: Boydell and Brewer, 1985.

Einhard, Hilduin. *The Life of Charlemagne*. Translated by Samuel Epes Turner. New York: Harper & Brothers, 1880. Reprinted in Fordham University Internet Medival Sourcebook. January 1999. Accessed 21 Apr. 2012.
http://www.fordham.edu/halsall/basis/einhard.asp.

---. *Royal Frankish Annals*. In Scholz, 35-126.

"Encyclopedia: Low Saxon Language." Nation Master. Accessed January 9, 2007.
http://www.nationmaster.com/encyclopedia/Low-Saxon-language.

Enright, Michael J. *Lady with a Mead Cup: Ritual, Prophecy, and Lordship in the European Warband from La Tène to the Viking Age*. Portland: Blackrock, Co. Dublin, 1996.

Evans, Stephen S.. *The Lords of Battle: Image and Reality of the Comitatus in Dark-Age Britain*. Woodbridge, Suffolk, UK: Boydell Press, 1997.

Fickett-Wilbar, David. "Ritual Details of the Irish Horse Sacrifice in Betha Mholaise Daiminse." *The Journal of Indo-European Studies* 40, no. 3 & 4, (Fall & Winter 2012): 315-43.

"The Fight at Finnsburh." In Hieatt, 133-134.

"Folk Memory," Oxford Dictionaries Online. Accessed July 4, 2014, http://www.oxforddictionaries.com/us/definition/english/folk-memory.

Foisel, John. *Saxons through Seventeen Centuries.* Cleveland, OH: The Central Alliance of Transylvanian Saxons of the United States, 1965.

Gardner, John. *Grendel.* New York: Vintage Books, 1971.

Gelling, Peter and Hilda Roderick Ellis Davidson. *The Chariot of the Sun, and Other Rites and Symbols of the Northern Bronze Age.* New York: Praeger, 1969.

Geoffrey of Monmouth. *British History*. In Giles, 87-292.

---. *The History of the Kings of Britain*. Translated by Lewis G. M. Thorpe. Harmondsworth: Penguin, 1966.

Giles, J. A., ed. *Six Old English Chronicles: Of Which Two Are Now First Translated From The Monkish Originals*. London: Elibron Classics, 2005.

Gildas. *The Works of Gildas*. In Giles, 293-380.

Göngu-Hrólfs Saga. Göngu-Hrólfs Saga. Accessed March 13, 2014. http://www.snerpa.is/net/forn/gonguhr.htm.

"The Gospel of Pseudo-Matthew." Wesley Center Online. Assessed January 9, 2007. http://wesley.nnu.edu/sermons-essays-books/noncanonical-literature/noncanonical-literature-gospels/the-gospel-of-pseudo-matthew/.

Gräslund, Bo, and Neil Price. "Twilight of the Gods? The 'Dust Veil Event' of AD 536 in Critical Perspective." *Antiquity* 86 (2012): 428-43. Accessed November 4, 2014.

http://antiquity.ac.uk/ant/086/ant0860428.htm.

Green, D. H., and Frank Siegmund. *The Continental Saxons from the Migration Period to the Tenth Century: An Ethnographic Perspective*. Rochester, NY: Boydell Press, 2003.

Grimm, Jacob. *Teutonic Mythology*. Vol. 1 and 4. Translated by James Steven Stallybrass. Mineola, NY: Dover Publications, 2004.

Gull-Þóris Saga. Icelandic Saga Database. September 13, 2007. Accessed February 15, 2014.
http://sagadb.org/gull-thoris_saga.

Guy. *The Carmen De Hastingae Proelio of Guy, Bishop of Amiens*. Edited by Catherine Morton and Hope Muntz. Oxford: Clarendon, 1972.

Hálfdanar Saga Eysteinssonar. Hálfdanar Saga Eysteinssonar. Accessed March 13, 2014.
http://www.snerpa.is/net/forn/half-e.htm.

Hall, John R. Clark. *A Concise Anglo-Saxon Dictionary: For the Use of Students*. Cambridge: University Press, 1916. Accessed January 18, 2014.
http://lexicon.ff.cuni.cz/texts/oe_clarkhall_about.html.

Hamer, Richard F. S., trans. In *A Choice of Anglo-Saxon Verse*. London: Faber, 1970.

"Hárbarðsljóð." *Poetic Edda*. Heimskringla. Accessed March 15, 2014.
http://www.heimskringla.no/wiki/Hárbarðsljóð

"Hávamál." *Poetic Edda*. Heimskringla. Accessed March 16, 2014.
http://heimskringla.no/wiki/Hávamál.

Hedeager, Lotte. "Scandinavia before the Viking Age." *The Viking World*. Edited by Stefan Brink and Neil S. Price. London: Routledge, 2008. 11-22.

Henderson, George. *The Norse Influence on Celtic Scotland*. Glasgow: J. Maclehose, 1910.

Herbert, Kathleen. *English Heroic Legends*. Norfolk, England: Anglo-Saxon Books, 2004.

Hieatt, Constance B., trans. In *Beowulf and Other Old English Poems*. New York: Bantam Books, 1988.

Holt, David H. "Did Extreme Climate Conditions Stimulate the Migrations of the Germanic Tribes in the 3rd and 4th Centuries? An Examination of Historical Data, Cimate Poxy Data, and Migration Events." Thesis, University of Arkansas, 2002. Accessed Apr. 16, 2012.
http://www.cast.uark.edu/research/research_theses/david_holt/

Hornklofi, Þorbjörn. "Hrafnsmál." Heimskringla. Accessed March 23, 2014.
http://www.heimskringla.no/wiki/Haraldskvæði_(Hrafnsmál)_ (B1).

Howarth, David. *1066: The Year of the Conquest*. 1978. Reprint, New York: Penguin Books, 1981.

Hucbald of St. Amand. *The Life of St. Lebuin*. In *The Anglo-Saxon Missionaries in Germany, Being the Lives of SS. Willibrord, Boniface, Leoba and Lebuin together with the Hodoepericon of St. Willibald and a selection from the correspondence of St. Boniface*. Edited and translated by C. H. Talbot. London and New York: Sheed and Ward, 1954. Reprinted in Fordham University Internet Medieval Sourcebook. October 1, 2000. Accessed January 9, 2007.
http://www.fordham.edu/halsall/basis/lebuin.html.

Ibn Fadlan, Ahmad. *Travel Report as it Concerns the Scandinavian Rûs*. Smithville, Texas: Rûna-Raven Press, 1998.

Jordanes. *The Origins and Deeds of the Goths*. Translated by Charles C. Mierow. Texts for Ancient History Courses: University of Calgary. Apr. 22, 1997. Accessed Apr. 16, 2012.
http://people.ucalgary.ca/~vandersp/Courses/texts/jordgeti.html.

Kershaw, Kris. *The One-Eyed God: Odin and the (Indo-) Germanic Männerbünde*. Washington, D.C.: Journal of Indo-European Studies, 2000.

Kristiansen, Kristian, and Carsten Müller. *New Directions in Scandinavian Archaeology Vol I*. Lyngby: The National Museum of Denmark, 1979.

Kristjánsson, Jónas, ed. *Viktors saga ok Blávus*. Reykjavík: Handritastofnun Íslands, 1964.

Kuijpers, Antoon, Niels Abrahamsen, Gerd Hoffmann, Veit Hühnerbach, Peter Konradi, Helmar Kunzendorf, Naja Mikkelsen, Jörn Thiede, and Wilhelm Weinrebe. "Climate Change and the Viking-age Fjord Environment of the Eastern Settlement, South Greenland." *Geology of Greenland Survey Bulletin* 183 (1999): 61-67. Accessed April 3, 2012. www.geus.dk/publications/review-greenland-98/gsb183p61-67.pdf.

Kurth, Godefroid. "Charles Martel." In *The Catholic Encyclopedia*. New York: Robert Appleton Company, 1908. Reprinted in New Advent. Accessed January 9, 2007.
http://www.newadvent.org/cathen/03629a.htm.

Lawrence, William Witherle. "The Dragon and His Lair in Beowulf." *PMLA* 33, no. 4 (January 01, 1918): 547-83. Accessed March 10, 2014.
http://www.jstor.org/stable/10.2307/456981?ref=search-gateway:829f2ed5c9dba2d8e50ba3f1bbd10bb4.

Larrington, Carolyne, trans. *The Poetic Edda*. New York, NY: Oxford University Press, 1999.

Mallory, J. P., and Douglas Q. Adams, eds. *Encyclopedia of Indo-European Culture*. London: Fitzroy Dearborn, 1997.

Marcellinus, Ammianus. *Res Gestae Libri XXXI*. Accessed January 9, 2007.
http://www.stephen.j.murray.btinternet.co.uk/barbarian.htm.

"Maxims I." Internet Sacred Text Online. 2011. Accessed July 28, 2014.
http://www.sacred-texts.com/neu/ascp/a03_13.htm.

"Maxims II." Internet Sacred Texts Archive. Accessed March 30, 2014.
http://www.sacred-texts.com/neu/ascp/a15.htm.

Murphy, G. Ronald S. J. *The Saxon Savior: The Germanic*

Transformation of the Gospel in the Ninth-Century Heliand. Oxford: Oxford University Press, 1995.

Nennius. *Historia Brittonum*. In *Six Old English Chronicles*. Edited by J. A. Giles. London: Henry G. Bohn, 1848. Reprinted in Fordham University Internet Medieval Sourcebook. August 1998. Accessed January 9, 2007.
http://www.fordham.edu/halsall/basis/nennius-full.html.

---. *History of the Britons*. In Giles, 381-416.

Nicholle, David. *Arthur and the Anglo-Saxon Wars*. Oxford: Osprey Publishing Ltd., 2003.

Nithard. *Histories*. In Scholz, 127-174.

Northouse, Peter G. *Leadership: Theory and Practice*. Thousand Oaks: Sage Publications, 2004.

Pálsson, Hermann and Paul Edwards, trans. *The Book of Settlements: Landnámabók*. Manitoba, Canada: University of Manitoba Press, 1972.

"Parallelism: Mary, Jesus and the Palm Tree." WikiIslam. Accessed Januray 9, 2007.
http://wikiislam.net/wiki/Parallelism:_Mary,_Jesus_and_the_Palm_Tree.

Paterculus, Velleius. *Compendium of Roman History*. Translated by F. W. Shipley. Loeb Classical Library 152. London and Cambridge, Massachusetts: Harvard University Press, 1924. Reprinted in LacusCurtius as *Roman History: Book II: Chapters 94-131*. Accessed January 9, 2007.
http://penelope.uchicago.edu/Thayer/E/Roman/Texts/Velleius_Paterculus/2D%2A.html.

Pálsson, Hermann and Paul Edwards, trans. *The Book of Settlements: Landnámabók*. University of Manitoba Press: Manitoba, Canada, 1972.

Paul the Deacon. *History of the Langobards*. Translated by William D. Foulke. University of Pennsylvania, 1907. Reprinted in *New Northvegr Center*. Accessed Apr. 16, 2012.
http://www.northvegr.org/histories%20and%20chronicles/history%20of%20the%20lombards/title.html.

Paulus Diaconus. *Historia Langobardorum*. New Northvegr Center. Accessed January 9, 2007. http://www.northvegr.org/lore/langobard/titles.php.

Pollington, Stephen. *Anglo-Saxon Burial Mounds: Princely Burial in the 6th and 7th Centuries*. Swaffham, Norfolk: Anglo-Saxon Books, 2008.

---. *Leechcraft: Early English Charms, Plant Lore, and Healing*. Norfolk, England: Anglo-Saxon Books, 2000.

---. *The Meadhall: The Feasting Tradition in Anglo-Saxon England*. 2nd ed. Little Downham, Ely, Cambs.: Anglo-Saxon Books, 2010.

Ptolemy, Claudius. *Claudius Ptolemy: The Geography*. Edited and translated by Edward Luther Stevenson. New York Public Library, 1932. Reprint, Dover Publications, 1991. Reprinted in LacusCurtius. Accessed January 9, 2007. http://penelope.uchicago.edu/Thayer/E/Gazetteer/Periods/Roman/_Texts/Ptolemy/home.html.

Rauer, Christine. *Beowulf and the Dragon: Parallels and Analogues*. Cambridge: D.S. Brewer, 2000.

Reclam, Phillipp, ed. *Widukind Von Corvey Res Gestae Saxonicae: Die Sachsengeshichte*. Ditzingen: Gesamtherstellung, 2002.

Robinson, Orrin W. *Old English and Its Closest Relatives: A Survey of the Earliest Germanic Languages*. Stanford, CA: Stanford University Press, 1992.

Rodrigues, Louis J., trans. *Anglo-Saxon Verse Charms, Maxims & Heroic Legends*. Pinner: Anglo-Saxon Books, 1994.

Russell, James C. *The Germanization of Early Medieval Christianity: A Sociohistorical Approach to Religious Transformation*. New York: Oxford University Press, 1994.

Savage, Anne, trans. *The Anglo-Saxon Chronicles: The Authentic Voices of England, From the Time of Julius Caesar to the Coronation of Henry II.* New York: Barnes & Noble, 2000.

Saxo Grammaticus. "Gesta Danorum." Det Kongelige Bibliotek. Accessed March 30, 2014. http://wayback-01.kb.dk/wayback/20101108105429/http%3A//www2.kb.dk/e

lib/lit/dan/saxo/lat/or.dsr/.

---. *The History of the Danes Books I-IX*. Translated by Peter Fisher. Cambridge: D. S. Brewer, 1996.

Schmidt, Martin and Uta Halle. "On the folklore of the Externsteine - or a centre for Germanomaniacs. In Archaeology and Folklore," 153-169. Edited by Cornelius Holtorf and Amy Gazin-Schwartz. London: Routledge, 1999.

Scholz, Bernard Walter, ed. *Carolingian Chronicles*. Ann Arbor, MI: University of Michigan Press, 2006.

Scott, S. P., trans. "The Visigothic Code: Forum Judicum." The Library of Iberian Resources Online. Accessed June 10, 2014. http://libro.uca.edu/vcode/visigoths.htm.

Schwyzer, Philip. *Literature, Nationalism and Memory in Early Modern England and Wales*. New York: Cambridge University Press, 2004.

Siegmund, Frank and Giorgio Ausenda. "Current Issues and Suggested Future Directions in the Study of the Continental Saxons." In Green and Siegmund, 329-350.

Smithers, G. V. "The Making of Beowulf; Inaugural Lecture of the Professor of English Language Delivered in the Applebey Lecture Theatre on 18 May, 1961." Durham, England: University of Durham, 1961.

Sörla Saga Sterka. Sörla Saga Sterka. Accessed March 13, 2014. http://www.snerpa.is/net/forn/sor-st.htm.

Sturluson, Snorri. *Edda*. Translated by Anthony Faulkes. Rutland, VT: Everyman, 2000.

---. *Egil's Saga*. In Thorsson and Scudder, 101.

---. *The Prose Edda*. Translated by Jean I. Young. Berkeley: University of California Press, 1954.

---. "The Prose Edda in Old Icelandic." New Northvegr Center. Accessed November 4, 2014. http://northvegr.org/old%20icelandic%20old%20english%20texts/the%20prose%20edda%20in%20old%20icelandic/.

---. "Skáldskaparmál." *Prose Edda*. Heimskringla. Accessed March 23, 2014. http://www.heimskringla.no/wiki/Skáldskaparmál.

---. "Ynglinga Saga." *Heimskringla, Or, the Lives of the Norse Kings*. Edited by Erling Monsen. Translated by A. H. Smith. New York: Dover Publications, 1990.

---. *Ynglinga Saga*. Heimskringla. Accessed March 23, 2014. http://www.heimskringla.no/wiki/Ynglinga_saga.

Sozomen. "Ecclesiastical History." *The Goths in the Fourth Century*. Edited by Peter Heather and John Matthews. Liverpool: Liverpool University, 2004.

Steinsland, Gro. "Origin Myths and Rulership. From the Viking Age Ruler to the Ruler of Medieval Historiography: Continuity, Transformations and Innovations." In *Ideology and Power in the Viking and Middle Ages: Scandinavia, Iceland, Ireland, Orkney, and the Faeroes*, 15-68. Leiden: Brill, 2011.

Tacitus, Cornelius. *The Agricola and the Germania*. Translated by H. Mattingly and S. A. Handford. Harmondsworth, Middlesex: Penguin Books, 1970.

---. *The Annals*. Translated by Alfred John Church and William Jackson Brodribb. London and New York: Macmillan, 1877. Reprinted in The Internet Classics Archive. Accessed January 9, 2007. http://classics.mit.edu/Tacitus/annals.html.

Thorpe, Benjamin. *Northern Mythology*. Hertfordshire: Wordsworth Editions, Ltd., 2001.

Thorsson, Örnólfur and Bernard Scudder, eds. *The Sagas of Icelanders*. London: Viking Penguin, 2000.

Tolkien, J. R. R. *Finn and Hengest*. Boston: Houghton Mifflin, 1983.

---. *The Monsters and the Critics: The Essays of J.R.R. Tolkien*. London: Harper Collins, 1997.

Tripp, Raymond P. *More about the Fight with the Dragon: Beowulf, 2208b-3182: Commentary, Edition, and Translation*. Lanham: University Press of America, 1983.

Turville-Petre, E. O. G. *Myth and Religion of the North*. Westport, Connecticut: Greenwood Press, 1975.

"Vafþrúðnismál." *Poetic Edda.* Heimskringla. Accessed November 4, 2014. http://www.heimskringla.no/wiki/Vaf%C3%BEr%C3%BA%C3%B0nism%C3%A1l.

Vatnsdæla Saga. Icelandic Saga Database. Accessed March 23, 2014. http://sagadb.org/vatnsdaela_saga.

"Vita Barbati Episcopi Beneventani." In *Monumenta Germaniae Gistorica: Scriptores Rerum Langobardicarum Et Italicarum: Saec. VI-IX*, 557-63. Hannover: Hahniani, 1878. http://books.google.de.

Völsunga Saga. Heimskringla. Accessed February 15, 2014. http://www.heimskringla.no/wiki/V%C3%B6lsunga_saga.

"The Wanderer." In Hieatt, 105-108.

Wang, Xunming, Fahu Chen, Jiawu Zhang, Yi Yang, Jijun Li, Eerdun Hasi, Caixia Zhang, and Dunsheng Xia. "Climate, Desertification, and the Rise and Collapse of China's Historical Dynasties." *Human Ecology* 38, no. 1 (2010): 157-72. Accessed April 3, 2012. doi:10.1007/s10745-009-9298-2.

Watkins, Calvert. *The American Heritage Dictionary of Indo-European Roots.* Boston, MA: Houghton Mifflin, 2000.

---. *How to Kill a Dragon: Aspects of Indo-European Poetics.* New York: Oxford University Press, 1995.

Wawn, Andrew, trans. "The Saga of the People of Vatnsdal." In Thorsson and Scudder, 205-211.

Wells, Peter. *The Battle that Stopped Rome.* New York, NY: W.W. Norton & Co., 2003.

The Wicker Man. Directed by Robin Hardy. Featuring Christopher Lee. DVD. British Lion Films. 1973.

Willibald. The Life of St. *Boniface*, chapter 5. In *The Anglo-Saxon Missionaries in Germany, Being the Lives of SS. Willibrord, Boniface, Leoba and Lebuin together with the Hodoepericon of St. Willibald and a selection from the correspondence of St. Boniface.* Translated by C. H. Talbot. London and New York: Sheed and Ward, 1954. Reprinted in Fordham University Internet Medieval Sourcebook. September 1, 2000. Accessed

January 9, 2007.
http://www.fordham.edu/halsall/basis/willibald-boniface.asp.

Wódening, Eric, *We Are Our Deeds: The Elder Heathenry, Its Ethic and Thew*. Watertown, NY: Theod, 1998.

Wood, Ian. "Beyond Satraps and Ostriches: Political and Social Structures of the Saxons in the Early Carolingian Period." In Green and Siegmund, 271-289.

Wood, Michael, perf. "Episode 7: "Penda"" In *The Essay - Anglo-Saxon Portraits*. BBC Radio 3. October 23, 2012. Accessed April 6, 2014.
http://www.bbc.co.u/iplayer/episode/b01ngr45.

Wood, Raymund F. "The Three Books of the Deeds of the Saxons." PhD diss., University of California, Berkeley, 1949. Accessed June 30, 2014.
http://search.proquest.com/docview/301830925.

Wright, Joseph. *An Old High-German Primer: With Grammar, Notes, and Glossary*. Oxford: Clarendon Press, 1888. Accessed January 18, 2014. http://lexicon.ff.cuni.cz/texts/ohg_wright_about.html.

ENDEMARC/ENDMARKS/ENDNOTES

[1] "Maxims I," line 160, Internet Sacred Text Online, 2011, accessed July 28, 2014, http://www.sacred-texts.com/neu/ascp/a03_13.htm. Translation by Þórbeorht Línléah.

[2] Raymond F. Wood, "The Three Books of the Deeds of the Saxons" (PhD diss., University of California, Berkeley, 1949), 161, accessed June 30, 2014, http://search.proquest.com/docview/301830925. This work is a translation of Widukind of Corvey's *Res Gestae Saxonicae* and will be cited as such for general references. This is from book I of Widukind's work.

[3] The borders of modern Sax-ony are different than those of ancient Saxony. Niedersachsen, however, does contain much of the original Saxland.

[4] Munro Chadwick, *Origin of the English Nation* (Washington: The Clivedon Press, 1983), 100.

[5] Orrin W. Robinson, *Old English and Its Closest Relatives: A Survey of the Earliest Germanic Languages* (Stanford, CA: Stanford University Press, 1992), 104.

[6] Wood, "The Three Books of the Deeds of the Saxons," 162. This is book 1, chapter 3 of Widukind's work.

[7] Ibid. This is book 1, chapter 4 of Widukind's work.

[8] Ibid., 162-163. This is book 1, chapter 5 of Widukind's work.

[9] Ibid., 165. "Warriors with long knives", an etymology of the name Sahson/Saxon, provided by Þórbeorht Línléah. This event is recounted in Widukind bk. 1, ch. 7.

[10] Claudius Ptolemy, *Claudius Ptolemy: The Geography*, ed. and trans. Edward Luther Stevenson (New York Public Library, 1932, repr. Dover Publications, 1991), repr. LacusCurtius, accessed January 9, 2007, http://penelope.uchicago.edu/Thayer/E/Gazetteer/Periods/Roman/_Texts/Ptolemy/home.html, bk. II, ch. 10: Greater Germany (Fourth Map of Europe).

[11] Robinson, *Old English and Its Closest Relatives*, 104.

[12] Ptolemy, *Claudius Ptolemy: The Geography*, http://penelope.uchicago.edu/Thayer/E/Gazetteer/Periods/Roman/_Texts/Ptolemy/home.html.

[13] John Foisel, *Saxons through Seventeen Centuries* (Cleveland, OH: The Central Alliance of Transylvanian Saxons of the United States, 1965), 4.

[14] Calvert Watkins, *The American Heritage Dictionary of Indo-European Roots* (Boston, MA: Houghton Mifflin, 2000), 74. The modern English "Saxon" is ultimately derived from the early Germanic "Sahson," meaning "warrior with knives."

[15] Robinson, *Old English and Its Closest Relatives*, 100.

[16] Cornelius Tacitus, *The Agricola and the Germania*, trans. H. Mattingly and S. A. Handford (Harmondsworth, Middlesex: Penguin Books, 1970), 165.

[17] Foisel, *Saxons through Seventeen Centuries*, 1.

[18] Tacitus, *The Agricola and the Germania*, 165.

[19] The Angrivarii later become known as the Angrarii.

[20] Tacitus, *The Agricola and the Germania*, 163.

[21] Peter Wells, *The Battle that Stopped Rome* (New York, NY: W.W. Norton & Co., 2003), 25-29.

[22] Ibid., 64.

[23] Velleius Paterculus, *Compendium of Roman History*, trans. F. W. Shipley, Loeb Classical Library 152 (London and Cambridge, Massachusetts: Harvard University Press, 1924), repr. LacusCurtius as *Roman History: Book II: Chapters 94-131*, accessed January 9, 2007, http://penelope.uchicago.edu/Thayer/E/Roman/Texts/Velleius_Paterculus/2D%2A.html.

[24] Tacitus, *The Agricola and the Germania*, 131.

[25] Robinson, *Old English and Its Closest Relatives*, 100.

[26] Ibid.

[27] Tacitus, *The Agricola and the Germania*, 130-131.

[28] Tacitus, *The Annals*, trans. by Alfred John Church and William Jackson Brodribb (London, New York: Macmillan, 1877), repr. The Internet Classics Archive, accessed January 9, 2007,

http://classics.mit.edu/Tacitus/annals.html, bk. II, ch. 19 and 22.

[29] Tacitus, *The Agricola and the Germania*, 129.

[30] Robinson, *Old English and Its Closest Relatives*, 101.

[31] Kevin Duerinck, "Germanic Tribes," Germanic Tribes Portal, February 3, 2007, accessed February 9, 2007, http://www.duerinck.com/tribes1.htm; Ian Wood, "Beyond Satraps and Ostriches: Political and Social Structures of the Saxons in the Early Carolingian Period," in *The Continental Saxons from the Migration Period to the Tenth Century: An Ethnographic Perspective*, eds. D. H. Green and Frank Siegmund (Rochester, NY: Boydell Press, 2003), 276. Compiled from these two sources.

[32] Hucbald of St. Amand, *The Life of St. Lebuin*, in *The Anglo-Saxon Missionaries in Germany, Being the Lives of SS. Willibrord, Boniface, Leoba and Lebuin together with the Hodoepericon of St. Willibald and a selection from the correspondence of St. Boniface*, ed. and trans. C. H. Talbot (London and New York: Sheed and Ward, 1954), repr. Fordham University Internet Medieval Sourcebook, October 1, 2000, accessed January 9, 2007,

http://www.fordham.edu/halsall/basis/lebuin.html.

[33] Ammianus Marcellinus, *Res Gestae Libri XXXI*, accessed January 9, 2007.

http://www.stephen.j.murray.btinternet.co.uk/barbarian.htm

[34] David Nicholle, *Arthur and the Anglo-Saxon Wars* (Oxford: Osprey Publishing Ltd., 2003), 3- 4.

[35] Nennius, *Historia Brittonum*, in *Six Old English Chronicles*, ed. J. A. Giles (London: Henry G. Bohn, 1848), repr. Fordham University Internet Medieval Sourcebook, August 1998, accessed January 9, 2007, http://www.fordham.edu/halsall/basis/nennius-full.html. Bede dates this to 449 CE.

[36] Ibid.

[37] Walter Dörfler, "Rural Economy of the Continental Saxons from the Migration Period to the Tenth Century," in Green and Siegmund, 143. Walter Dörfler cites pollen levels which indicate that there was a vast decrease in the population of Saxony beginning around 450 CE. The gist of his evidence is that cultivated fields were abandoned and subsequent reforestation occurred.

[38] Nicholle, *Arthur and the Anglo-Saxon Wars*, 4.

[39] Adam of Bremen, *History of the Archbishops of Hamburg-Bremen* (New York, NY: Columbia University Press, 2002), 8.

[40] Paulus Diaconus, *Historia Langobardorum*, New Northvegr Center, accessed January 9, 2007, http://www.northvegr.org/lore/langobard/titles.php, bk. 2, ch. 6.

[41] Ibid., bk. 3, ch 6.

[42] Paulus Diaconus actually leaves off with the Saxons being defeated, yet history shows that the Saxons did indeed take their homeland once again.

[43] Luke 19:27. King James Version

[44] Ibid., 22:49, 50. This is but one example in which Jesus' followers are described as armed. It is quite unusual for mere fishermen to have swords in their possession and even more unusual for wandering preachers. It is not unusual, however, for political revolutionaries to

carry arms. Nor was it unusual during Roman times for such revolutionaries to be executed, sometimes by crucifixion.

[45] Ibid., 19:11.

[46] Acts 17:6.

[47] Matthew 10:35.

[48] Hilduin Einhard, *Royal Frankish Annals*, in *Carolingian Chronicles*, ed. Bernard Walter Scholz (Ann Arbor, MI: University of Michigan, 2006), 51.

[49] Godefroid Kurth, "Charles Martel," in *The Catholic Encyclopedia* (New York: Robert Appleton Company, 1908), repr. New Advent, accessed January 9, 2007, http://www.newadvent.org/cathen/03629a.htm. Dates taken from here.

[50] Benjamin Thorpe, *Northern Mythology* (Hertfordshire: Wordsworth Editions Ltd., 2001), 169.

[51] The afterworld inhabited by oath breakers, adulterers, and murderers.

[52] Adam of Bremen, *History of the Archbishops of Hamburg-Bremen*, 11.

[53] This is not a typo. At this point in time, there was no agreed upon beginning and ending of the year amongst the Christians. Whereas the Germans began the year at Yuletide around the twenty first of December and the Romans began it on the first day of January, the Christian Franks were beginning the year on the twenty fifth of March, which coincided with the feast of the Annunciation.

[54] This is probably the same as the Astfali.

[55] It is not recorded whether or not Widukind was actually raised as war-king. Though *heritogo* was once denoted a war-king, it was eventually used as term for "duke," a Frankish misinterpretation of the role of an Alderman.

[56] Einhard, *Royal Frankish Annals*, in Scholz, 60.

[57] Charlemagne, *Capitulary for Saxony*, in *Translations and Reprints from the Original Sources of European History*, vol. VI, ch. 5, trans.

D. C. Munro (Philadelphia: University of Pennsylvania Press, 1900), repr. Fordham University Internet Medieval Sourcebook, January 1996, accessed January 9, 2007,

http://www.fordham.edu/Halsall/source/carol-saxony.asp.

[58] Adam of Bremen, *History of the Archbishops of Hamburg-Bremen*, 12.

[59] Einhard, *Royal Frankish Annals*, in Scholz, 75.

[60] Ibid., 81.

[61] Matthew 10:35-36.

[62] Adam of Bremen, *History of the Archbishops of Hamburg-Bremen*, 15.

[63] Nithard, *Histories,* in Scholz, 167. Whereas most of the dates concerning the Frankish-Saxon conflicts have come from the *Royal Frankish Annals*, my source for this account came from Nithard.

[64] Nithard actually used the term *lazzi*, Old High German for *latti*, slave. It is very doubtful that Nithard would have appealed to slaves for help. It is more likely that Lothair intended *liti*, freedmen, as *latti* were generally considered an insignificant element of society and would have had no training in even the most rudimentary use of arms.

[65] Nithard, *Histories*, 167.

[66] Carl E. Anderson, "Formation and Resolution of Ideological Contrast in the Early History of Scandinavia" (PhD diss., University of Cambridge, 1999), 11, accessed January 9, 2007, http://www.carlaz.com/phd/AndersonCE_1999_PhD.pdf.

[67] Adam of Bremen, *History of the Archbishops of Hamburg-Bremen*, 87.

[68] Jacob Grimm, *Teutonic Mythology*, trans. James Steven Stallybrass (Mineola, NY: Dover Publications, 2004), 1:154.

[69] Frank Siegmund and Giorgio Ausenda, "Current Issues and Suggested Future Directions in the Study of the Continental Saxons," in Green and Siegmund, 350.

[70] "Encyclopedia: Low Saxon Language," Nation Master, accessed January 9, 2007,

http://www.nationmaster.com/encyclopedia/Low-Saxon-language.

[71] Thorpe, *Northern Mythology,* 168. See Massmann, *Abschwörungsformeln* No. 1. Translation by Þórbeorht Línléah.

[72] Grimm, *Teutonic Mythology,* 1:203.

[73] Ibid., 4:1714.

[74] E. O. G. Turville-Petre, *Myth and Religion of the North* (Westport, Connecticut: Greenwood Press, 1975), 100.

[75] Georges Dumézil, *Gods of the Ancient Northmen,* trans. The Regents of the University of California (Berkeley, CA: University of California Press, 1973), 19-20.

[76] Carolyne Larrington, trans., *The Poetic Edda* (New York, NY: Oxford University Press, 1999), 167.

[77] Grimm, *Teutonic Mythology,* 1:197.

[78] Ibid., 216.

[79] Among modern mythologists, this theory has been rejected for some time. Of those who still cling to it, Hilda Davidson is the most well-known. Though Davidson's early works on the afterlife and the Anglo-Saxon sword are second to none, her more popular mythological works such as *Gods and Myths of Northern Europe* were largely built upon mythological theories that had long been rejected by her peers. Nevertheless, as her mythological works were printed in paperback and were penned for public consumption rather than peer review, they have long remained in print, being readily available at any large chain bookstore. This has led to their popularity among contemporary Heathens, who are often faced with a dearth of informational material to begin with. This is one reason why the modern Heathen has become more and more out of touch with serious scholarly mythological studies, having been sold discarded nineteenth century theory without the resources to know any better.

[80] Grimm, *Teutonic Mythology,* 1:216.

[81] Larrington, trans., *The Poetic Edda,* 78.

[82] Snorri Sturluson, *Edda,* trans. Anthony Faulkes (Rutland, VT: Everyman, 2000) 76. The most popular version of the *Prose Edda* in

print today is an abridgement published by the University of California. The Everyman publication, in contrast, contains the entirety of the *Prose Edda*. If the Heathen reader is unable to readily find this reference to Tiuu, this may be the explanation.

[83] Ibid., 156.

[84] Georges Dumézil, *From Myth to Fiction: The Saga of Hadingus*, trans. Derek Coltman (Chicago, IL: University of Chicago Press, 1973), 136. From the *Corpus Carminum Faeroensium*, a collection of Faeroes ballads compiled in 1840, lines 191-192 as quoted by Dumézil.

[85] Snorri Sturluson, "Ynglinga Saga," *Heimskringla or the Lives of the Norse Kings*, trans. Erling Monsen and A.H. Smith (New York, NY: Dover Publishing, 1990), 8.

[86] Sturluson, *Edda*, 21.

[87] Grimm, *Teutonic Mythology*, 4:1714.

[88] E. O. G. Turville-Petre, *Myth and Religion of the North*, 100.

[89] Saxo Grammaticus, *The History of the Danes Book I-IX*, trans. Peter Fisher (Cambridge: D. S. Brewer, 1996) VIII: 240.

[90] Translation by Þórbeorht Línléah.

[91] William A. Chaney, *The Cult of Kingship in Anglo-Saxon England* (Manchester: Manchester University Press, 1970), 20-21.

[92] Sturluson, "Ynglinga Saga," 19.

[93] Georges Dumézil, *Archaic Roman Religion*, vol. 1, trans. Philip Krapp (Baltimore, MD: John Hopkins University Press, 1996), 161.

[94] For those interested in exploring this matter further, *Gods of the Ancient Northmen* and *Mitra-Varuna* are among Dumézil's foremost writings on the subject.

[95] Adam of Bremen, *History of the Archbishops of Hamburg-Bremen*, 207.

[96] Snorri Sturluson, "Egil's Saga," in *The Sagas of Icelanders*, trans. Bernard Scudder, ed. Örnólfur Thorsson and Bernard Scudder, (London: Viking Penguin, 2000), 101.

[97] Larrington, trans., *The Poetic Edda*, 66, line 33.

[98] Dumézil, *Gods of the Ancient Northmen*, 6. From "Hallfreðar Saga Vandræðaskálds" as quoted by Dumézil.

[99] Ibid., 19-20.

[100] Dumézil, *Archaic Roman Religion*, 161.

[101] Adam of Bremen, *History of the Archbishops of Hamburg-Bremen*, 11.

[102] Einhard, *Royal Frankish Annals*, in Scholz, 49.

[103] Martin Schmidt and Uta Halle, "On the Folklore of the Externsteine - or a centre for Germanomaniacs" in *Archaeology and Folklore*, ed. Cornelius Holtorf and Amy Gazin-Schwartz (London: Routledge, 1999), 161.

[104] Gerhard Hess, "Kreuz und Palmbaum-Idol am Externstein" Glaubensgemeinschaft – Oding – Deutschland, accessed January 9, 2007, http://oding.org/index.php/irminsul-irrtum/458-dattel-palme-am-extern-stein. The source for the diagrams used in this section is Gerhard Hess' *Irminsul Dattelpalme Weltenbaum* [Irminsul, Date palm, World Tree] and *Kreuz und Dattelpalme* [Cross and Date Palm]. Herr Hess's permission was granted for the use of these images.

[105] "The Gospel of Pseudo-Matthew," Wesley Center Online, assessed January 9, 2007, http://wesley.nnu.edu/sermons-essays-books/noncanonical-literature/noncanonical-literature-gospels/the-gospel-of-pseudo-matthew/.

[106] Parallelism: Mary, Jesus and the Palm Tree," WikiIslam, accessed Januray 9, 2007, http://wikiislam.net/wiki/Parallelism:_Mary,_Jesus_and_the_Palm_Tree.

[107] Bonanus of Pisa, *Fugeine Giptup*, ca.1150, bronze sculpture on cathedral door, Pisa, Italy, accessed Jan. 9, 2007, http://faculty.maryvillecollege.edu/scripts/as_web4.exe?Command=Doc&File=Apocicon.ask&DocID=553350.

[108] Daniel Anlezark, trans., *The Old English Dialogues of Solomon and Saturn* (Woodbridge, Suffolk: D.S. Brewer, 2009), 67, lines 39-42.

[109] James E. Cathey, ed., *Hêliand: Text and Commentary*, (Morgantown: West Virginia University Press, 2002), 65, line 1595. Translation by Þórbeorht Línléah.

[110] G. Ronald S. J. Murphy, *The Saxon Savior: The Germanic Transformation of the Gospel in the Ninth-Century Heliand* (Oxford: Oxford University Press, 1995), 90.

[111] Anlezark, trans., *The Old English Dialogues of Solomon and Saturn*, 71, lines 161-169.

[112] Sebastian Münster, *Irminsul*, ca. 1590, woodcut on single sheet in *Cosmography*, Rolf Speckner, Hamburg, Germany, accessed January 9, 2007, http://de.wikipedia.org/wiki/Datei:Irminsul_nach_Sebastian_M%C3%BCnster.Ca._1590.JPG.

[113] Grimm, *Teutonic Mythology*, 1:116. From the *Kaiserchronik* as quoted by Grimm.

[114] The Norse word *tyr* simply had the meaning of "god." Þórr is similarly referred to as Chariot-tyr.

[115] Ahmad Ibn Fadlan, *Travel Report as it Concerns the Scandinavian Rûs*, (Smithville, Texas: Rûna-Raven Press, 1998), 7.

[116] Dumézil, *Gods of the Ancient Northmen*, 35.

[117] Chadwick, *The Origin if the English Nation*, 227. From Widukind of Corvey's *Res Gestae Saxonicae* as quoted by Chadwick.

[118] Adam of Bremen, *History of the Archbishops of Hamburg-Bremen*, 207.

[119] Ibid., 11.

[120] Sturluson, *Edda*, 17.

[121] Davidson, H. R. Ellis, *Gods and Myths of the Viking Age* (New York, NY: Barnes & Noble Publishing, 2006), 194.

[122] Larrington, trans., *The Poetic Edda*, 34, lines 138-139.

[123] Tacitus, *The Agricola and the Germania*, chap. 34.

[124] Willibald, *The Life of St. Boniface*, chap. 5, in *The Anglo-Saxon Missionaries in Germany, Being the Lives of SS. Willibrord, Boniface, Leoba and Lebuin together with the Hodoepericon of St. Willibald and a selection from the correspondence of St. Boniface*, trans. C. H. Talbot (London and New York: Sheed and Ward, 1954), repr. in Fordham University Internet Medieval Sourcebook, September 1, 2000, accessed January 9, 2007, http://www.fordham.edu/halsall/basis/willibald-boniface.asp.

[125] Grimm, *Teutonic Mythology*, 1:74

[126] Hermann Pálsson and Paul Edwards, trans., *The Book of Settlements: Landnámabók* (Manitoba, Canada: University of Manitoba Press, 1972), 45.

[127] Translation by Þórbeorht Línléah

[128] Andrew Wawn, trans., "The Saga of the People of Vatnsdal," in Thorsson and Scudder, 205.

[129] Ibid., 207.

[130] Ibid., 211.

[131] Adam of Bremen, *History of the Archbishops of Hamburg-Bremen*, 207.

[132] Ibid., 208.

[133] Grimm, *Teutonic Mythology*, 1:190. From the "*Hist. Caroli Magni*, Hildesh. 1603, chap. 18 end" related by Letzner and quoted by Grimm.

[134] Ibid.

[135] Thorpe, *Northern Mythology*, 168. See Massmann, *Abschwörungsformeln* No. 1. Translation by Þórbeorht Línléah.

[136] Tacitus, *The Agricola and the Germania*, 134.

[137] Larrington, trans., *The Poetic Edda*, 21, verse 49.

[138] For those who read the footnotes, there is an embryonic article contained therein, which may be subtitled "An Anglo-Saxon Tale of Mead, Myth, and Human Sacrifice." At some point, this thread of

Heathen theology will be properly explored. The ideas, contained in the follow footnotes, will, however, be more fully expounded in a forthcoming work.

[139] See "Betwixt Blood Bespattered Benches" Appendice III: Reckoning the Lore

[140] Caxton wrote the preface to Sir Thomas Malory's *Le Morte Darthur* and described Arthur as one of the "nine worthy" men in (pre)Christian history who deserved special praise for their merit. "Arthur-worshipping" here follows the older meaning of the term "worship" as used by Malory. It means, "to hold someone to be of worth, to honor them."

[141] Robert Wace, Laymon, Sir Thomas Malory, and Sir Alfred Lord Tennyson have all expounded upon the importance of the historically obscure Arthur while largely ignoring the historical importance of Hengest.

[142] "Folk Memory," Oxford Dictionaries Online, accessed July 4, 2014, http://www.oxforddictionaries.com/us/definition/english/folk-memory. "Folk memory" is, according to the *Oxford British and World English Dictionary*, "a recollection or body of recollections of the past that persists among a particular group of people."

[143] Such as *John Barleycorn* or the *Derbyshire Ram*.

[144] Chaney, *The Cult of Kingship in Anglo-Saxon England*, 7.

[145] Bede, *Ecclesiastical History of the English People: With Bede's Letter to Egbert and Cuthbert's Letter on the Death of Bede*, trans. Leo Sherley-Price (Harmondsworth: Penguin Books, 1990), 63.

[146] Hengest's and Horsa's arrival is dated to the year 449 CE by both Bede (731 CE) and the *Anglo-Saxon Chronicle* (latter 9th century). The Welsh monk Nennius in his *Historia Brittonum* (828 CE) provided a date of 447 CE. For the purpose of this chapter, the date provided by Bede is accepted.

[147] The terms Teutonic and Germanic are nearly synonymous. The "Teutons" and the Norse of the Migration Era can be thought of as

kindred/cognate in language, religion, and custom with the former being descended from the latter by an earlier migration.

[148] Philip Schwyzer, *Literature, Nationalism and Memory in Early Modern England and Wales* (New York: Cambridge University Press, 2004), 1-48.

[149] A German word, used in philosophy, to indicate a cultural and historical worldview.

[150] Eric Wódening, *We Are Our Deeds: The Elder Heathenry, Its Ethic and Thew* (Watertown, New York: Theod, 1998). The quoted material is actually the subtitle of the book.

[151] James C. Russell, *The Germanization of Early Medieval Christianity: A Sociohistorical Approach to Religious Transformation* (New York: Oxford University Press, 1994), 11.

[152] Northouse, *Leadership: Theory and Practice* (Thousand Oaks: Sage Publications, 2004), 238.

[153] Ibid., 242-244.

[154] Ibid., 242.

[155] Tacitus, *The Agricola and the Germania*, 113.

[156] Literally, a "shaper". A *scóp* was an Anglo-Saxon skald/bard/poet.

[157] Kathleen Herbert, *English Heroic Legends* (Norfolk, England: Anglo-Saxon Books, 2004), 235.

[158] J. R. R. Tolkien, *Finn and Hengest* (Boston: Houghton Mifflin, 1983), 159.

[159] The *Finnesburh Fragment* states that there were *sixtig sigebeorna*, "sixty victory-bairns" (author's translation).

[160] Northouse, *Leadership: Theory and Practice*, 242.

[161] Folcwald literally means, "Folk-wielder," i.e. "the ruler." Rather than a personal name, Folcwald may, instead, indicate that Finn was the son of the Frisian *folcwald*/king. This would mean that he, like Hengest, was a Wóden-sprung noble.

[162] An Anglo-Saxon word for a noble.

[163] Wódening, *We Are Our Deeds*, 7.

[164] Constance B. Hieatt, trans., *Beowulf*, in *Beowulf and Other Old English Poems*, (New York: Bantam Books, 1988), 30. Hieatt's prose translation of *Beowulf* is a perfect example of this. While her translation of the text is, for the most part, brilliant, it is painfully apparent that she was perplexed when it came to the use of *eoton* in the Finnesburh episode, translating it as "giant" rather than as "Jute."

[165] Seemingly because, as will be seen in the footnotes which follow, the hall-slaughters may very well incorporate parts of the Norse myth regarding the Mead of Inspiration. If so, use of such an ambiguous word may have been an intentional choice, an Anglo-Saxon style riddle, on the part of the fragment's *scóp*.

[166] The mention of wolves, carrion-birds, and the spear – each animated and each lending voice to the din of battle – is important in dating the tradition upon which this poem is based. Wóden, the god from which Hengest is said to be descended, is the Anglo-Saxon cognate of the Norse god, Óðinn (NE: Odin). In the Norse *Eddas*, Óðinn is said to wield a spear and to keep, as his companions, wolves and ravens. He is also said to be the discoverer of the runes, a myth that may be alluded to in the *Anglo-Saxon Rune Poem's* passage for the *ós* rune, a word which means both "mouth," as the source of speech (creation), and god (cognate to the Old Norse *áss*, one of the *Æsir*, one of the gods).

[167] Richard F. S. Hamer, trans., in *A Choice of Anglo-Saxon Verse* (London: Faber, 1970), 34-40.

[168] Asser, *Annals of the Reign of Alfred the Great, From A. D. 849 to A. D. 887*, in *Six Old English Chronicles; Of Which Two Are Now First Translated From The Monkish Originals*, ed. J. A. Giles (London: Elibron Classics, 2005), 44; Tacitus, *The Agricola and the Germania*, chapters 9, 39. The thane referred to as Ordláf in the *Finnesburh Fragment* is later referred to as Ósláf in *Beowulf*. While this may represent a divergent tradition, this difference could also be explained as a scribal error in the *Beowulf* manuscript. The name Ósláf would translate as "the god's leaving" (as in left over, what remains). Ordláf, however, translates as "the leavings of the weapon's point," i.e., slaughter. This mirrors Guðláf, the "the leavings of battle." In other words, weapon-slaughter and war-slaughter were

within the hall. Given the shared suffix of –láf it may be assumed that Ordláf and Guðláf were brothers.

An alternate theory, put forward by this author, is that Ósláf is the original form with "the god's leaving" referring to a sacrifice made to Wóden as a god of victory and war. Tacitus' in *The Germania* (98 CE) made special note of the prevalence of human sacrifice in this god's cult, a practice which endured through the Migration Era and until the end of the Viking age.

If Ósláf is the correct form, then it may be that the *guð* prefix in Guðláf relates to the Proto-Germanic **guð*, "god" (Old English: *god*, Gothic: *guþa*; Old Norse *goð*). It is from this root that Gautr, an Old Norse byname for Óðinn, is derived. Geat, an Anglo-Saxon cognate of Gautr, appears in Asser's *Annals* as an ancestor of Wóden. Of Geat, Asser recorded that he had been "long worshipped as a god." Such would suggest that the names Ósláf and Guðláf allude to a Wódenic sacrifice. Furthermore, it could be argued that they, like Hengest and Horsa, represent reflexes of the Indo-European twin horse gods. The suggestion that the Finnesburh massacres may have been sacrifices intended to win the favor of the war-god Wóden will have to be explored further in another work.

[169] Northouse, *Leadership: Theory and Practice*, 242.

[170] The name Friðuwulf does not appear in either the *Finnesburh Fragment* or *Beowulf*. Tolkien discovered the name in Asser's aforementioned genealogy of King Alfred the Great. There a king named Finn is said to have had a son named Friðuwulf. Friðuwulf, Finn, Wóden, and Guð-Geat all appear in Alfred's genealogy.

[171] Sigeferþ is another Wódenic name. Sigðir (Victory giver), Sigföðr (Victory father), Sigföðr (Victory Geat), and Sigtýr (Victory god) are all bynames for Óðinn found in Old Norse poetry. The prefix of sig- also appears in the names of the Wóden-sprung Volsungs, of which Sigmund and Sigurðr (Sigurd) are remembered in the Icelandic *Völsungasaga*, the medieval German *Nibelungenlied*, and Richard Wagner's opera, *Der Ring des Nibelungen*.

[172] The name Eaha may be derived from the Old English word *eah-*, "eye." If so, the name, rendered as "the eyed one," may refer to

Wóden who in Norse literature is said to have sacrificed one of his eyes.

[173] Gárulf means "spear wolf," further pointing to Wóden's involvement in the massacre.

[174] Guðere, see the discussion on Guðláf.

[175] In the original text, the words *forgyldan* and *guldan* are used to describe the repayment of the mead. In keeping with this author's theory that the hall-slaughters of Finnesburh relate to mythological events, it should be noted that the root of these words, *geld*, means both "payment" and "worship." *Godgild* is, in Old English, a term for Heathen worship. This further supports the idea that Finnesburh is a late remembrance of what was originally understood to be a sacrifice to Wóden.

[176] "The Fight at Finnsburh," in Hieatt, 136.

[177] Tacitus, *The Agricola and the Germania*, 113.

[178] Larrington, trans., *The Poetic Edda*, 29; Snorri Sturluson, *The Prose Edda*, trans. Jean I. Young. (Berkeley: University of California Press, 1954), 100-103. Mead, the sacred drink of the gods, lay at the heart of Heathen belief. In Norse mythology, mead is said to have come from the blood of Kvasir, a god of wisdom who was created as part of a truce between the Æsir and Vanir, two warring tribes of gods. Later, Kvasir was murdered in the hall of two dwarves, Fjalar and his brother Galar, who then used Kvasir's blood to brew the Mead of Inspiration. The mead eventually fell into the hands of the giants who, as enemies of the Æsir, would have used its insight against them. Ultimately, however, Óðinn/Wóden, through deception and the swearing of a false oath, stole the mead from the giants and returned its power to the gods. Along the way, a few drops were said to have spilled out of Wóden's mouth; these, having fallen to the earth, become the scóp's share. It is tempting to see the Finnesburh hall-slaughters as reflexes of this very myth. In the mead hall, Finn and his Frisian/Jute thanes murder Hnæf, much as the dwarves slew Kvasir, a guest in their own hall. Hengest, like Wóden, must break an oath in the hall to repay/regain the mead and avenge the death of Hnæf/Kvasir.

[179] Tacitus, *The Agricola and the Germania*, 113.

[180] "The Battle of Maldon," in Hieatt, 116.

[181] Ibid., 114.

[182] I have used the less common variant, *scild*, rather than the more frequent form of *scyld,* so as to not confuse the reader when the Scyldings are mentioned; the etymology is different though the spelling is the same.

[183] Wódening, *We Are Our Deeds*, 52.

[184] *Beowulf*, in Hieatt, 30.

[185] An open air cremation, in keeping with Heathen practice.

[186] Northouse, *Leadership: Theory and Practice*, 242.

[187] "The Wanderer," in Hieatt, 106.

[188] *Beowulf*, in Hieatt, 31.

[189] A nod to the Middle English song, *Sumer Is Icumen In* (Summer is Coming In).

[190] *Bældæg* means "balefire day" and is thus cognate to the Celtic *Beltane* and the Old High German *Pholtag*. Phol is mentioned in the second *Merseburg Charm* as being Wóden's son. Bældæg appears as a person, rather than as a date, in the Anglo-Saxon royal genealogies. Bældæg, also known as Bealdor, was the mythic son of both Hengest and Finn's common mythic forefather, Wóden. It may not be entirely ironic then that the summer before, perhaps on this very occasion, Hnæf was slain in the mead-hall. In Norse mythology, Bealdor's Norse cognate, Baldr, was himself murdered in the hall of the gods. In fact, a euphemized version of this story survives in *Beowulf* lines 2424-2471, with the Norse Baldr and his kinsman/slayer Höðr appearing as Herebeald and Hæðcyn. Tolkien's kinsman against kinsman reading of the Finnesburh hall-slaughter may hold a deeper religious significance than the scholar suspected.

There are several elements to this story that hint of Finn's attack on Hnæf as being born of more than a quarrel between Jutish factions. As discussed throughout the footnotes, Finn may have intended Hnæf to be a sacrifice to Wóden. In fact, there are several elements in the Finnesburh hall-slaughters which mirror, albeit imperfectly, events in

Norse mythology. In religion, ritual is often intended to magically recall or reenact a myth; a comparative example of this is the Mass.

[191] Mead, a wine made with honey, water, and yeast, was the drink *par excellence* of the Teutonic tribes, comparable to the *ambrosia* of the Greeks and the sacred *soma* of the Indo-Iranians.

[192] The drinking vessel of choice for this day and age was the bull's horn, hollowed out and lined with beeswax. Thus, "a toast" was synonymous with "a horn."

[193] Those seeking to understand this rite and its metaphysical significance in pre-Christian Teutonic belief more thoroughly should seek out copies of Paul C. Bauschatz's *The Well and the Tree: Word and Time in Early Germanic Culture* and Michael Enright's *Lady with a Mead Cup: Ritual Prophecy and Lordship in the European Warband from La Tene to the Viking Age*. The latter has just recently returned to print.

[194] Northouse, *Leadership: Theory and Practice*, 244.

[195] See Chapter 7: "Lore and Landscape"

[196] Geoffrey of Monmouth, *British History*, in Giles, 183.

[197] Anglo-Saxon goddess or goddesses of fate, recalled in Shakespeare's *Macbeth* as the Weird Sisters.

[198] Spear-man. The Anglo-Saxon god of the sea was known as Garsecg. "Garsecg's arm" is a kenning used in poetry for the English Channel.

[199] Gildas, *The Works of Gildas*, in Giles, 310.

[200] Ibid.

[201] Geoffrey of Monmouth, *British History*, in Giles, 184.

[202] Ibid., 186-187.

[203] Ibid., 188.

[204] Gildas, *The Works of Gildas*, in Giles, 312.

[205] Geoffrey of Monmouth, *British History*, in Giles, 188.

[206] Tacitus, *The Agricola and the Germania*, 108.

[207] Geoffrey of Monmouth, *British History*, in Giles 189.

[208] Ibid., 186.

[209] Nennius, *History of the Britons*, in Giles, 406.

[210] An Anglo-Saxon title for a warlord or ruler, often applied to divinities, particularly the Christian god, in poetry.

[211] The Anglo-Saxon word *dóm*, from which the modern English word "doom" springs, meant both "judgment," as in Doomsday, and "reputation." It is in the latter sense that this conclusion is titled.

[212] Wódening, *We Are Our Deeds*, 61-63.

[213] Northouse, *Leadership: Theory and Practice*, 243.

[214] "Hengest has not fallen far from the tree" refers to his Wóden-sprung lineage. Yggdrasill is the World Tree in Norse mythology that Óðinn is said to have hung from.

[215] Larrington, trans., *The Poetic Edda*, 20.

[216] John Gardner, *Grendel* (New York: Vintage Books, 1971).

[217] "The Battle of Finnsburh," Georgetown University, lines 3-4, accessed April 6, 2014, http://web.archive.org/web/20131029210649/http://www8.georgetown.edu/departments/medieval/labyrinth/library/oe/texts/a7.html. Commonly referred to as the *Finnesburh Fragment*. Translation by Þórbeorht Línléah.

[218] Calvert Watkins, *How to Kill a Dragon: Aspects of Indo-European Poetics* (New York: Oxford University Press, 1995), 10.

[219] Ibid., 10. Reworded slightly to pluralize.

[220] Ibid., 301.

[221] The most notable examples of Anglo-Saxon poems that may contain Heathen elements but which make no mention of dragons are *The Dream of the Rood*, the *Æcer Bót*, and the *Old English Rune Poem*.

[222] Paul Acker, "Dragons in the Eddas and in Early Nordic Art," in *Revisiting the Poetic Edda: Essays on Old Norse Heroic Legend*, 53-75, ed. Carolyne Larrington (New York: Routledge, 2013), 55.

[223] Ibid., 55-56.

[224] Christine Rauer, *Beowulf and the Dragon: Parallels and Analogues* (Cambridge: D.S. Brewer, 2000), 32.

[225] "Beowulf in Anglo-Saxon," Internet Sacred Texts Archive, lines 2711b-2715a, accessed March 30, 2014, http://www.sacred-texts.com/neu/asbeo.htm.

[226] Possibly tines of the god Wuldor (ON: Ullr). As the tines of a Germanic deity, these may have been magical wands, inscribed with runic symbols, such as those described by Tacitus in chapter 10 of *Germania*.

[227] Stephen Pollington, *Leechcraft: Early English Charms, Plant Lore, and Healing*. (Norfolk, England: Anglo-Saxon Books, 2000), 217, lines 30-35. This passage, from an Old English text called the *Lacnunga*, is commonly referred to as "The Nine Herbs Charm." Translation by Þórbeorht Línléah.

[228] ON: *móðr* is cognate with OE: *mód*. Mód is often translated as "heart" or "courage" though in ON: *móðr* seems to be more often translated as "wrath."

[229] Sophus Bugge, ed., "Völuspá," in *Sæmundar Edda*, (1867), verses 55-57, accessed January 18, 2014, http://etext.old.no/Bugge/. Translation by Þórbeorht Línléah.

[230] Russell, *The Germanization of Early Medieval Christianity*, 182-205. While not addressing dragons directly, James C. Russell's *The Germanization of Early Medieval Christianity* provides excellent insight into the persistence of Heathen BABV (beliefs, attitudes, values, and behaviors) in the early medieval Christian religion. In the work, Russell explores the underlying continuity of a worldview that persisted prior to, during, and for some time after, the conversion of the Germanic peoples from Heathendom to Christianity.

[231] Wight is an archaic English word, derived from the OE: *wiht*, a word which could refer to any kind of being, living, undead, natural, or supernatural. While it is not often used in day to day dialogue, it is regularly used in Anglo-Saxon and Norse studies and is therefore used throughout this book.

[232] The entire line: *Filistina, freond Nebrondes*, "of the Philistines,

friend of Nimrod" is easily omitted. Given that this one line is all that makes this poetic passage a Christian text, it may very well represent an early, half-hearted, attempt to Christianize Heathen lore.

[233] An Old Norse poetic term, related to the archaic Modern English "hight," "to name/call." A *heiti* is a poetic-name, a by-name or kenning, given to a god, hero, wight, or materially significant item in Germanic poetry.

[234] The author's own poetic pun or *heiti*, intended to relate Wóden's association with wolves (or werewolves) to his offspring, Þunor.

[235] Anlezark, trans., "Solomon and Saturn II," in *The Old English Dialogues of Solomon and Saturn*, lines 33-46. Translation by Þórbeorht Línléah. Referred to hereafter in the chapter as *Solomon and Saturn II*.

[236] A recently archaic word, used in print as late as 1915, with the meaning of "punishment".

[237] This author is aware of only the two, though room has been left to account for others should they have been overlooked.

[238] The name Jǫrmungandr is derived from the Old Norse *jǫrmun* "great (in size)" and *gandr*, "magic staff."

[239] Midgarðsormr is another name for Jǫrmungandr that is found in Norse mythological writings. It is derived from the Old Norse *Midgarð* "Middle Earth" and *ormr* "*wyrm.*"

[240] *Hálfdanar Saga Eysteinssonar*, Hálfdanar Saga Eysteinssonar, chapter 20, accessed March 13, 2014, http://www.snerpa.is/net/forn/half-e.htm. "*Þá varð Hárekr at flugdreka ok sló Skúla með sporðinum*" translated by Þórbeorht Línléah.

[241] ON for berserker. Berserkers will be discussed in more detail in the next few pages.

[242] *Göngu-Hrólfs Saga*, Göngu-Hrólfs Saga, chapter 33, accessed March 13, 2014,

http://www.snerpa.is/net/forn/gonguhr.htm. *Hafði hann verit stundum flugdreki, en stundum ormr, göltr ok griðungr eða önnur skaðsamlig skrípi* translated by Þórbeorht Línléah.

[243] Jónas Kristjánsson, ed., *Viktors Saga Ok Blávus* (Reykjavík: Handritastofnun Íslands, 1964), 31. *Bregzt hann jflugdreka liki* translated by Þórbeorht Línléah.

[244] An archaic English word which means "form, body, corpse."

[245] Gustaf Cederschiöld, *Baerings Saga*, in *Magus Saga Jarls, Konraś Saga, Baerings Saga, Floverts Saga, Bevers Saga* (Lund: F. Berlings Boktryckeri, 1884), 191, accessed March 13, 2014, http://books, google.com/books. Translation and standardization of the following text by Þórbeorht Línléah. *Idrekaliki, svá ógvrlegs, at engi þeirra, er a landi váru, þorað egn at sia.*

[246] *Sörla Saga Sterka*, Sörla Saga Sterka, chapter 8, accessed March 13, 2014,

http://www.snerpa.is/net/forn/sor-st.htm. *Brást hann þá í dreka líking, af því at hann var mjök hamrammaðr* translated by Þórbeorht Línléah.

[247] Anlezark, *The Old English Dialogues of Solomon and Saturn*, 70. Translated from the Old English by Þórbeorht Línléah.

[248] *Völsunga Saga*, Heimskringla, chapter VIII, accessed February 15, 2014, http://www.heimskringla.no/wiki/V%C3%B6lsunga_saga. *Því at úlfahamir hengu í húsinu yfir þeim* translated by Þórbeorht Línléah.

[249] Þorbjörn Hornklofi, "Hrafnsmál," Heimskringla, line 8, accessed March 23, 2014,

http://www.heimskringla.no/wiki/Haraldskvæði_(Hrafnsmál)_(B1).

[250] *Vatnsdæla Saga*, Icelandic Saga Database, chapters 9 and 47, accessed March 23, 2014,

http://sagadb.org/vatnsdaela_saga.

[251] The etymology components of *berserk* are commonly believed to be *ber-* "bear" and *serk* "shirt" though alternate etymologies have been put forward.

[252] Literally "to go berserk."

[253] Kris Kershaw, *The One-Eyed God: Odin and the (Indo-) Germanic Männerbünde* (Washington, D.C.: Journal of Indo-European Studies, 2000), 61. For a more detailed analysis of the Óðinn/ *úlfahamir/ berserker* connection as it relates to the aforementioned episode in the

Völsunga Saga, see 59-61.

[254] The idea of the hero being placed within a gigantic glove could bring to mind a Norse parallel from the *Prose Edda*. In the *Gylfaginning* portion of the text, the god Þórr and his traveling companions stop for the night, taking refuge and rest within a cave that turns out to be the glove of the giant Skrýmir.

[255] "Beowulf in Anglo-Saxon," lines 2085-2088.

[256] Snorri Sturluson, "Skáldskaparmál," *Prose Edda*, Heimskringla, chapter 6, accessed March 23, 2014,

http://www.heimskringla.no/wiki/Skáldskaparmál.

[257] The author has coined this phrase to mirror the idea of *textus receptus*, "received text," a phrase used in Biblical textual criticism. *Verbum receptus* would thus mean "received word."

[258] Also, the maxim "Drake shall dwell in the low (burial mound), ancient (*fród*), of treasures proud" ("Maxims II," lines 26b-27a) reads almost as an abridgement to the fire-drake's second introduction in *Beowulf*. As it appears there, "Hoard-joy found the old twilight-scather standing open, he who, burning, barrows seeketh. The naked hate-drake who by night flieth . . . he shall seek the hoard in the earth. There he, Heathen gold, wardeth, old (*fród*) in winters." (lines 2270b-2277a) Translations by Þórbeorht Línléah

[259] "Maxims II," Internet Sacred Texts Archive, lines 42b-43a, accessed March 30, 2014, http://www.sacred-texts.com/neu/ascp/a15.htm. Translation by Þórbeorht Línléah.

[260] One who walks about the marches, the borderlands.

[261] "Beowulf in Anglo-Saxon," lines 102-105.

[262] Ibid., line 426.

[263] Vampire in the original pre-Bram Stoker sense.

[264] G. V. Smithers, "The Making of Beowulf; Inaugural Lecture of the Professor of English Language Delivered in the Applebey Lecture Theatre on 18 May, 1961" (Durham, England: University of Durham, 1961), 8.

[265] George Henderson, *The Norse Influence on Celtic Scotland*

(Glasgow: J. Maclehose, 1910), 106.

[266] Jón Hnefill Aðalsteinsson, *A Piece of Horse Liver: Myth, Ritual and Folklore in Old Icelandic Sources*, trans. Terry Gunnell and Joan Turville-Petre (Reykjavík: Háskólaútgáfan, 1998), 144-145.

[267] Ibid., 147.

[268] Ibid., 146.

[269] Saxo Grammaticus, "Gesta Danorum," Det Kongelige Bibliotek, Book V, accessed March 30, 2014, http://wayback-01.kb.dk/wayback/20101108105429/http%3A//www2.kb.dk/elib/lit/dan/saxo/lat/or.dsr/.

[270] A fourteenth century Icelandic manuscript containing several sagas and histories.

[271] H. R. Ellis Davidson, *Patterns of Folklore* (Ipswich: D. S. Brewer, 1978), 107-108.

[272] "Beowulf in Anglo-Saxon," line 1331.

[273] Stephen Pollington, *Anglo-Saxon Burial Mounds: Princely Burial in the 6th and 7th Centuries* (Swaffham, Norfolk: Anglo-Saxon Books, 2008), 21.

[274] "Beowulf in Anglo-Saxon," line 2139. Literally a "ground-hall."

[275] Ibid., lines 2232, 2410, 2515.

[276] Ibid., line 1006.

[277] Particularly when it may be that multiple oral traditions surrounding the story are preserved in a single text. It is worth noting that, of Beowulf's battles with Grendel and Grendel's mother, there are three versions given in the text. The first is that of the narrator describing the action as it unfolds. The second is that of Beowulf recounting his deeds to king Hroðgar in the meadhall. The third is that of Beowulf, upon returning home, recounting his adventure to his own king, Hygelác. The differences in these versions might be accounted for by the poet having multiple traditions and variations of the story to draw upon. Those familiar with Biblical textual criticism will no doubt find this idea familiar.

[278] "Beowulf in Anglo-Saxon," lines 2312, 2699.

[279] *Völsunga Saga*, chapter 14.

[280] *Gull-Þóris Saga*, Icelandic Saga Database, September 13, 2007, chapter 3, accessed February 15, 2014, http://sagadb.org/gull-thoris_saga. Translation by Þórbeorht Línléah.

[281] Ibid., chapter 20.

[282] Raymond P. Tripp, *More about the Fight with the Dragon: Beowulf, 2208b-3182: Commentary, Edition, and Translation* (Lanham: University Press of America, 1983), ix.

[283] Ibid., 24.

[284] Christine Rauer, *Beowulf and the Dragon*, 39.

[285] "Beowulf in Anglo-Saxon," lines 2230-2269.

[286] William Witherle Lawrence, "The Dragon and His Lair in Beowulf." *PMLA* 33, no. 4 (January 01, 1918): 558, accessed March 10, 2014, http://www.jstor.org/stable/10. 2307/456981?ref=search-gateway:829f2ed5c9dba2d8e50ba3f1bbd10bb4.

[287] Ibid., 558.

[288] Hilda R. Ellis Davidson, "The Hill of the Dragon," *Folklore* 61, no. 4 (December 1950): 169-85, doi:10.1080/0015587X.1950.9718012.

[289] Smithers, "The Making of Beowulf," 11.

[290] Ibid., 22.

[291] J. R. R. Tolkien, *The Monster and the Critics: The Essays of J. R. R. Tolkien* (London: Harper Collins, 1977), 20. In all fairness, it should be mentioned that the dating of *Beowulf* is by no means an open and shut case and that other, later, dates have been proposed by other academics.

[292] Although "laid low" is a slang expression, this author has employed it as a poetic pun. The Old English *hlǽw,* "grave" survives in English as the archaic "low" used in the sense of "burial mound."

[293] "Hárbarðsljóð," *Poetic Edda*, Heimskringla, verse 23, accessed March 16, 2014,

http://www.heimskringla.no/wiki/Hárbarðsljóð. *Brúðir bölvísar* translated by Þórbeorht Línléah.

[294] "Beowulf in Anglo-Saxon," line 556. A battle in Beowulf's past.

[295] Ibid., lines 732, 739, 1000.

[296] Ibid., line 1259. *áglǽcwíf,* 1269, 1520.

[297] Ibid., line 1512.

[298] Ibid., line 2534, 2557, 2905.

[299] Ibid., line 893.

[300] Ibid., line 2592.

[301] An intentional allusion to the idea of Max Müller's infamous assertion that mythology was a "disease of language."

[302] "Beowulf in Anglo-Saxon," line 892.

[303] Chaney, *The Cult of Kingship in Anglo-Saxon England*, 2.

[304] Prohibitions against the pagan practice of burning grain as an offering to the dead that they might furnish the living with renewed health is found in numerous Medieval penitentials, including that of Theodore, a 7th century Archbishop of Canterbury.

[305] "Beowulf in Anglo-Saxon," line 2330.

[306] Ibid., lines 2208b-2211.

[307] Ibid., line 2211.

[308] G. K. Chesterton, "The Ethics of Elfland," in *Orthodoxy* (Chicago: Moody Publishers, 2009), 74. In his work "The Ethics of Elfland" Chesterton wrote that "Tradition means giving votes to the most obscure of all classes, our ancestors. It is a democracy of the dead. Tradition refuses to submit to the small and arrogant oligarchy of those who merely happen to be walking about. All democrats object to men being disqualified by the accident of birth; tradition objects to them being disqualified by the accident of death." Chesterton's idea of "Tradition" is here compared to the Anglo-Saxon idea of *ealde riht*.

[309] "Beowulf in Anglo-Saxon," line 2557. *Fréode*, a variant of *friþ*, is a word which means "security, protection, peace" and is a concept that is closely connected to the idea of sacral kingship.

[310] Smithers, "The Making of Beowulf," 22.

[311] "Beowulf in Anglo-Saxon," lines 885-889. Translation by Þórbeorht Línléah.

[312] Ibid., lines 2250-2253.

[313] Cathey, ed., *Hêliand: Text and Commentary*, lines 4899b-4900. Translation of an Old Saxon text (as opposed to Anglo-Saxon) by Þórbeorht Línléah.

[314] Snorri Sturluson, *Ynglinga Saga*, Heimskringla, chapter 8, accessed March 23, 2014, http://www.heimskringla.no/wiki/Ynglinga_saga. Translation by Þórbeorht Línléah.

[315] "Hávamal," *Poetic Edda*, Heimskringla, line 72, accessed March 16, 2014, http://www.heimskringla.no/wiki/ Hávamal. Translation by Þórbeorht Línléah.

[316] Acker, "Dragons in the Eddas and Early Nordic Art," 53-75.

[317] Guy, *The Carmen De Hastingae Proelio of Guy, Bishop of Amiens*, eds. Catherine Morton and Hope Muntz (Oxford: Clarendon, 1972), 38. Translation by Þórbeorht Línléah.

[318] David Howarth, *1066: The Year of Conquest* (1978; repr., New York: Penguin Books, 1981), 187.

[319] Guy, *The Carmen*, xliv.

[320] "Beowulf in Anglo-Saxon," lines 2802b-2808.

[321] Sturluson, *Ynglinga Saga*, chapter 12.

[322] Tacitus, *The Agricola and the Germania*, 102.

[323] Guy, *The Carmen*, xliv.

[324] Phillipp Reclam, ed., *Widukind Von Corvey Res Gestae Saxonicae: Die Sachsengeshichte*. (Ditzingen: Gesamtherstellung, 2002), 44.

[325] Geoffrey of Monmouth, *The History of the Kings of Britain*, trans. Lewis G. M. Thorpe (Harmondsworth: Penguin, 1966), 171.

[326] "Vita Barbati Episcopi Beneventani," in *Monumenta Germaniae Gistorica: Scriptores Rerum Langobardicarum Et Italicarum: Saec,*

VI-IX (Hannover: Hahniani, 1878), 557, http://books.google.de. Translated by Þórbeorht Línléah.

[327] Michael Wood, perf., episode 7, "Penda"" in *The Essay - Anglo-Saxon Portraits*, BBC Radio 3, October 23, 2012, accessed April 6, 2014,

http://www.bbc.co.u/iplayer/episode/b01ngr45.

[328] *The Annals of St. Neots* is an English account of the *Visio Eucherii*. The *Visio* is a vision that Hincmar of Reims attributed to Saint Eucherius of Orléans.

[329] David Dumville, Simon Keynes, and Michael Lapidge, eds., *The Anglo-Saxon Chronicle: The Annals of St. Neots with Vita Prima Sancti Neoti* (Cambridge: Boydell and Brewer, 1985), 37.

[330] Gro Steinsland, "Origin Myths and Rulership. From the Viking Age Ruler to the Ruler of Medieval Historiography: Continuity, Transformations and Innovations," in *Ideology and Power in The Viking and Middle Ages: Scandinavia, Iceland, Ireland, Orkney, and the Faeroes* (Leiden: Brill, 2011), 32.

[331] Hålogaland was the northernmost province in Viking Age Norway.

[332] Steinsland, "Origin Myths and Rulership," 32.

[333] David Fickett-Wilbar, "Ritual Details of the Irish Horse Sacrifice in Betha Mholaise Daiminse," *The Journal of Indo-European Studies* 40, no. 3 & 4 (Fall & Winter 2012): 316.

[334] Ibid., 317.

[335] *The Wicker Man*, directed by Robin Hardy, featuring Christopher Lee. (British Lion Films, 1973), DVD.

[336] A reference to the 10th century Anglo-Saxon charm *Æcer Bót/Acre Remedy*.

[337] David W. Anthony, *The Horse, the Wheel, and Language: How Bronze-Age Riders from the Eurasian Steppes Shaped the Modern World*. (Princeton: Princeton University Press, 2007), 367-368.

[338] Peter Gelling and Hilda Roderick Ellis Davidson, *The Chariot of the Sun, and Other Rites and Symbols of the Northern Bronze Age* (New York: Praeger, 1969), 2.

[339] Björn E. Berglund, "Human Impact and Climate Changes—Synchronous Events and a Causal Link?" *Quaternary International* 105, no. 1 (2003): 9, accessed April 3, 2012. doi:10.1016/S1040-6182(02)00144-1.

[340] Gelling and Davidson, *The Chariot of the Sun*, 3.

[341] Watkins, *How to Kill a Dragon*, xii.

[342] Kristian Kristiansen and Carsten Müller, *New Directions in Scandinavian Archaeology Vol I*. (Lyngby: The National Museum of Denmark, 1979), 180.

[343] Ibid.

[344] Gelling and Davidson, *The Chariot of the Sun*, 181.

[345] Tacitus, *The Agricola and the Germania*, 139.

[346] Jordanes, *The Origins and Deeds of the Goths*, trans. Charles C. Mierow, Texts for Ancient History Courses: University of Calgary, Apr. 22, 1997, accessed Apr. 16, 2012, http://people.ucalgary.ca/~vandersp/Courses/texts/jordgeti.html, IV: 2.

[347] Paul the Deacon, *History of the Langobards*, trans. William D. Foulke (University of Pennsylvania, 1907), repr. in *New Northvegr Center*, accessed Apr. 16, 2012, http://www.northvegr.org/histories%20and%20chronicles/history%20of%20the%20lombards/title.html.

[348] Tacitus, *The Agricola and the Germania*, 109.

[349] Jón Hnefill Aðalsteinsson, *Under the Cloak: A Pagan Ritual Turning Point in the Conversion of Iceland*, (Reykjavík: Háskólaútgáfan, Félagsvísindastofnun, 1999), 128.

[350] Lotte Hedeager, "Scandinavia before the Viking Age," in *The Viking World*, ed. Stefan Brink and Neil S. Price (London: Routledge, 2008), 13.

[351] Tacitus, *The Agricola and the Germania*, 134.

[352] U. Büntgen, W. Tegel, K. Nicolussi, M. Mccormick, D. Frank, V. Trouet, J. O. Kaplan, F. Herzig, K.-U. Heussner, H. Wanner, J. Luterbacher, and J. Esper, "2500 Years of European Climate Variability and Human Susceptibility," *Science* 331, no. 6017 (2011):

578, accessed April 3, 2012, doi:10.1126/science.1197175.

[353] Ibid., 579.

[354] Folk-wandering

[355] Xunming Wang, Fahu Chen, Jiawu Zhang, Yi Yang, Jijun Li, Eerdun Hasi, Caixia Zhang, and Dunsheng Xia, "Climate, Desertification, and the Rise and Collapse of China's Historical Dynasties," *Human Ecology* 38, no. 1 (2010): 164, accessed April 3, 2012, doi:10.1007/s10745-009-9298-2.

[356] J. B. Bury, *The Invasion of Europe by the Barbarians* (New York: Russell & Russell, 1963), 26-27.

[357] Holt's research is tremendously insightful, but in his thesis he, most likely as the result of a typographical error, places Sozomen's writing a full century earlier than it occurred.

[358] Aþanareiks, a 4th century Thervingian Gothic king

[359] Sozomen, "Ecclesiastical History," in *The Goths in the Fourth Century*, eds. Peter Heather and John Matthews (Liverpool: Liverpool University, 2004), 101.

[360] David H. Holt, "Did Extreme Climate Conditions Stimulate the Migrations of the Germanic Tribes in the 3rd and 4th Centuries? An Examination of Historical Data, Climate Poxy Data, and Migration Events," thesis, University of Arkansas, 2002, sec. Implications, accessed Apr. 16, 2012, http://www.cast.uark.edu/research/research_theses/david_holt/.

[361] Athanaric's name literally translates in Old Gothic to "Year-King" with "year" carrying with it the connotation of harvest.

[362] Translated from the German by Þórbeorht Línléah: Luck-vessel

[363] William A. Chaney, "Paganism to Christianity in Anglo-Saxon England," *Harvard Theological Review* 53, no. 03 (1960): 209, accessed April 3, 2012, doi:10.1017/S0017816000027012.

[364] Ing was erst, mid the East Danes, seen by sedge-dwellers. Then he went eft over the wave. His wain ran after him. Thus the Heardings named the hero. (Author's own translation, 4/21/12).

[365] Hilda R. Ellis Davidson, *Gods and Myths of Northern Europe*

(Baltimore, MD: Penguin, 1964), 93.

[366] The name Lýtir is believed to be derived from the Old Norse *hlut* "lot" as in the casting of lots for divination.

[367] Hilduin Einhard, *The Life of Charlemagne*, trans. Samuel Epes Turner (New York: Harper & Brothers, 1880), repr. in Fordham University Internet Medieval Sourcebook, January 1999, accessed April 21 2012, http://www.fordham.edu/halsall/basis/einhard.asp.

[368] Holt, "Did Extreme Climate Conditions,"sec. Conclusions.

http://www.cast.uark.edu/research/research_theses/david_holt/.

[369] Luck, favor, magic

[370] Sturluson, *Ynglinga Saga*, 15.

[371] Olaf Tree-feller

[372] Sturluson, *Ynglinga Saga*, 32.

[373] Holt, "Did Extreme Climate Conditions,"sec. Implications.

[374] Ibid.

[375] Literally, "world-outlook". This term is used to denote the way a people perceive the world and their place within it.

[376] Steinsland, "Origin Myths and Rulership," 33.

[377] For whatever reason, Wóden is oft depicted as a "usurper" or "latecomer" by academic revisionists such as Philip A. Shaw and Richard North and by Heathens who think that said revisionism somehow equates to reconstruction. That is not the belief nor is it the intention of this author. That the popularity of various god-cults waxed and waned throughout history is no great scandal. That Wóden's cult surged in its political importance by the end of the Migration Era has no bearing on the sacred-timeless-spaceless-being of any of the gods. History is profane whereas the gods exist in the realm of the sacred. This said, more information regarding the rise of Wóden's cult during the Migration Era may be found Kris Kershaw's *The One-eyed God: Odin and The Indo-Germanic Männerbünde*. Furthermore, Jón Hnefill Aðalsteinsson's *A Piece of Horse Liver: Myth, Ritual, and Folklore in Old Icelandic Sources* explores the inherent tension in Heathen belief that existed between the cults of

Ing and Wóden. Lastly, Gro Steinsland's *Origin Myths and Rulership: From the Viking Age Ruler to the Ruler of Medieval Historiography: Continuity, Transformations and Innovations* provides a well-wrought and thoughtful narrative surrounding the cultic changes which occurred among Norse kings.

[378] A line from *Beowulf*

[379] Tacitus, *The Agricola and the Germania*, 107, 111.

[380] Ibid., 118.

[381] Kershaw, *The One-eyed God,* 108; S. P. Scott, trans., "The Visigothic Code: Forum Judicum," The Library of Iberian Resources Online, Books 3 and 4, accessed June 10, 2014, http://libro.uca.edu/vcode/visigoths.htm. Kershaw cites twenty as being the age by which most Irish Celts were married. The *Forum Ludicum*, a 7th century Visigothic law code, also ascribes twenty as a suitable age for marriage.

[382] Anne Savage, trans., *The Anglo-Saxon Chronicles: The Authentic Voices of England, From the Time of Julius Caesar to the Coronation of Henry II* (New York: Barnes & Noble, 2000), 83.

[383] This assumes that they were twins.

[384] Less rigid than Modern English in its word order due to a greater abundance of noun and adjective declensions.

[385] The craft of the *scóp* (shaper), poet-singer-performer.

[386] For a firsthand experience of this, I highly recommend one procure a copy of Benjamin Bagby's performance of *Beowulf*. I've only seen part of this, but it is truly amazing.

[387] For more on the role of the mead-hall in ancient Anglo-Saxon society, I highly recommend *Lords of Battle: Image and Reality of the Comitatus in Dark-Age Britain* by Stephen S. Evans, particularly chapter 7, and *The Mead-Hall: Feasting in Anglo-Saxon England* by Stephen Pollington.

[388] An oath of fealty to one's lord.

[389] Literally a harp, or perhaps, to be more historically honest, a lyre. A musical instrument of this type was found in the famous Sutton Hoo ship burial.

[390] Compare to *frætwe* in the story of Sigimund

[391] unknown, strange

[392] Sigemund the son of Wæl

[393] Are equipped without knowledge (do not know)

[394] Seamus Heaney translates this as "feuds and foul doings." Benjamin Slade translated it as "feuds and feats of arms." *Fyren* (*Firen*) has only negative connotations. Bosworth-Toller defines it as "wicked deed, sin, crime." T'would seem as if Sigemund was not without fault.

[395] Literally, "war's hard" with hard being a noun meaning "hard object."

[396] *Wrætlic* from *wræt*, "ornament, work of art, jewel" and *líc* (-like). Most translations render this as "wondrous" for the purpose of alliterating with Wyrm. I have expounded upon this some to keep the alliteration yet convey the beauty of the beast.

[397] This conveys the image of the dragon pinned through, like a butterfly, against the wall.

[398] Drighten (warlord)-like, becoming of a warlord, becoming of a noble.

[399] The OE: *sweltan* originally meant "to die".

[400] *Áglæca* is generally translated as "monster" or "demon." Its etymology is disputed. It is generally agreed that *ág* means "wicked" yet *læca* could mean "leech," an old world use for a healer, or it could possibly be a variant of *lác*, a word which means "play, sport, dance" but which also means "sacrifice."

[401] The lee of warriors, the shelter of warriors, a lord.

[402] Literally "male waning in silliness." Though the author generally provides literal translations, the meaning of this half-line is lost if translated in such a fashion. From *won/wan* comes the Modern English "wane". *Sǽlig* means "blessed, happy" but in Modern English

is preserved as "silly." *Wer*, for "male" can still be found in the word "werewolf."

[403] *Biorn/beorn* is traditionally translated as warrior. The etymology of the word is not entirely agreed upon though it may be related the Old Norse *bjǫrn*, "bear." The imagery of a bear-warrior brings to mind the notion of the Norse *berserkr*.

[404] Compare to *mærost* in the story of Sigemund slaying the dragon

[405] ON: *móðr* is cognate with OE: *mód*. *Mód* is often translated as "heart" or "courage" although in ON: *móðr* seems to be more often translated as "wrath."

[406] Aldnari is a difficult word to translate and is generally glossed as "fire." The word appears to be derived from the ON: *eld*, "fire" and Nari (alternate Narfi), the name of one of Loki's sons who is turned into a wolf by the gods, torn asunder, and whose bowels are then used to bind Loki. Rudolf Simek traces the etymology to *nár* "corpse" (Simek 228). As such I have chosen to translate this as "corpse-fire" which invokes the dual imagery of the world and the inhabitants within it burning up, but also that of either Þórr burning upon a pyre or the Wyrm itself burning up.

[407] A recently archaic word, used in print as late as 1915 with the meaning of "punishment".

[408] "Vafþrúðnismál," *Poetic Edda*, line 44, Heimskringla, accessed November 4, 2014, http://www.heimskringla.no/wiki/Vaf%C3%BEr%C3%BA%C3%B0nism%C3%A1l. Translation by Þórbeorht Línleah.

[409] Snorri Sturluson, "The Prose Edda in Old Icelandic," chap. 51, New Northvegr Center, accessed November 4, 2014, http://northvegr.org/old%20icelandic%20old%20english%20texts/the%20prose%20edda%20in%20old%20icelandic/. Translation from Old Icelandic by Þórbeorht Línleah.

[410] Ibid.

[411] J. P. Mallory and Douglas Q. Adams, eds., *Encyclopedia of Indo-European Culture* (London: Fitzroy Dearborn, 1997), 180-183.

[412] Bo Gräslund and Neil Price, "Twilight of the Gods? The 'dust Veil Event' of AD 536 in Critical Perspective," *Antiquity* 86 (2012): 431, accessed November 4, 2014, http://antiquity.ac.uk/ant/086/ant0860428.htm.

[413] Ibid., 433.

[414] Ibid., 440.

[415] Bede, *Ecclesiastical History of the English People*, 231.

[416] This is covered in the chapter "Layers in the Well."

FÓREFINGER/FOREFINGER/INDEX

Abrenuntiatio, 30, 31, 41, 42, 44

Adam of Bremen, 14, 25, 26, 35, 42, 61, 67, 68, 175, 192, 193, 194, 196, 197, 198, 199

áglæca, 106, 107, 108, 110

Ahnenerbe, 47

Alaric, 12

Amesbury, 73, 80, 85, 133, 135, 136, 141, 142, 143, 146

Ammianus Marcellinus, 12, 192

Angles, 13, 31, 40, 72, 74, 81, 88, 123, 124, 125

Anglo-Saxons, 2, 13, 28, 30, 31, 56, 81, 82, 83, 84, 87, 88, 96, 113, 114, 126, 136, 137

Angrivarii, 8, 11, 20, 190

Arminius, 9, 10, 24

Ásatru, 28

Athanaric, 126, 129, 219

Austrasia, 16

Avars, 23

Badon Hill, 13

Baldr, 36, 205

baptism, 21, 22, 26, 30, 69, 114, 128, 167

Bede, 71, 72, 106, 110, 133, 134, 140, 176, 192, 200, 223

Beowulf, 3, 42, 71, 75, 76, 77, 78, 81, 88, 89, 91, 92, 93, 94, 95, 97, 98, 99, 100, 101, 102, 103, 104, 105, 106, 107, 108, 109, 110, 111, 112, 113, 115, 117, 141, 150, 152, 153, 154, 155, 156, 157, 176, 181, 182, 184, 185, 186, 202, 203, 205, 208, 211, 212, 213, 214, 215, 220,

221

berserker, 96, 117, 210, 211

Boniface, 17, 18, 25, 64, 65, 181, 187, 191, 199

Britannia, 12, 13, 14, 23, 31, 72, 81, 83, 88, 125, 139, 140, 141

Britons, 12, 13, 81, 82, 83, 84, 133, 136, 137, 141, 183, 207

Bructeri, 11

Cædmon's Hymn, 66

Capitulary of Carloman, 16

Carloman, 16, 17, 18, 30, 31, 69

Carmen de Hastingae Prolio, 112

Carolingian, 17, 115, 128, 185, 188, 191, 193

Carolingians, 16, 17, 18

Chaney, 39, 71, 107, 114, 127, 177, 196, 200, 214, 219

Charlemagne, 6, 15, 18, 26, 27, 46, 47, 51, 58, 63, 67, 69, 177, 178, 193

Charles Martel, 16, 17, 115, 167, 182, 193

Chauci, 8, 10, 11

Cherusci, 8, 9, 10, 11, 24

Childeric III, 128

Christianity, 15, 16, 17, 22, 23, 26, 27, 29, 30, 33, 36, 51, 54, 64, 68, 73, 112, 126, 177, 184, 201, 208, 219

Chronicon ex chronicis, 31

Dómaldi, 129

draca, 89, 103, 107, 147, 152, 155

draugar, 100

Dumézil, 33, 37, 38, 41, 42, 44, 178, 195, 196, 197, 198

East Saxon, 30, 31, 32, 41

Egil's Saga, 43, 185, 196

Eresberg, 45

Eresburg, 18, 20, 46, 63, 69

Essex, 31, 32, 38, 40, 127

Externsteine, 46, 47, 48, 51, 52, 53, 54, 55, 60, 69, 185

Fáfnir, 89, 103, 104, 105, 106, 107, 110, 160

Finn, 74, 75, 76, 77, 78, 79, 80, 134, 186, 201, 203, 204, 205

Finnesburh, 73, 74, 75, 76, 77, 80, 81, 84, 85, 87, 88, 134, 135, 140, 145, 146, 147, 201, 202,

203, 204, 205, 207

Finnesburh Fragment, 81, 145

Fjörgyn, 90, 94, 117, 162

Flateyjarbók, 101, 127

Florence of Worcester, 31

Fosite, 119

Frankish Royal Annals, 21

Franks, 5, 14, 15, 16, 17, 18, 19, 20, 21, 22, 23, 24, 25, 30, 31, 33, 128, 193

Freyja, 34, 95

Freyr, 31, 33, 35, 36, 38, 39, 41, 42, 43, 44, 66, 67, 113, 127, 161

frið, 75, 78, 80, 82

Frisia, 16, 18, 75, 78, 134

Frisians, 6, 16, 17, 22, 64, 78, 79

Frô, 33, 34, 35, 36, 37, 38, 39, 40, 41, 42, 44, 66, 67, 69

Frûa, 34

Gárman Lord, v, 1, 28

gást, 99, 100, 103, 104, 106, 110

Geoffery of Monmouth, 81

Gerald of Wales, 119

Germania, 7, 8, 9, 10, 11, 58, 63, 64, 82, 113, 186, 190, 191, 199, 201, 202, 203, 204, 206, 208, 216, 217, 218, 220

Germanische Heiligtumer, 47, 57

Gesta Danorum, 101, 184, 212

Gesta Hammaburgensis Ecclesiae Pontificum, 45

Getae, 34

ghost, 3, 99, 101, 102, 108, 116, 152, 156

Gildas, 82, 86, 133, 139, 179, 206

godpoles, 60, 66

Gǫngu-Hrólfs Saga, 95

Gospel of Pseudo-Matthew,, 53, 197

Goths, 12, 34, 122, 123, 125, 126, 131, 181, 186, 217, 218

Grendel, 86, 95, 97, 99, 100, 101, 102, 103, 104, 106, 152, 153, 179, 207, 213

Grettis Saga, 101, 102

Grifo, 17

Grimm, 26, 31, 34, 35, 36, 42, 44, 47, 65, 68, 180, 194, 195, 196, 198, 199

Guy of Amiens, 112

Hadeln, 6, 14, 23, 28

Hadugato, 14

Hálfdanar Saga Eysteinsson, 95

Hávamál, 57, 63, 70, 86, 180

Hêliand, 56, 111, 177, 198, 215

Hengest, 3, 12, 71, 72, 73, 74, 75, 76, 78, 79, 80, 81, 82, 83, 84, 85, 86, 133, 134, 135, 136, 137, 139, 140, 141, 142, 143, 146, 186, 200, 201, 202, 203, 204, 205, 207

Hermann Hamelmann, 46, 57

Hermes, 61

Herulians, 39, 40

Hessian, 17, 18, 64

Hessians, 17, 64, 65

Hildeburh, 75

Hildegar, 17, 18, 25

Historia Brittonum, 13, 71, 141, 183, 192, 200

Hnæf, 74, 75, 76, 77, 78, 79, 80, 134, 204, 205

Horsa, 12, 72, 81, 82, 84, 133, 135, 136, 140, 141, 200, 203

Hrafnsmál, 96, 181, 210

Hucbald of St. Amand, 12

Huns, 12, 125, 130, 131

Ibn Fadlan, 59, 64, 68, 181, 198

Indra, 41

Ing, 39, 108, 113, 126, 127, 131, 219, 220

Ingmund, 66, 67

Irmin, 19, 35, 58, 60, 61, 62, 63

Irminfrid, 14

Irminsûl, 2, 18, 19, 20, 21, 24, 42, 45, 46, 47, 48, 51, 53, 57, 58, 59, 60, 61, 62, 63, 66, 67, 68, 69

Jesus, 15, 19, 24, 25, 48, 50, 51, 53, 54, 56, 183, 192, 197

Jǫrmungandr, 90, 91, 94, 209

Jupiter, 41, 58, 61, 64, 65

Jupitersäule, 58

Jutes, 13, 72, 74, 76, 79, 80, 81, 125

King Arthur, 13

Kvasir, 97, 204

Lambton Worm, 94

Langobards, 11, 14, 15, 114, 167, 183, 217

Loki, 94, 95, 103, 222

Lothair, 25, 26, 194

Lýtir, 127, 128, 219

Marcomanni, 10

Marklo, 12

Marklosahson, 28

Mars, 34, 41, 61

Mary, 53, 54, 183, 197

Massacre of Verden, 21

mead, 37, 73, 75, 77, 78, 79, 80, 84, 85, 86, 97, 98, 145, 204, 205, 221

Mercury, 31, 61

Merovingian, 17, 128

Mitra-Varuna, 41, 196

Mûspelli, 92, 93, 165

Nāsatya, 41

Nennius, 13, 71, 80, 84, 133, 141, 183, 192, 200, 207

Neo-Pagan, 28, 61

Nerthus, 117, 119, 124, 127

Neustria, 16

Nibelungenlied, 106, 203

Niorðr, 35, 36

Nordliudi, 11, 21, 23, 24, 25

Nordmannia, 6, 21

Northalbingia, 6, 8

Northalbingians, 7

Obodrites, 23, 24, 25

Odin, 31, 33, 36, 43, 63, 129, 181, 202, 211, 220

Óðinn, 19, 31, 35, 36, 38, 41, 42, 56, 59, 63, 70, 96, 97, 98, 103, 111, 127, 130, 143, 202, 203, 204, 207, 211

Ólafr Geirstaðaálfr, 108, 113

Óláfr Trételgja, 129

Old Saxons, 2, 5, 13, 28, 30, 56

Oldenburgisch Chronicon, 46

palm tree, 53, 55, 58, 60

Pater Noster, 56, 57

Pepin, 16, 17, 18, 22, 25

Picts, 12, 13, 81

Procopius, 39

Prose Edda, 34, 36, 37, 38, 62, 94, 97, 122, 143, 185, 186, 196, 204, 211

Ptolemy, 7, 8, 184, 190

Quirinus, 41, 44

Qur'an, 54

Radbod, 16, 17, 18

Res Gestae Saxonicae, 5, 6, 61, 114, 167, 184, 189, 198, 216

Rouran, 125

Rudolf of Fulda, 45, 58, 62

sacral kingship, 39, 94, 109, 127, 215

sahs, 7, 32

Sahsnôt, vii, 1, 2, 16, 29, 30, 31, 32, 33, 34, 35, 36, 38, 41, 42, 44, 66, 69

Sahsono, 7

Salian Franks, 6

Saxo Grammaticus, 39, 101, 184, 196, 212

scild, 78, 79, 80, 84, 86, 205

scóp, 66, 74, 77, 78, 106, 108, 115, 116, 140, 146, 201, 202, 204, 220

Scythians, 34

seax, 7, 32

Seaxnéat, 2, 16, 30, 36, 127

Sigemund, 106, 107, 110, 150, 151, 221, 222

Sigifrid, 20

Sigurd, 34, 203

Skáldskaparmál, 97, 160, 186, 211

Snorri Sturluson, 62, 113, 143, 196, 204, 211, 215

Solomon and Saturn, 56, 88, 91, 93, 95, 97, 98, 149, 175, 198, 209, 210

Sörla Saga Sterka, 95, 185, 210

Sozomen, 126, 186, 218

Stellinga, 25, 26

stirps regia, 40, 71

Suavi, 14, 15

Suebi, 15, 70, 74

Suebic, 8, 9, 11, 119

Swǽfe, 15

symbel, 66, 79, 83, 84, 145, 146

Tacitus, 7, 8, 10, 11, 63, 64, 67,

70, 74, 77, 83, 113, 122, 124, 127, 133, 186, 190, 191, 199, 201, 202, 203, 204, 206, 208, 216, 217, 218, 220

Teutoburger Wald, 8, 9

The Battle of Maldon, 77, 176, 205

þéaw, 84, 86

Þéodisc Geléafa, v, 1, 28

Theodish Belief, 28

Theodoric, 14, 16

Þing, 7, 12, 20, 21, 32, 40

Thor, 31, 33, 35, 36, 42, 43, 65, 90

Thracians, 34

Þunar, 16, 17, 18, 30, 31, 33, 34, 35, 42, 44, 61, 64, 65, 66, 67, 69

Þunor, 16, 90, 92, 117, 122, 209

Thuringian, 6, 17

Thuringians, 7, 14, 17, 32, 61

Tiuu, 33, 34, 35, 36, 38, 40, 60, 61, 196

Topographia Hibernica, 119

Tuisto, 119

Turville-Petre, 32, 38, 44, 175, 186, 195, 196, 212

Týr, 33, 38, 40, 60

úlfhéðnar, 96, 117

Ulphilas, 126

Unwan, 26

Uuôden, 16, 18, 19, 26, 30, 31, 33, 34, 35, 36, 37, 38, 39, 40, 41, 42, 44, 59, 60, 61, 63, 64, 66, 67, 69

Varus, 9, 10

Vatnsdæla Saga, 66, 187, 210

Viking, 3, 32, 47, 65, 67, 77, 112, 122, 123, 124, 127, 178, 180, 186, 197, 198, 203, 206, 216, 218, 220

Vita Lebuini Antiqua, 12

Völsunga Saga, 96, 103, 106, 110, 160, 187, 210, 211, 213

Völuspa, 90, 93, 94, 162

Vortigern, 13, 72, 81, 82, 83, 84, 136

Vortimer, 82, 83, 133, 136

wearg, 91, 93

weltanschauung, 73, 85, 116, 128, 130

wéoh, 69, 70

Weser, 8, 9, 11, 16, 20, 21

Westfali, 11, 20, 21, 22, 24

Widsið, 74

Widukind of Corvey, 5, 6, 61, 114, 189, 198

Wilhelm Teudt, 47, 58, 60

Witan Þéod, 28

Wóden, 16, 36, 56, 57, 71, 72, 85, 90, 91, 92, 96, 98, 108, 115, 117, 127, 130, 143, 148, 201, 202, 203, 204, 205, 207, 209, 219

Wyrd, 81, 120, 131, 157

wyrm, 89, 90, 91, 92, 93, 94, 95, 97, 98, 103, 106, 110, 149, 151, 152, 160, 162, 209

Yggdrasill, 19, 62, 63, 64, 68, 85, 207

Ynglinga Saga, 37, 38, 40, 111, 113, 160, 161, 186, 196, 215, 216, 219

Yngvi, 31, 36, 38, 39, 41, 113, 126